PRAISE FOR *FASHION BRAND MANAGEMENT*

'Sustainability and digitalization are radically transforming the fashion industry. The rise of online platforms, social media, 3D product development, AI and the circular economy are changing the industry on all levels, from marketing and product development to supply chains and business models. In all areas, old knowledge needs to be replaced while new practices lead us forward. This book addresses all these changes brilliantly, highlighting some amazing examples. A wonderful guide for students with entrepreneurial ambitions.'
José Teunissen, Dean, School of Design and Technology, London College of Fashion, UAL

'When it comes to practical advice about surviving and thriving in the world of fashion, one need look no further than the clear insight of Alison Lowe. A hands-on professional to her fingertips, Alison brings to the table an unbeatable combination of years of experience and an accessible writing style which addresses fashion's issues with admirable directness. An indispensable guide'.
Maurice Mullen, Head of Fashion & Luxury Goods, *Evening Standard*

'Provides a fresh, contemporary approach to the subject of fashion business, fusing both core academic theory and practical tips. This will be an invaluable addition to our course reading lists. A must-read for all budding fashion entrepreneurs.'
Alexandra Hill, Course Leader, Norwich University of the Arts

'Provides a thorough introduction to all aspects of fashion management while maintaining a clear strategic focus. Covering a wide range of topics, this book is filled with relevant examples and case studies from around the world and is written in an approachable and engaging style. Alison Lowe has managed to include a high level of critical analysis, making it appropriate for both undergraduate and postgraduate students. It's wonderful to see such an informative and inspiring book about current fashion management practice!'
Sennait Ghebreab, Programme Leader for Business BA Courses, Istituto Marangoni School of Fashion, London

'Alison Lowe has written a must-read primer for anyone considering fashion business and management. Packed with plenty of useful information and engaging yet relevant case studies, it is now on the essential reading list for all my undergraduate and graduate students. Read this book and learn from one of the best.'

Kent Le, Programme Leader for International Fashion Business, University of East London and Adjunct Professor, Business of Fashion, Fordham University, New York

'Gives unique insights into how to plan, scale and market successfully in the fashion industry. The book is clearly laid out and defines key terms for fashion branding, business, marketing and communication. It contains sections that illustrate pertinent and ethical implications of fashion, such as sustainability, fashion innovation and how newer digital business practices affect fashion. It is a crucial textbook for fashion studies and will be an important reference point for those working in fashion branding, fashion businesses and their related industries. I highly recommend this book.'

Ram Shergill, Editor in Chief, *The Protagonist Magazine*

Fashion Brand Management

Plan, scale and market
a successful fashion business

Alison Lowe

KoganPage

First published in Great Britain and the United States in 2023 by Kogan Page Limited

2nd Floor, 45 Gee Street
London
EC1V 3RS
United Kingdom

8 W 38th Street, Suite 902
New York, NY 10018
USA

4737/23 Ansari Road
Daryaganj
New Delhi 110002
India

www.koganpage.com

Kogan Page books are printed on paper from sustainable forests.

ISBNs
Hardback   978 1 3986 0902 0
Paperback   978 1 3986 0900 6
Ebook   978 1 3986 0901 3

British Library Cataloguing-in-Publication Data
A CIP record for this book is available from the British Library.

Library of Congress Cataloging-in-Publication Data
Names: Lowe, Alison, author.
Title: Fashion brand management : plan, scale and market a successful
    fashion business / Alison Lowe.
Description: 1 Edition. | New York, NY : Kogan Page Inc, 2023. | Includes
    bibliographical references and index.
Identifiers: LCCN 2022052630 (print) | LCCN 2022052631 (ebook) | ISBN
    9781398609006 (paperback) | ISBN 9781398609020 (hardback) | ISBN
    9781398609013 (ebook)
Subjects: LCSH: Fashion merchandising. | New products. | Branding
    (Marketing) | Strategic planning. | Customer relations. | Consumer
    behavior.
Classification: LCC HD9940.A2 L69 2023 (print) | LCC HD9940.A2 (ebook) |
    DDC 687.068/8–dc23/eng/20221103
LC record available at https://lccn.loc.gov/2022052630
LC ebook record available at https://lccn.loc.gov/2022052631

Typeset by Integra Software Services, Pondicherry
Print production managed by Jellyfish
Printed and bound by CPI Group (UK) Ltd, Croydon CR0 4YY

CONTENTS

ABOUT THE AUTHOR

Alison Lowe MBE has built a reputation over the past 20 years as one of the leading supporters of emerging fashion. She is passionate about supporting creative talent and preparing them for the challenges of balancing creativity and commerciality. Renowned for her practical, realistic approach to running a creative business, Alison acts as a consultant to brands across the globe from start-ups to established fashion businesses, supporting fashion brands, retailers, manufacturers and training providers.

As a serial entrepreneur, Alison has a natural talent for discovering a gap in the market and creating a business solution to meet the need, leading her to start several businesses including 'Chameleon', a creative recruitment agency, and 'Road Runners', an express courier business. Alison's move into fashion came from a freelance consultancy role with a fashion week platform, which resulted in her discovering that emerging fashion labels lacked support and advice in developing long-term, successful businesses. In 2003, she established Felicities, a specialist business incubator for start-up and emerging fashion and creative brands. Over the past 20 years the agency has worked with over 2,000 labels, supporting them in developing their brands and providing them with advice and opportunities to build their labels and introduce their businesses into new markets.

The agency had increasing interest from brands around the world who wanted support to build their businesses, however Felicities had limited capacity for the number of brands it could work with, as the in-depth approach meant that it needed to restrict the number of brands it could work with each year. In looking at ways to resolve this, Alison identified a new opportunity to offer support options to more brands and launched an online platform Start Your Own Fashion Label. This platform offers up-to-date industry information on subjects that brands need, such as how to contact buyers, talk to press, work with manufacturers and how to create a line sheet – to name a few. This information is presented in easy to understand, downloadable guides and templates that provide easy ways for start-up brands to implement the learning straightaway. Start Your Own Fashion Label also offers mentoring and membership options to both UK and international designers.

Alongside running her two businesses and consultancy roles with a range of brands in the UK and internationally, Alison also develops and teaches business courses for fashion universities around the world including London College of Fashion, University of the Arts London, Emlyon Business School and British School of Fashion. Alison is regularly invited to be a guest speaker at international conferences, fashion weeks, events and universities. She is a founding member of the Centre for Entrepreneurs, an ambassador for Retail Weeks Be Inspired programme, a fellow of the RSA (royal society for arts, manufactures and commerce), and on the judging panel of the Great British Entrepreneurs competition.

Alison has won numerous awards and honours, the highlight of which was being awarded an MBE for services to the fashion industry in HRH the Queen's Birthday Honours 2017. Alison was also nominated and awarded as one of the Maserati 100 in 2016. This award was created by the luxury car manufacturer to recognize 100 game-changing entrepreneurs who are disrupting the business world. The Maserati 100 is dedicated to celebrating the positive impact entrepreneurs have on the economy and society as a whole; Alison was named alongside dynamic entrepreneurs such as Richard Branson; Julie Deane from the Cambridge Satchel Company; Sir Charles Dunstone, founder of Carphone Warehouse; and Pret a Manger founders Sinclair Beecham and Julian Metcalfe.

Instagram: @alisonlowembe

LinkedIn and Facebook: Alison Lowe MBE

FOREWORD

When I initially met Alison Lowe two things stood out. First, she is a generous person who gives you her undivided attention, asking thought-provoking questions and creating a safe space in which to hold conversations, where the dispensing of knowledge was done with the goal of growth for all involved. Second, she knows the field of fashion business like the back of her hand.

Even better, after years of training and teaching, she is just as interested in learning and expanding her own understanding of the ever-evolving world of fashion as she is in sharing her expertise with others. Alison teaches not only with compassion, she also does it in a way that never alienates or makes those who turn to her feel less than, for not knowing what they don't know. In other words, she is a fashion industry life coach, and often a lifeline, for nascent designers who don't know where to start, brand builders looking to create a rock-solid foundation and individuals who just want to get a better grasp of this global community.

Over the past 20 years, the fashion industry has gone through some radical transformations. There has been the growing dominance of online commerce, the paradigm shift caused by the arrival of powerful social media platforms, and now the advent of the metaverse and Web3. All of this has shifted or made obsolete many of the old-school ways of doing business in fashion. Not to mention the new consumer mindset of millennials and zoomers who, unlike previous generations, are looking for much more out of their purchases. They want accountability, traceability, inclusivity and sustainability all incorporated into what they buy, where they shop and the brands they support.

Creating a flourishing fashion label today has become as much about a company's brand storytelling, environmental impact and DEI (diversity, equity and inclusion) as it is about the products they sell. And in a climate run rampant with cancel culture and ever-shortening attention spans, threading the needle of success has only become that much more difficult.

I have no doubt that in the coming years this book will be turned to and referenced over and over again by fashion students and experts alike – a touchstone in an industry with surprisingly few concrete guideposts to help give both a macro and micro insight into a world that is famous for putting on a happy facade and does everything it can to distract from what is going on behind the curtain.

To sum it all up, Alison is a positive force for good in an industry that can be brutal, unforgiving and difficult to navigate. She gives her students, and the readers of her books, the critical tools they need to map out a road to success in an ever-shifting creative industry that is also an ever-expanding billion-dollar global business. Having Alison in your corner from the start is the best first step anyone can take when they decide to take on fashion.

Jessica Michault
Deputy Editor, *Harper's Bazaar Arabia*

ACKNOWLEDGEMENTS

This book is based on research and many years of working with phenomenally talented people in the fashion industry who have inspired me to continually learn more about the industry and find ways to deal with the constant challenges. I want to thank all my industry colleagues, and the designers and brands who have always been open to my hundreds of questions, tolerated my demands to try things a different way, and trusted me to help them find new solutions to current challenges.

I have gathered research and consulted with many international fashion industry bodies and trade press to ensure information included is relevant and up-to-date, and I am thankful for the access to a wide range of sources of information that will be important for the future development of the industry and fashion brands.

I am really grateful to the purpose-driven brands and organizations who have agreed to be included as case studies in this book and thank them for sharing insights into their businesses. I selected each of them as they are inspirational brands who are pushing the fashion industry to do things differently and take greater consideration towards people and the planet.

I am extremely grateful to have been given the opportunity to write this book and thank Kogan Page and the editorial team for their faith in me to write an academic textbook. I want to say a special thank you to the extremely talented fashion creative Gabriela Wieckowska, who created all the graphics in this book.

Finally, I would like to acknowledge the support and love of my family, in particular my daughters Josie and Mollie, who have always been the motivation and inspiration to keep going, achieve more and try to be a role model they deserve. I must also add a final dedication to my father David Lowe, who whilst sadly no longer with us, would be immensely proud to see me complete a book with his own publishers Kogan Page.

Introduction

The changing reality of the fashion industry

LEARNING OBJECTIVES

After reading this chapter you should be able to:

- Understand the challenges the fashion industry has faced over the past two decades
- Explain the changing reality of the fashion industry
- Know why fashion brands have to consider new business models in order to survive
- Describe how fashion brands can work towards a visionary future

The fashion industry has always marched to its own beat, insisting on using its own business models rather than traditional management processes, and rigid schedules that the whole industry was compelled to adhere to. It has not though always been the dynamic, disruptive, glamorous and bold industry that it likes to proclaim. The global fashion industry has for decades adhered to a very prescriptive business model, with dutiful brands all following the same system and timings in making, showing and selling their collections. By following the same calendar, trends, business models and methods, many brands were putting themselves at a disadvantage economically and environmentally, as well as having limited competitive advantage due to doing things the same as everyone else. Even before the Covid-19 pandemic disrupted the whole world, the global industry was facing bleak concerns about the social and environmental impact of fashion. The fashion industry was broken, and brands needed to do things differently to survive in a dynamic and volatile environment.

The sector has been discussing the 'broken fashion industry' for decades (BBC, 2018), and whilst cracks have appeared throughout the industry, with unmissable clues everywhere that there is something wrong, many within the fashion world are still clinging to outdated business models and ways of working. The fashion industry is renowned for its smoke and mirrors approach, hiding behind a carefully engineered image, to only show the glamorous and successful side of the business that generates consumer interest and sales. However, brands need to face what is really happening and build their businesses with the knowledge and understanding of the new paradigm that is taking shape in the fashion industry. In an ever-changing, volatile market, the old fashion industry rules just don't work any more.

This book will address the challenges the industry needs to address, gain an understanding of the reality of the fashion industry, consider the advantages of new business models and practices, and investigate a future, more entrepreneurial approach to designing, producing, selling and marketing fashion.

A broken fashion industry

There are many areas of the fashion industry that have been declared as broken, including too much designer competition, overproduction, seasonal collections, changing consumer demand, climate change, environmental and social problems as well as macro-environmental challenges. As Josie Warden wrote in a blog post in 2019 for the RSA, 'the fashion industry is having an existential crisis' (Warden, 2019).

Behind the glamorous images that appear in the fashion magazines, the beautiful clothes hanging in the stores and the influencers inspiring us to purchase the latest new things, there have been wide-ranging discussions about the environmental and social harm the industry is causing. Newspaper headlines have called out child labour and poor working conditions, as well as the climate and environmental impacts of textile production, including depleting and poisoned water supplies, soil degradation and pollution. The Rana Plaza factory crash in 2013 brought the evidence of labour abuses to the eyes of the world, but still, as Warden (2019) declared, 'for a long time, fashion has been the darling – beautiful, seductive and always one step ahead – elegantly side-stepping the challenges about its less attractive side'.

There are many reasons that fashion brands have not changed the way they run their businesses for decades. For some, it is because they are still holding on to the concept that fashion is 'art' not business, therefore they don't need to consider successful business models used in other sectors, or that the larger established labels are part of huge corporations that can be inflexible or slow to pivot to new methods. For others, it could be fear of the unknown, their belief that the old system still works for them, or that they are working on the theory that if their sales are still strong why fix something that isn't broken. Part of the blame for newer brands following old business models can be due to outdated education and learning, with some academic courses or tutors, despite their best intentions, lacking up-to-date industry experience or knowledge of latest business changes.

Those looking to start a fashion brand would need to review all the broken systems in the fashion industry in order to understand the challenges and avoid the pitfalls that others are currently wallowing in.

Too many designers and brands

There is a saturated market of fashion design graduates all competing in a cut-throat jobs market to secure employment in design. Universities and colleges are filled with great talent but there are not enough jobs for the number of design students who graduate, and the issue is global. In a Business of Fashion article about fashion graduates, Sophie Soar (2018) quoted a survey by the Council of Fashion Designers of America (CFDA) of 23 US schools, which revealed that only 10 per cent of fashion design students were going into design jobs. In comparison to the number of students learning design, very few study the practical skills of pattern making and sewing skills, with factories all over the world struggling to recruit high-quality, technically trained staff to make fashion.

For fashion design students to succeed they need to stand out from the crowd – the industry is still seeking genius designers who have a unique design aesthetic, vision, construction or fresh concept. While previous graduate talents such as John Galliano and Alexander McQueen relied on their creative vision and instinct, most graduates today also need to come to the jobs market with a great understanding of the operational side of the industry. There has also always been a debate about whether fashion schools should prepare students for the 'real' commercial world or encourage them to push the boundaries of their creativity. Don-Alvin Adegeest (2015) considered this argument in an article for Fashion United, 'with saturated markets, overflowing fashion week calendars and store shelves piled to the hilt with fashion brands, it would be fair to say the world is no longer waiting for another designer'.

While there are not enough job vacancies to employ the number of fashion design graduates, there are also few opportunities for them to start their own fashion labels. The industry is already saturated with new brands that are all struggling to succeed. Designer Olivier Theyskens told Dezeen in 2015 that 'the fashion industry is unable to cope with the surplus of young designers starting their own labels'. He went on to explain how at New York fashion weeks the shows by young designers had barely one-third of their seats taken due to the over-offering of new brands that were all struggling to get noticed but failing to get the attention they need from the industry (Howarth, 2015).

There is fierce competition between the fashion brands that are already established, and getting attention and sales is harder than ever, particularly as so many of the fashion brands have the same or similar product offer. Differentiation is essential in business, and too many fashion labels just follow other more successful companies, resulting in a world full of mediocre fashion brands that fail to specialize in a new area. Today's consumer seeks brands that offer unique products, storytelling and experience, therefore fashion brands that want to succeed need to step out from the crowd.

Seasonal collections

It could be said in fashion that seasons are so last season! The subject of seasons has been a controversial topic for a long time, as many people in the industry challenge whether the concept is still relevant. For many brands and particularly the consumers, the seasonal model no longer makes sense. However, the season model has been so firmly embedded in the industry that a whole supply chain has lived in fear of stepping off the treadmill or missing a season.

The seasonal concept was developed in an era when customers needed appropriate clothing for different weather conditions, such as the necessity of warm clothing for the winter and lighter fabrics for summer. That concept has become less relevant as the modern world developed and the consumer became economically empowered with more disposable income, and clothing moved from being a necessity to fashion (Evans, 2022). Seasons in the fashion industry were a vehicle to compel consumers to buy more, by classifying clothing by set times of year, but customers no longer want or need to purchase seasonal clothing in this manner. Purchasing behaviours have been affected by climate change and the reality of residing and working in artificially heated or cooled buildings, thanks to high-tech air conditioning and heating systems. Consumers are also now global travellers who seek different clothing for varying climates at different times of year. Even in countries with clear seasonal changes, younger consumers rarely have separate summer and winter wardrobes any more, instead layering pieces in different weathers.

For fashion brands the seasonal concept has been a way of life, with every part of the industry – from trade shows, retail buying and design cycles to marketing – all rigidly following this same model instead of considering category nuances, supply chain logic or competitive advantage. Most brands were pulled into this seasonal web, forcing them to behave in ways that led to inefficient inventory planning, over-forecasting and overproduction (Evans, 2022).

The fashion week circus has been a major driver of the seasonal model system, forcing brands to create collections a season ahead to show to press and buyers. This system then became the DNA for retailers too, with the buyers placing seasonal orders from designers or manufacturers months in advance and then placing it in store at the same set time of year as their competitors. They would then hope that it would sell through at full price rather than sit for months, being ever more discounted until the new season collections arrive.

The consumer is eternally confused by this seasonal model, unsure why they are unable to purchase the designs that they have seen widely circulated images of online. If they see a product on the catwalk, they want it now. They also want to shop for garments for different climates at the time they need them. The customer no longer thinks about buying a product now to wear later! If it's hot they want a cotton shirt now; if it's cold they want a woollen top to wear immediately.

Whether it is looked at from the brand or the consumer perspective, the premise of seasons is obsolete, and fashion brands and retailers need to move on to newer, more efficient business models.

The end of the wholesale model

Fashion retail has been suffering monumental problems, struggling to adapt to changing consumer behaviours and the diminishing footfall into bricks-and-mortar stores. The business model of buying fashion products months in advance in mass quantities, managing the logistics to get the product on the shop floor at the right time, promoting the products and trying to sell them to a customer who can now access similar product from a myriad of places, is just not working any more.

As Jing Daily reported in 2020, 'Pressure on retailers to usurp its competitors has resulted in a macro-focus on brand exclusivity agreements, price sensitivities, implementation of luxury experiences, and leadership in reputation. The downside of this has resulted in a number of often unattainable requirements for brands that can make logistics and operations unworkable' (Davy, 2020). The relationships between buyers and brands have become untenable, as the stores pass the pain on to the brands as they move to a model where they take less risk and stock their shops in different ways. This means that the wholesale 'buying' process no longer exists for many brands, as stores take brands on a consignment or sale-or-return basis or want to place short orders that the brand must deliver in approximately three weeks. The short order or consignment model is a risky strategy for brands, as they would need to put the collection into production and hold it, in the hope that a short order or consignment is requested by a store. For start-up or emerging labels, the wholesale market terms are not feasible with their limited resources to produce and finance collections in advance. These labels are also less attractive to store buyers, as they seek brands with a good-sized customer base that they can drive into the store, and smaller brands usually don't have a significant database of their own consumers.

In a 2015 article on Business of Fashion, Doug Stephens, founder of Retail Prophet, argued that the 'future of retail is the end of wholesale'. He explained that with the stores struggling to compete with an expanding mosaic of online competitors, which can even include the brands they work with, it seems inevitable that retailers will have to define a new model, one better suited to the fragmented market they find themselves in (Stephens, 2015). For a brand, the wholesale model has become less attractive as the risk versus margin paradigm means that the direct-to-consumer model would reflect better on their bottom line.

Changing consumer demands

The fashion industry has been accused of becoming disconnected from reality due to having little or no understanding of today's customer. Consumer buying behaviours changed and the fashion industry faced growing disruption as the customer developed new priorities and desires. The customer was now in the driving seat, demanding that they want it all and they want it now. With more choice, more information, more access and greater expectations, the customer is looking for brands that offer more than product, they want a great shopping experience online and in-store, easy delivery and returns processes, greater transparency and sustainability, as well as a brand that connects with them through social media. A Mintel Designer Fashion UK report in 2021 advised luxury retailers that they would have to 'work hard on translating the in-store experience online to deliver the same level of staff expertise and focus on making digital experiences equally as high-end as those found in stores' (Mintel Store, 2021). Brands that were still using outdated methods, such as relying purely on wholesale, to sell fashion products started losing market share to brands that were being more disruptive and entrepreneurial in attracting the customer.

Customers no longer simply walk into a store and ask an assistant for help, they research, read reviews, conduct online price comparisons and look for the perfect items to match their personality (Chan, 2021). The consumer changed from looking just for product, to looking for experience, as they would rather 'do' something than 'buy' a possession. The effect of this is that consumers now spend more of their disposable money on experiences, or even buying food or drink, when they fail to find a great experience in a fashion retail environment. Customer experience is different to customer service, as explained by retail expert Neil Hamilton in an interview for Retail Insight Network, in that customer service focuses on a singular transaction between customer and brand, whereas customer experience encompasses the customer's entire journey across every touchpoint of the brand, in-store, online and on social media (Paige, 2020). Fashion brands needed to start putting the experience first in the customer journey. If the customer has a great experience, they will want to buy a product to remind themselves of the great time they had.

Environmental and social issues

Many parts of the industry have been ignorant of, or are simply avoiding, the impact that fashion is creating in our world and are not acknowledging that the way we make, use and throw away clothes is unsustainable. The statistics about fashion consumerism and disposal are horrendous, with millions of tonnes of clothes produced, worn and thrown away every year (MacArthur Foundation, 2022). In a House of Commons (2019) environmental audit, it was reported that textile production contributes more to climate change than international aviation and shipping combined, consumes lake-sized volumes of fresh water and creates chemical and plastic pollution. This audit also expressed concern that some of the biggest retailers produce in countries that have the lowest pay conditions, using child and forced labour with little trade union representation, as well as in areas that have weak environmental protection. Jack Hesketh in a feature on Fashions Finest questioned whether the fashion industry is really broken and discussed how aggressive consumerism has generated an industry that is already stretching natural resources and people to their limits: 'We now consume and dispose of clothing faster than ever before. We want what we see, and we want it for a price that's simply unsustainable. Behind the haze of branding and carefully curated narratives, there are products, and what really matters is how these products are sourced, manufactured and disposed of at the end of life' (Hesketh, 2022).

> The equivalent of a rubbish truck load of clothes is incinerated or buried in landfill every second of every day (Business of Fashion and McKinsey & Company, 2022).

Adding to the issues of sustainability is the internationally documented problem of overproduction in the fashion industry. Many fashion brands, both mass market and luxury powerhouses, have reportedly disposed of millions of pounds' worth of fashion product by either burning it or sending it to landfill, and both options cause huge environmental damage. One well-reported incident in 2017 was when Burberry incinerated unsold clothes, accessories and perfume worth £28.6 million in order to protect its brand, choosing to destroy unwanted items to prevent them being stolen or sold cheaply through outlets. A BBC feature on the incident reported that while Burberry declared that the energy generated from burning its products was captured, making it environmentally friendly, they received considerable backlash for the lack of respect for their own products as well as the hard work of their team and natural resources that were used to make them (BBC News, 2018). The growing amount of overstock points to poor management, with brands choosing to incinerate perfectly good products rather than slow down their production. For the lower end of the market, some fast-fashion brands find that the costs of reprocessing returns of their lowest price products are not realistic, so rather than make them available again for sale they dispose of them by incineration or sending to landfill. In a Vogue India article Emily Chan (2020a) talked about the broken fast-fashion system and how 'fast-fashion brands must also drastically rethink their business models, which are reliant on selling mass volumes of clothes at low prices. An estimated 150 billion garments are now produced annually, while around 87 per cent of the material used for clothing production ends up being landfilled or incinerated'.

Overproduction occurs because of poor seasonal buying decisions, lack of understanding of the customer, as well as brands being forced by manufacturers to produce higher order quantities to reach the price point they feel the market will accept. Outrage started to grow, as more overproduction scandals became public knowledge and fashion brands started facing mounting pressure from both consumers and the industry to clean up their acts.

Alongside the issues of overproduction and the disposal methods of unsold inventory, there have been numerous concerns with sustainability in the fashion industry, with the huge environmental costs of producing clothes at its very core. Fast fashion is perceived to be a fundamental cause of many of the sustainability problems in the industry, due to the consumer's constant desire for new and different; however, all fashion brands at all levels cause damage to the environment. Campaigning body Fashion Revolution is concerned that the mainstream fashion industry is built upon the exploitation of labour and natural resources: 'Wealth and power are concentrated in the hands of a few, and growth and profit are rewarded above all else. Big brands and retailers produce too much too fast and manipulate us into a toxic cycle of overconsumption. Meanwhile, the majority of people that make our clothes are not paid enough to meet their basic needs, and already feel the impacts of the climate crisis – which the fashion industry fuels' (Fashion Revolution, 2022).

The environmental impact from the processes of making fashion include depleting water sources due to the extreme levels of water needed to produce clothes, as well as water pollution in countries where garments are produced, leading to poisonous rivers in places like Bangladesh and Indonesia. Toxic substances, such as lead and mercury from the dyeing process, pollute the water, which is harmful to both aquatic and human life. Fashion is also one of the major contributors of plastic microfibres entering our oceans (MacArthur Foundation, 2022). Synthetic garments release microfibres every time clothes are washed, which introduces plastic into our food chain. Heavy chemicals are used in cotton farming as well as during fabric production, with dyeing and bleaching not only adding to water pollution but also soil degradation and deforestation coming from the use of wood-based fibres such as rayon. On top of this, the fashion industry accounts for a large percentage of global carbon emissions due to the amount of energy used in the production and transporting of clothing. In an article in the *New Stateman*, Tansey Hoskins (2014) described how 'The glossy idea of "fashion" hides the labour of millions of deeply exploited labourers. It hides the terrifying environmental impact of fashion, and the sexism, racism and alienation enshrined in the industry'.

Many brands declare they are making great strides to become more sustainable, in reality they are simply 'greenwashing' as a marketing approach to sell more clothes.

In *Vogue* in 2020, Emily Chan discussed the issue of greenwashing, a phrase coined in 1986 by environmentalist Jay Westervelt, who declared that greenwashing – or 'green sheen' – is when a company uses misleading or false claims to suggest it is doing more for the environment than it actually is (Chan, 2020b). In the fashion industry many words have been thrown around including eco-fashion, sustainability, green fashion, environmentally conscious fashion, but the buzzwords often belied the reality. Fashions Finest declared that the problem lies with the fashion industry pulling the wool over our eyes, 'dressing up' products to make us believe that all is fair and humane, while falling short on supply chain transparency, fabric choice, quality, human rights and recycling (Hesketh, 2022).

Fashion works at an incredibly fast pace and the impact of that is often felt in the health and wellbeing of people working in the industry. Along with the unethical labour practices and lack of fair wages in many areas of the industry, there is also the high level of stress that fashion professionals are under to meet demanding deadlines, discover the next trend and work the long anti-social hours needed to deliver the next collection. Mental health issues have risen from the constant pressure to deliver creativity, innovation and a strong bottom line. There is a well-used phrase in the fashion industry that you are only as good as your last collection. When John Galliano had his infamous breakdown in 2011, he was overseeing 32 collections a year and a show every four weeks (Gorton, 2015). It is this kind of working environment that cultivates unhealthy working practices among creatives.

Whichever way you turned, the reality was that the fashion industry needed to start acting more responsibly and start taking positive steps to clean up its act, moving beyond talking about sustainability to meeting the customer demand to act more ethically and transparently.

The impact of the global Covid-19 pandemic

While the fashion industry was starting to debate how to address its ethical and sustainability issues, react to a changing consumer demand and respond to an ever-changing macro-environment, no one could have predicted that the world would face one of the greatest health crises in modern history. The Covid-19 pandemic in 2020 made the world stop and, as Tamsin Blanchard (2020) wrote in the *Guardian*, 'While sections of the fashion industry already knew they could not continue on their current trajectory, it was inconceivable that brands could be forced to slow down, let alone stop production altogether'. Around the world every fashion brand had to deal with international lockdowns, supply chain issues and logistical nightmares. This unprecedented interruption to business caught the industry out, with seasonal collections in various states of disarray as access to international sourcing and manufacturing was temporarily halted, and physical bricks-and-mortar stores shut down, with huge amounts of seasonal product left on the shop floor. The fashion industry was thrown into panic and, as Devieka Gautam (2020) rightly stated in The Quint, 'the fashion industry isn't built for agility, and the pandemic proved it'. While some brands turned their production lines to making face masks, surgical gowns and hand sanitizers, others found themselves having to furlough their staff and hibernate their businesses until 'normal' life resumed. For some factories though, as orders dried up, their low-paid workers suddenly found themselves cast out with no notice or financial support. Millions of garment workers suffered because of the pandemic, with the Bangladesh Garment Manufacturers and Exporters Association declaring that more than $3.18 billion worth of orders were cancelled or suspended in Bangladesh alone (BGMEA, 2022).

Global shutdowns resulted in a 'work from home' scenario that meant consumers were spending more time online than ever before and this accelerated the shift to a digital world. Brands rushed to improve their online presence as consumers turned to e-commerce not only to shop but seek experiences to engage with. Some brands reacted quickly to the changing market, pivoting to meet new customer demands, while others waited for 'life to return to normal', resulting in many brands not surviving the pandemic. During this time, as well as dressing differently for life online, the consumer became community focused, knowledgeable and enquiring, taking more time to research and read about brands they purchased from, as well as seeking brands that offered them empathy, connection and engagement rather than just selling them products.

The Covid-19 pandemic did not totally break fashion, but it did expose the challenges of a broken industry and highlighted that new business models were needed to build a more sustainable future.

The new reality

There is a new reality in the fashion industry, and the fashion rulebook has been ripped apart and thrown away. The new dawn for the industry means that fashion labels do not need to adhere to the rules of the past, they can now build the brand and follow a business model that is best for their label, rather than doing the same thing as everyone else.

The pandemic gave the industry some much needed time to slow down and re-evaluate industry practices, and for many fashion brands it was time out to consider new business models, streamline their organizations and take bold steps forward towards a new, more sustainable future. Astute brands took the opportunity to consider where they stood in the market, what their point of difference and purpose was, and how they could run their businesses with more focus on the triple bottom line of people, profits and the planet. It also accelerated innovation, digital and sustainability trends, and while some business leaders felt that these might be fleeting changes,

PWC's Global Consumer Insights Pulse Survey, conducted in March 2021, revealed that the changes were sticking, signifying a historic and dramatic shift in consumer behaviour. The research also showed the continuous growth of online shopping and an increasing sensitivity to the environmental impact of purchases (PWC, 2021).

There will, however, be a period of transition, as the industry recovers and adapts. The fallout from the pandemic will continue for a while as brands recuperate and deal with the challenges in the supply chain, as well as the huge amount of out-of-date, unsold product from their closed stores. The market environment will remain complex for the foreseeable future, with logistical bottlenecks, manufacturing delays, high shipping costs, material shortages and increasing costs. 'Fashion as a system is in a state of flux right now', says Giorgio Armani in a *Vogue* article in 2020, 'But this is a unique opportunity to fix what was wrong – which is a lot – and create something new, more meaningful' (Thomas, 2020). It is important that the surviving brands keep moving forward with new business models and not slip back into old habits. Sociologist Werner Sombart declares that the industry needs new economic models that better reflect the relationship humans have with the natural world, and warns that we must make sure these ideas are not watered down and interpreted as yet more opportunities to tweak an existing system. He insists that fashion brands should fully explore the potential of circular economy models as it is time for a change, not more tweaks (Warden, 2019).

Popular business models that are emerging include 'see now buy now' shows, or a move away from the traditional fashion calendar to copy the 'drop' model, which is successfully used by streetwear labels to release smaller and more frequent collections that create rarity value and elevate anticipation. Many brands supported an open letter to the industry from Dries Van Noten calling for a realignment of the delivery schedule to end or delay price markdowns, as well as a reconfiguration of the supply chain into something more respectful towards humanity and the planet (Thomas, 2020). It is now time to see action on these issues and for brands to take an entrepreneurial approach, building unique businesses with points of difference and competitive advantage in the products they create, the way they sell their collections or engage with their customers. 'It will be increasingly important to adopt more agile ways of working and depart from the traditional operating model' (Amed et al, 2019). In an overpopulated market, the brand must stand out with a point of difference, which can come from a unique feature, product, story, greater transparency in the supply chain, unique brand experience or more importantly a sense of purpose and meaning that is authentic and connects and engages with the consumer.

The new reality of the fashion industry comes from brands shaking off the negative elements of the past and working together to build a new positive system, with successful fashion brands putting the customer, innovation, technology and ethical issues at the heart of everything they do.

A visionary future

The hope for the future is that there will be a rebirth of fashion, with an industry that puts people and the planet if not ahead, then alongside profit. Though there will be some changes, it will take a major cultural as well as economic change to make a drastic difference. Therefore, fashion needs industry leaders to make bold moves towards circular business models, take action on environmental and social priorities, and focus on greater diversity, equality and inclusion across the industry (Luxury Communications Council, 2020).

There is already evidence of brands taking visionary steps forward with the adoption of new creative and commercial technologies and innovation including the development of non-fungible tokens (NFTs), avatars and computer-generated imagery, digital collections and showcasing. There is also more of a push towards blockchain technology giving products digital passports that will increase transparency and authenticity as well as add value.

Fashion brands must remain vigilant and keep their businesses agile to have the flexibility to respond to an ever-shifting macro-environment and build strategies to deal with future challenges and adapt to changing consumer demand. The industry also has a responsibility to educate and lead customer behaviours away from constant consumption towards new rent, repair and recycle options.

A visionary brand leader will constantly look at the bigger picture, seeking new ways to push the company forward, identifying new and innovative products and processes that meet the consumer's needs. The new ways forward include the elements below, which will also be discussed in future chapters.

The end of ownership

Fashion product has a changing lifespan as new business models evolve, with more brands developing pre-owned, rental, circular, repair and upcycle models. Brands are tapping into these markets as opportunities to connect with new customers, as there is a new generation of consumers who care less about what they own and more about what they do. The future may result in consumers moving away from permanently owning their clothing.

Increasing awareness

As younger generations of consumers have an increasing awareness of social and environmental causes, they seek fashion labels that are more purpose-driven, have stronger opinions and greater social and environmental brand values.

Speed to consumer

The consumer will become more demanding and impatient to immediately purchase and receive the products they discover. Brands will need to increase their speed to market, offering shorter lead times and ensuring any products that are advertised or promoted are immediately available. Creating small batch product drops and achieving just-in-time production can improve the speed to consumer.

Authenticity and transparency

Brands will need to build even greater consumer trust by sharing information and having high-level brand transparency around price, quality, and production. Brands will need to focus on communicating their authenticity to build more genuine connections with the consumer rather than just promoting products.

Omnichannel

Consumers will demand a more seamless consumer experience across all the brand's channels. Consumers will switch between in-store and online, from web to mobile, desktop to tablet, store to web. They will need brands to develop the right experience at the right time and the brands need to understand and leverage the omnichannel opportunities. An effective omnichannel strategy improves customer experience and can encourage them back to the bricks-and-mortar store, as well as helping a brand increase efficiency and revenue and reduce costs. The shift to online shopping will continue, with many workers expected to continue working from home at least some of the time, and as identified in the PWC last Pulse survey, the at-home cohort are significantly less likely to shop in physical stores than the cohort working away from home, so online shopping will continue to rapidly gain ground on in-store shopping (PWC, 2021).

Technology

Visionary brands will keep up-to-date with changing technology and the new opportunities it offers. This will include new social media channels, apps, in-store technology, blockchain and RFID (radio frequency identification) as well as smart fabrics and wearable technology. Artificial intelligence will help brands use data for predictive forecasting, planning and merchandising, as well as offer the consumer better browsing and personalization. Augmented reality will advance from the basic QR code to wider image or facial recognition to offer an enhanced customer experience and opportunities.

Summary

The fashion industry has some huge historic challenges to overcome as well as dealing with future market volatility, uncertainty, continuing geopolitical conflicts and shifts in the global economy. The reality of the fashion industry with all its nuances, internal processes and dirty secrets will need to be challenged and dealt with, as it cannot continue with old business models or return to the 'normal' patterns of the past. The visionary future will involve the industry building new systems and models that encourage genuine, authentic businesses with new business models, goals, values and ethics.

Key terms

augmented reality	fast fashion	retail
authenticity	greenwashing	saturated market
blockchain	landfill	seasonal collections
buyer	macro-environment	see now buy now
consignment	NFT – non-fungible token	supply chain
consumer		sustainability
differentiation	omnichannel	transparency
drop model	overproduction	wholesale

Chapter review questions

- Explain the challenges the fashion industry has been struggling with.
- Give examples of the new areas of development in the fashion industry.
- Describe some of the reasons why the fashion industry needs to be more sustainable and ethical.

Activity

Find an example of a fashion brand that has changed its business model away from seasonal collections to the drop model.

References

Adegeest, D (2015) Should fashion schools focus on creativity or business?, *Fashion United*, https://fashionunited.com/news/fashion/should-fashion-schools-focus-on-creativity-or-business/201508267970 (archived at https://perma.cc/HRV8-6UZM)

Amed, I, Beltrami, M, Berg, A, Hedrich, S and Rolkens, F (2019) Self-disruption in the fashion industry, *McKinsey.com*, www.mckinsey.com/industries/retail/our-insights/self-disruption-in-the-fashion-industry (archived at https://perma.cc/X2MT-URQK)

BBC (2018) Can the 'broken' fashion industry be fixed?, *BBC News*, www.bbc.co.uk/news/business-46347337.amp (archived at https://perma.cc/3QY3-UVDY)

BBC News (2018) Burberry burns bags, clothes and perfume worth millions, *BBC News*, www.bbc.co.uk/news/business-44885983 (archived at https://perma.cc/CS8T-86SS)

BGMEA.com.bd (2022) www.bgmea.com.bd/ (archived at https://perma.cc/RZ9S-3PST)

Blanchard, T (2020) 'Put Earth first': can a greener, fairer fashion industry emerge from crisis, *Guardian*, www.theguardian.com/fashion/2020/mar/27/put-earth-first-can-a-greener-fairer-fashion-industry-emerge-from-crisis (archived at https://perma.cc/8CYQ-7NVX)

Business of Fashion and McKinsey & Company (2022) The State of Fashion 2022

Chan, E (2020a) The fast-fashion system is broken – so what happens next?, Vogue India, www.vogue.in/fashion/content/the-fast-fashion-system-is-broken-so-what-happens-next (archived at https://perma.cc/4CVJ-WJBN)

Chan, E (2020b) 6 ways to be greenwashing vigilant, *British Vogue*, www.vogue.co.uk/news/article/greenwashing-in-fashion (archived at https://perma.cc/B8UC-CUDM)

Chan, J (2021) Consumer insights for fashion industry, [Blog] *Linkfluence*, www.linkfluence.com/blog/consumer-insights-for-fashion-industry (archived at https://perma.cc/2XDK-VL68)

Davy, I (2020) Is this the end of wholesale?, *Jing Daily*, https://jingdaily.com/is-this-the-end-of-wholesale/ (archived at https://perma.cc/GM39-3DMN)

Evans, S (2022) Are seasons relevant in fashion anymore, *ClothesOneDay.com*, www.clothesoneday.com/are-seasons-relevant-in-fashion-anymore (archived at https://perma.cc/FH5K-37AM)

Fashion Revolution (2022) FRW 2022, www.fashionrevolution.org/ (archived at https://perma.cc/Y2BK-UYZL)

Gautam, D (2020) Covid didn't break fashion industry – it exposed a broken system, *The Quint*, www.thequint.com/voices/opinion/fashion-industry-malpractices-broken-system-environmental-damage-wastage-covid-pandemic-impact-learnings#read-more (archived at https://perma.cc/CX5M-GEWS)

Gorton, T (2015) Galliano speaks out about alcoholism, addiction and recovery, *Dazed Digital*, www.dazeddigital.com/fashion/article/26739/1/galliano-speaks-out-about-alcoholism-addiction-and-recovery (archived at https://perma.cc/FB3N-2N38)

Hesketh, J (2022) Is the fashion industry really broken?, *Fashionsfinest.com*, www.fashionsfinest.com/fashion/item/6408-is-the-fashion-industry-really-broken (archived at https://perma.cc/8D4L-KJLT)

Hoskins, T (2014) 'Fashion' is just an excuse for the rich to exploit the poor, *New Statesman*, www.newstatesman.com/culture/2014/05/fashion-just-excuse-rich-exploit-poor (archived at https://perma.cc/37EL-LB6V)

House of Commons (2019) Fixing fashion: clothing consumption and sustainability, House of Commons Environmental Audit Committee

Howarth, D (2015) The fashion industry is saturated, *Dezeen*, www.dezeen.com/2015/01/30/olivier-theyskens-interview-fashion-industry-saturated-seoul-design-week-2014/ (archived at https://perma.cc/UK9P-KGEM)

Luxury Communications Council (2020) Why luxury brands aren't giving up on fashion month, www.luxurycommunicationscouncil.com/why-luxury-brands-arent-giving-up-on-fashion-month/ (archived at https://perma.cc/NE3Z-AZVD)

MacArthur Foundation, E (2022) Fashion and the circular economy, *Ellenmacarthurfoundation.org*, https://ellenmacarthurfoundation.org/topics/fashion/overview (archived at https://perma.cc/M93U-UECB)

Mintel Store (2021) Designer fashion – UK – 2021: consumer market research report, *Mintel*, https://store.mintel.com/report/uk-designer-fashion-market-report (archived at https://perma.cc/2G8V-PKY7)

Paige, J (2020) Improving customer service and experience: Q&A with Neil Hammerton, *Retail Insight Network*, www.retail-insight-network.com/analysis/improving-customer-service-and-experience-qa-with-neil-hammerton/ (archived at https://perma.cc/FWK6-KYRM)

PWC (2021) The global consumer: changed for good, www.pwc.com/gx/en/consumer-markets/consumer-insights-survey/2021/gcis-june-2021.pdf (archived at https://perma.cc/5VQR-ZE8W)

Soar, S (2018) The fashion school graduates: where are they now?, *The Business of Fashion*, www.businessoffashion.com/articles/news-analysis/the-fashion-school-graduates-where-are-they-now/ (archived at https://perma.cc/M9FA-8EBU)

Stephens, D (2015) The future of retail is the end of wholesale, *The Business of Fashion*, www.businessoffashion.com/opinions/retail/future-retail-end-wholesale/ (archived at https://perma.cc/C3UX-8KJ5)

Thomas, D (2020) What will it really take to fix fashion?, *British Vogue*, www.vogue.co.uk/fashion/article/fashion-after-coronavirus (archived at https://perma.cc/9UEJ-UYJE)

Warden, J (2019) Fashion is broken: where can it go from here? *RSA*, www.thersa.org/blog/2019/09/fashion-is-broken-where-can-it-go-from-here (archived at https://perma.cc/PM34-34GA)

Putting the customer first

1

LEARNING OBJECTIVES

After reading this chapter you should be able to:

- Explain why it is important to put the customer first
- Understand the process of consumer segmentation
- Discuss changing consumer behaviours
- Create detailed consumer profiles for specific customer groups

Introduction

Many fashion brands make the mistake of running their businesses and producing collections without up-to-date, in-depth research and information on who their customer is, what they need, want or care about. It is only when the brand discovers that sales are non-existent that they panic and realize the importance of understanding the customer. This situation happens for fashion brands of all sizes whether they are a start-up or an established label.

Start-up fashion brands often don't know who their customer is due to the designer coming from a fashion school that encourages pushing the boundaries of design without consideration of commerciality. Some fashion schools advise design students to be as creative as possible, without considering the customer, competitors or the realities of trying to sell their creations. This attitude sets up designers for failure and can cause conflict between a brand and wholesale store buyers, who define start-up designers as hopeless idealists. For the designer who wants to focus on the shape, construction and aesthetic of their design they can feel that the buyers lack imagination, creativity and are only interested in profit. Both points of view are true in some ways. Designers are often misled into thinking that if they create extreme designs that get attention from the press, then this will lead the customer to wanting their brand more than other labels. However, the stores and customers want wearable garments at the right prices, not art pieces.

For more established brands, their lack of understanding of customers is due to losing connection with them, failing to research changes in the market or failing to anticipate changing consumer behaviours and needs. These brands rely on assumptions rather than fact. Consumers are no longer tolerant of brands that make no attempt to understand them, and with access to thousands of brands around the world they can easily take their business elsewhere. This lack of understanding can mean brands don't pay enough attention to representation, diversity and inclusion, which leads to a disconnect with today's consumer.

An outstanding talent for design and fabulous products is a great start, but to turn passion into a business means a brand has to learn how to either persuade the customer to buy their designs or adapt their design philosophy to meet the customer's needs. Either way, every brand must understand who the customer is and what they want.

In many books the customer is included in the general marketing section or comes after the design and manufacturing processes. However, the subject is too important to lose within a general marketing chapter. There is no business without a customer, therefore in this book the chapter comes early as the customer must always come first.

This chapter will discuss the methods to research and identify the customer, look at segmentation, changing consumer trends and buying behaviours. The knowledge gained in this chapter will inform the rest of the development and management of a brand, including product design, sales, marketing, branding and promotion.

Consumer behaviours

Consumer behaviour is the study of how individual customers buy and use products and services to satisfy their needs and wants. The process of identifying consumer behaviours involves investigating their actions and why they behave in certain ways, such as why they buy a particular product, how often they buy fashion products and where they buy them. Consumer behaviour is a process that starts with a desire or recognition of a problem, research for solutions, evaluation of alternatives before taking action to purchase, then evaluation of decision. All customers do not behave in the same way through this process – they will respond according to their nature, lifestyle or cultural factors (Chand, n.d.a).

> The success of a fashion business relies on its ability to understand consumer needs and offer merchandise that will satisfy those needs.

Consumer behaviours change over time and new behaviours, attitudes and opinions form the basis of new consumer trends. These are different to fashion trends, which focus on seasonal products, colours and fabrics. Consumer trends can be more abstract, relating to underlying values or opinions that drive customers to specific products or services, such as health, materialism, sustainability (Solomon, n.d.). Consumer trend forecasting is big business, as brands seek to be innovative and adapt to new business opportunities.

Many of the changes happening in the fashion industry have arisen due to the changing buying behaviours of consumers. Today's customer has access to a global market at the click of a button. They have access to more information than ever before about products and brands, and they can purchase product in numerous ways. This has led to a change in the relationship between brands and consumers, with the customer having much more control over what they want and when they want it.

Knowledge of consumer behaviour and trends enables a brand to make the right business decisions in every part of the brand, including product, packaging, manufacturing, pricing, brand positioning and promotion. A brand that understands what motivates a consumer to buy can then create the right product, present it in a way that appeals to the customer's motivations and ensures they buy their product not the competitor's.

Psychology of fashion

The starting point for looking at consumers is to acknowledge the importance psychology plays in how and why they behave in certain ways. Psychology is the scientific study of influence of thoughts, beliefs, values, feelings and perceptions, which each affect how consumers select, purchase, experience and use fashion. Fashion brands need to consider psychology as it is based on evidence not assumptions and is essential for brands that want to get inside the mind of their consumers and understand how emotional triggers can affect sales and customer loyalty.

The psychology of fashion changes over time, as identified by Kodžoman: 'In early civilizations, the key purpose of clothing was to keep us warm and relatively dry. In the 21st century we should be aware that protection is only one function of clothing (along with identification, modesty, status and adornment). This means that clothing allows people to be recognized as members of a specific group; it covers the body in a proper way; shows position or rank within a group; and it helps people express their uniqueness and creativity' (Kodžoman, 2019).

Clothing heavily influences the impressions others have of us, leading them to make judgements about who we are from what we wear. Damhorst (1990) states that 'dress is a systematic means of transmission of information about the wearer'. Clothing therefore is a powerful communication tool, but judgements may not be based on fact, or even be a conscious decision, they are usually an automatic snap judgement based on past experiences, education or familial upbringing. Clothing also affects the wearer's own self-perception and feelings of self-worth. It is widely understood that what we wear affects us psychologically, affecting our mood and feelings of self-worth. Adam and Galinsky (2012) coined the phrase 'enclothed cognition' to describe the influence that clothes have on the wearer's psychological processes, through two factors – the symbolic meaning of the clothes and the physical experience of wearing them.

Brands need to consider why people buy fashion and how psychological facts can inform the decisions customers make when buying fashion products, such as dressing to impress a potential boss, a potential partner or to wow their friends. There can be conscious and subconscious psychological factors and emotional triggers that draw customers to products, such as self-esteem, satisfaction or power. Psychological factors also incorporate emotional processing, and a lot of fashion is bought on an emotional basis triggered by the five senses. Brands and stores that incorporate experiential retailing look at how they can appeal to all the senses by creating immersive experiences that generate emotional responses in their customers. A customer may think they favour a brand because of the quality or price, but it is more likely that it is their emotional response, how they 'feel' about the brand, that has a greater influence.

The subject of psychology is revisited in the section on neuromarketing, which is a process of promoting a brand based on the psychological traits of a target audience.

The changing consumer

The past decade has brought unprecedented change around the world through a combination of social, economic, political and public health crises occurring simultaneously. Times of crisis and uncertainty have a significant impact on us as individuals and as consumers. Consumers change when the environment around them evolves, resulting in economic constraints such as a rise in living costs, healthcare or education expenses, or due to new competitive options available through technology. The modern consumer is a construct of growing economic pressure and increasing competitive options, they are more capricious, less loyal, have less time but are more conscientious, they shy away from stores and prefer experiences over products (Lobaugh, Stephens and Simpson, 2019).

There has been a lot of research into how the consumer has changed during and post-pandemic and all results show that it is more important than ever to understand what the consumer will want to buy in the short-, mid- and long-term. WGSN (2022) identified that fear was an overwhelming sentiment affecting purchasing behaviour: 'A quick glance at a daily news feed (political unrest, environmental crises, fluctuating economies and, most recently, the global pandemic) and it's little surprise that fear is on the rise globally'. Market intelligence agency Mintel investigated the future global consumer and found that consumers were less trusting than ever, and their expectations of brands were evolving, leading to their need to see more transparency and progress in ethical initiatives (Mintel, 2022). In agreement with this research PWC's June 2021 Global Consumer Insights Pulse Survey agrees that consumers are expressing increased interest in sustainability. However, their data also shows that although consumers are saying they are eco-friendly, there are still many who say they are not. Their research indicates that Generation Z might be mostly aspirational about eco-friendly behaviours; their ideals often do not translate into spending (PWC, 2021). A Deloitte survey identified that brands who want to stand out and connect with future customers need to recognize the diversity of their consumer base, by race, ethnicity, LGBTQ status or differences in ability, so that the brand can authentically reflect a range of backgrounds and experiences in their organization, messaging and product development (Brodzik, 2020).

Many of the changes that occurred during the Covid-19 pandemic – including greater use of social media to discover and shop for fashion – are sticking, which signifies a historic and dramatic shift in consumer behaviour. McKinsey and Company research identified that 74 per cent of consumers say they are now more influenced to shop via social media than they were before the pandemic, and 70 per cent cite clothing as one of the product categories they shop for most on social media (McKinsey & Company, 2022). Alongside being more digital and eco-conscious, consumers are also more price-oriented, as well as focused on health, wellness, inclusivity and experiences. Customer experience expert Dan Gingiss advises that companies need to realize that they are no longer competing against the brand that sells similar products, they are competing with every other experience a customer has (Afshar, n.d.).

Consumer motivations

It can be difficult to identify what motivates consumers today, but it is known that as individuals we have conscious and unconscious desires and needs that make us choose or buy products. Maslow's hierarchy of needs framework is often used to explore motivations with brands trying to meet all the consumer's physiological, safety, social and esteem needs (Positive Psychology, 2019). There are other motivations that have also been identified (UKEssays, 2018) that make customers buy fashion, including:

- **Getting a bargain:** Today the high street is renowned for having constant sales, which has resulted in a generation of bargain hunters. Consumers are aware that the brands and stores will have sales and discounts at the end of the season, if not continually, so there is no reason to pay full price. These consumers are motivated to track products, seek discounts and follow the sales.

- **Standing out from the crowd:** Some customers want to create unique looks that express their personality. They will seek statement pieces or latest trend looks that they can style in their own way. This customer is an innovator, wanting to buy fashion pieces before they become widely available or get copied by fast-fashion brands.

- **Fitting in and belonging:** Many customers use fashion as a way of fitting in and belonging to a peer group. They are less confident in their ability to style their own looks, so seek guidance from the brand, peers and media to advise them how to put an outfit together. Peer pressure in dressing happens at all life stages, whether it is a child wanting to wear the same trainers as their friends, or the city worker who chooses to wear the same suit brand as his or her colleagues.

- **Trying to avoid clothes shopping:** Some customers don't enjoy clothes shopping so instead choose a 'uniform' such as jeans and t-shirts, which they can easily and quickly purchase and replace. They will choose to shop in stores that offer a consistent style or shopping experience, such as John Lewis, Next or Gap.

- **Looking like a celebrity:** For young females, one of the biggest drivers for fashion sales over the past decades has been celebrity. Many brands take advantage of the power that celebrities and influencers have over young consumers by collaborating with celebrities on campaigns. Young consumers want to buy fashion pieces that they feel will make them look like their favourite influencer or celebrity. The influence of celebrity has less impact on a mature consumer.

For all types of fashion product, three core motives have been identified as reasons that make consumers act and react in a particular way when purchasing (Chand, n.d.b). These product buying motives are:

- *Rational*: A rational motive is when the customer considers factors such as price, care, serviceability, practicality and warranties when making a purchase. If the customer has limited money, then they are likely to be more rational in their purchasing behaviour. They will ensure that they are spending their money wisely and either getting something at a good price or garments that will last well.

- *Emotional*: Fashion purchases are often emotionally motivated for female consumers. The customer seeks products that they feel will fulfil their emotional need for prestige, status, romance and social acceptance. The process of promoting fashion uses emotional triggers that draw the consumer into the brand's lifestyle. This is managed through stunning aspirational imagery, using celebrities in their campaigns or creating an inspirational in-store display.

- *Patronage*: Patronage motives relate to brand loyalty. A customer chooses to return to a particular retailer or store because they believe the company will offer them the best experience, price, customer service, personal shopping availability, convenience and product assortment. The more of these features a retailer or brand offers, the more likely it is that shoppers will return to the business in the future.

Future consumer trends

While it has been acknowledged that the consumer has changed considerably, the changes are still ongoing and it is necessary that brands continue to monitor, research and adapt to future trends. Research agencies such as Mintel have already predicted future global consumer trends in numerous reports, including identifying seven key drivers of consumer behaviour for the future: wellbeing, rights, value, identity, experience, surroundings and technology (Mintel, 2022).

Having reviewed research into consumer behaviours from a range of consumer insight sources, I developed a framework for fashion brands to easily take into consideration what consumers now seek from a fashion brand. The PACE framework for consumer expectations captures their demands under four headings of protection, acceptance, connection and engagement, as detailed in Figure 1.1.

Protection

Consumers now look for brands that take responsibility in protecting the planet, people, animals as well as the consumers themselves. These consumers actively seek brands that have socially and environmentally responsible practices in their supply chain so that they produce their product sustainably and ethically. Fashion Revolution's 2020 consumer survey evidenced that consumers are calling on fashion brands and governments to ensure transparency for human rights and the environment along the supply chain (Fashion Revolution, 2020).

The Fashion Revolution consumer survey also identified that people want to buy clothes made without harming the environment, animals, workers or consumers. Survey respondents said it was important that clothing is produced without using harmful chemicals, and one out of three people said it is important to buy clothing

Figure 1.1   PACE model

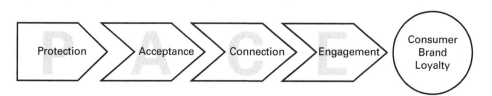

made by workers paid a fair living wage. From the 5,000 people across Europe surveyed, 29 per cent want to buy clothes made without harming animals and 45 per cent said it was important that clothing is made without child labour, while most people think it is important that fashion brands have ethical (72 per cent) and sustainability (80 per cent) certifications (Fashion Revolution, 2020).

Fashion's impact on the environment is rising in the public's consciousness with social justice and human rights issues gaining traction, and demands are increasing for the industry as a whole to improve its sustainability credentials. While public awareness has grown, it is anticipated that in the future consumer attitudes will translate into tangible changes in purchasing behaviour (BOF Team, 2020).

Acceptance

Acceptance relates to the consumer wanting to accept or trust that information given to them is honest and correct. The customer process of acceptance involves them considering if their perceptions of the brand, the product and the manufacturing process is 'as advertised'. As noted above, the consumer is seeking brands that offer protection across people, planet and animals, however they are now more aware of the huge amount of greenwashing that many brands practise, where they falsely promote their environmental efforts without the implementation of business practices that back up these claims (We Are Zeitgeist, n.d.). The fashion industry has exploited the lack of universal standards to use and abuse phrases like sustainability, green, ethical, eco and conscious to define their practices. Consumers have fallen prey to these marketing tactics due to a lack of knowledge and understanding, however, they are now becoming more educated. It is no longer acceptable to keep customers in the dark or try to manipulate them with low marketing strategies. The future consumer will continue to have greater access to information through online channels and will seek more knowledge about the brands they purchase from, and will therefore demand greater transparency from them. These consumers also seek more humanized brands, as to build trust they want to know more about the people behind the brand not just about the products. The consumer seeks brand storytelling that humanizes an otherwise faceless brand, and they want to know the people behind the brands doing the posting or communicating (Sprout Social, n.d.). The storytelling also needs to be authentically inclusive, reflecting a range of backgrounds and experiences that connect with consumers. The customer wants to support brands that represent them and their values, including metrics on equity, diversity and inclusion (ETBrandEquity, 2021).

The future consumer will be more demanding; therefore, businesses will need to stay informed about these customers' evolving needs. They have to maintain and build their brand integrity to help customers have the best experience (Afshar, n.d.).

Connection

The future customer will want more from a fashion brand than product, they also want connection, a sense of community and to feel valued. The consumer wants a highly personalized journey, with personal connections with the brand, a feeling of belonging and an engaging community (Retail Week, 2021). Sprout Social surveyed more than 1,000 consumers to understand their desire for greater connection with the brands they love as well as with each other and how brands can benefit when they facilitate connection. The report evidenced that consumers see brands as ideal facilitators of connection and that the labels should act as connectors first and sellers second (Sprout Social, n.d.). The consumer wants brands to foster connections not only directly with the business, but to bring together people with different perspectives. The Sprout Social research reported that brands emerging as leaders focus on building genuine relationships among their consumers, moving away from an emphasis on just selling product, and this approach further differentiates the brand from their competitors (Sprout Social, n.d.).

Consumers want to take a more active part in the relationship with brands, rather than being a passive partner who is just 'sold to or talked at'. Community is more than a database or list of customers, it is a common factor that unites a group of people through a common interest, shared values, a love of something or a passion for a particular style of fashion. Humans are pack animals and from early childhood they try to fit in with groups of people, by playing the same games, carrying the same lunch box, or wearing the same trainers. Even as they become adults they still try to fit in with social groups, work colleagues or even the neighbours. Brands need to tap into this idea by finding the elements that unite groups of their customers, so that they can start the conversations and build the engagement based on these elements. Brands need to build a positive impression that reaches the consumer on a subconscious level; this can be through representation, images and stories that build positive associations with the brand in their minds. This will ensure that subconsciously when the customer looks at the brand, they have favourable experiences and feelings that pop into their minds (Forbes, 2018).

Social media is one of the main channels for brand connections and a Sprout Social survey of over 1,000 people showed that more than half (55 per cent) of consumers want brands to use social to help connect like-minded people with each other, while more than one-third (36 per cent) are looking for communities they can belong to (Sprout Social, n.d.).

To support the development of a community a brand will need to have a strategy to ensure they stay in touch with their customers, with consistent engagement and interaction with them across all the brand's touchpoints.

Engagement

Consistently engaging with customers through a variety of channels helps brands build and strengthen human-to-human connection that adds value beyond just a transactional relationship. This results in benefits including increased sales, brand loyalty and brand perception. Amanda Gaid (2019) defines customer engagement as 'the level of interest people have to voluntarily interact with your brand. It goes beyond just buying your products or services – it's an emotional connection'. Customer engagement has never been more important, and brands need to know and anticipate their customers' needs and interests as consumers expect brands to know them and serve them only the content and products they want (Afshar, n.d.).

The days of a brand just pushing out information through advertising and press releases is over. Today the buzz is all about brands having direct engagement with the consumer. Brand engagement is the process of creating an emotional connection between a consumer and the brand. Engagement can be achieved through various channels and can be something as simple as a mention on social media, a consumer opening your newsletter or a conversation in-store. The ultimate purpose of engagement is to connect with the consumer through seamless experiences that build trust, which leads them to become loyal customers of the brand (Afshar, n.d.).

Engagement has become more important as the traditional marketing approaches of the past such as newspaper and magazine features and advertising no longer work. The consumer is bombarded with advertising from all angles and has become immune to its effects. They no longer purchase or consume magazines in the same way and the magazines generate little response or drive to action. Engagement is at the core of social media and social networking. These channels are about communication on a personal level, making a connection and bringing the consumer into the brand's lifestyle, and influencing their purchasing decisions. Engagement on social media relies on great content and images that connect with the consumer, who now trust more informal and authentic posts and user-generated content rather than glossy high-fashion-style imagery (Scott, 2020).

Engagement also involves developing impeccable customer service processes for customers who want a tailored experience as they progress from brand awareness to buying, seeking concierge-like engagement from customer service (Afshar, n.d.). High-level customer service involves brands participating in and encouraging two-way conversation, publicly showing they care about their customers by responding quickly to enquiries, positive and negative comments, and complaints.

The fashion industry focus on the metaverse as the new frontier for consumer engagement will enable brands to connect with consumers who are spending more time online. There will be new opportunities to capture untapped value streams, and the potential of non-fungible tokens, gaming and virtual fashion all offer fresh routes to creativity, community building, engagement and commerce (McKinsey & Company, 2022).

McKinsey & Company (2022) also identified that consumers will seek out opportunities for co-creation and will expect brands to engage with digital assets in a format that is native to the spaces they inhabit, rather than content that repeats across channels.

Consumer insight trend mapping

Consumer trends will continue to change, and these changes will influence what fashion products consumers want or need. Consumer buying behaviours are affected by evolving micro- and macro-environmental changes and all the changing social, demographic, environmental, retail, design and innovation trends will influence what and how the customers will buy in the future (Trend Monitor, 2021).

Figure 1.2   Consumer insight trend mapping

	Trend 1	Trend 2	Trend 3
Review – Who is the customer for this trend? – What do they need/expect? – Why do they follow this trend? – When do they want to adopt it? – What are their challenges around it?			
Competitor review of this trend			
Action – What innovation can the brand develop in this trend? – Which customer will it appeal to? New or current? – What customer needs does it meet?			

Trends that emerged from the Covid-19 pandemic were the result of fear, confusion and lack of control, such as the focus on basic needs, health and wellness concerns, and demand for hygiene and cleaning. Trend Monitor believe that behaviours that are forced on us in this way usually don't stick, they are just reactions, whereas true changes in behaviours happen over a long period of time, slowly changing our attitudes and habits (Trend Monitor, 2021). There seems to be a consensus from all the major trend and consumer insight companies that the priorities for the near future are based on sustainability, digital transformation, flexible living, personalization, and health and wellness.

Fashion brands will need to continually monitor consumer trends and identify the ones that are relevant to their consumer in order to future-proof their businesses. The consumer insight trend map shown in Figure 1.2 is a tool for brands to review upcoming trends to determine if they are relevant and how they will affect their consumers, as well as reviewing how their competitors are responding to the trend. Having researched and reviewed the trend, the brand can then act on their innovation strategy to meet their consumers' needs around the trend.

Research

Fashion brands cannot work on assumptions or gut feelings about their customers. With comprehensive research to understand the customer, a brand will be able to create the right product, uncover the language needed to communicate with the customers, determine the best way to sell to them and will guide the whole brand development. There can be no shortcut in this process, as business success is reliant on identifying and selling to unique customer segments relevant to the brand rather than taking a scattergun approach. In a Latana article on consumer research, Lauren Hamilton of Digital Narrative was quoted about the importance of brands having a true, deep knowledge of their target market, their lifestyle problems and what motivates them at the heart of a brand strategy – and that a scattergun approach wastes valuable budget, leaves consumers cold and fails to achieve the brand's objective (Prokopets, 2021). Research gives a brand the intelligence, insight, data and analysis they need to make decisions about every aspect of their brand. Brands are reliant on selling product to consumers, so they need to know what their customers want and the sentiments and trends that drive purchasing decisions. Consumer insights research is a primary element in a business model to keep the customer first in all developments of the label. 'Consumer research is the process of collecting information to first identify the target audiences and then zoom in on their preferences, perceptions, attitudes and purchasing drivers for a product, service or brand. Data collection and analysis are the key steps of consumer research.

To ensure accurate and unbiased results, marketers leverage an array of qualitative and quantitative research methods, alongside tools for interpreting the obtained input' (Prokopets, 2021). Global brands are investing heavily in market research so that they can react quickly to behaviour changes, stay informed about customers' evolving needs, maintain and build their brand integrity, and keep ahead of the competition.

There are two types of research that brands can conduct: primary research when they study the market themselves by running focus groups, customer surveys and reviewing their own sales data; and secondary research when they use other people's research such as industry trend reports and case studies. As many fashion brands sell their products to two different customer channels, they need to research both wholesale and direct customers. If looking for wholesale orders, the brand may have the buyer of the store as their customer, or maybe the sales agent who they must persuade to sell their collection to the stores on their behalf. Selling direct to consumer means the brand produces, packs, sells and distributes their products directly to the customer. Whichever approach the brand takes, they need to do comprehensive research to understand what that customer wants and needs.

Wholesale customer research

If a brand seeks wholesale customers they may be working directly with the store, or through an agent or a distributor. These third parties are all customers of the brand and have their own needs and wants from the brand and its product. A brand will need to conduct research into each store, agent or distributor to understand what other brands they sell and to whom. If a brand works with an agent or a distributor, they not only give the brand exposure to a wider market, they can also provide guidance and advice to ensure the product offer is right for the intended market (Wicker, 2020).

Wholesale accounts and international stores are not all the same, nor do they have the same customer base. Brands often list a wide range of department stores and say they want to be stocked in all of them, but that is not realistic. Each store will have a specific customer base and the brands and product they carry is different. They will be looking for brands that will help them attract their target customer. Brands often do not conduct adequate research on the store, so waste their time pursuing a shop or its buyer when it is not the right retailer for their brand – therefore primary research is needed to answer some initial questions (see Table 1.1). While in-store, the brand should also take advantage of talking to the shop assistants, as they are a valuable source of information on what works well in-store, what their customers look for, and which products are most popular and why.

Table 1.1   Wholesale account research

Store name	
Store buyer's name and contact	
Customer demographic	
Customer buying behaviour – are they buying one item or several, are they just browsing, do they have bags from other stores?	
Brands carried	
Product categories carried (formal, denim, lingerie, etc)	
Amount of stock carried for each brand	
Size ranges carried	
Price ranges	
Colour ranges carried	
Fabrics carried such as silks, cottons, knitted	
Predominantly plain or printed/patterned materials	
General silhouette or shape	
Merchandizing styles	
In-store experiences	

Direct customer research

A fashion brand can sell direct to the customer through their own e-commerce or physical store or through pop-up shops and events. The direct customer is the person who will wear the brand's garments, and this is the customer they really need to understand, to get inside their minds to find out what they buy and why, what types of brands they like and follow, as well as the type of content they engage with. At the most basic level, the brand needs to consider the 5 Ws of customer profiling: who their customer is, what they want, why they want it, when they want it and where they want it (Figure 1.3).

Gathering research on direct customers can be daunting as it involves a combination of primary and secondary research. Primary research could include hosting a focus group, visiting competitor stores or watching their customer in action. It can also involve following potential customers on social media to understand their values, lifestyle and brand preferences, as consumers now vocalize their opinions and thoughts openly on social media and are much more eloquent in sharing their feedback, likes and dislikes. Through platforms such as Instagram and Facebook you have access to authentic information and insights into the demographics, geography,

Figure 1.3   5 Ws of customer profiling

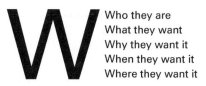

Who they are
What they want
Why they want it
When they want it
Where they want it

lifestyle, buying behaviour and brand loyalty of customers. Secondary research can be found through commercial sources and industry publications such as Mintel and WGSN; public sources through libraries and government departments who share industry statistics and research; and through fashion-school libraries.

A brand will not gain any advantage in the market by skimming over the research. Success comes from conducting intensive primary and secondary research to get an in-depth understanding of potential customers.

Segmentation

Having conducted significant research, a brand needs to analyse the information they have gathered in order to select appropriate customer groups to target. A mistake made by many fashion brands is that they try to compete in the mass market rather than picking a niche segment in which they can gain ground. Most brands cannot compete in a broad market, as fashion products cannot be all things to all people. Fashion brands need to develop their businesses by understanding who the best customers are that they can serve (440 Industries, 2019). Traditional business theory uses segmentation, targeting and positioning frameworks to identify the space that a brand wants to take up in their customer's mind. Segmentation is the process of dividing a broad target market into smaller groups of customers who are perceived to have the same needs, interests and priorities. The most used segmentation categories in fashion are based on geographic, demographic, behavioural and usage, and psychographic segmentation (see Figure 1.4).

Geographic

Geographic refers to where the customer is based, the country they live in, whether they reside in an urban or rural environment, in a hot or cold climate, as well as their housing type and location. The purpose of this research is to confirm that the product is suitable for different climates and living conditions. Customers from different locations can have different needs, such as a customer who lives in a rural area is less likely to buy trend-focused product than someone who lives in an urban area.

Figure 1.4   Consumer segmentation

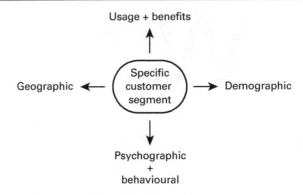

Demographic

This is the simplest type of segmentation and sometimes the only one that fashion brands use, as they only look at their customer according to age. Demographics need to consider more than just age, also grouping customers by gender, occupation, income, religion, nationality and race. Demographics will also include the life stage of the consumer, and whether they are a dependant or have a family, as this impacts on the disposable income they may have. Marketing specialists define customers into generational groups such as Generation X, Y, Z, Millennials or Generation Next, which is the consumer who looks for experience over product as well as authenticity and transparency from brands.

Usage and benefits

This segment divides the consumer by their behaviour in how they use the products and what benefits they seek from it. This could be used to divide customers who buy a lot of occasion wear, from someone who buys an occasion dress once every few years. This segment would also look at pricing consistencies, brand loyalty and volume of purchases, as well as how the customer wears the product.

Psychographic and behavioural

Psychographic segmentation is important in today's digital world, as this is the segment that will impact on how you connect and engage with your customers. Psychographics refers to lifestyle and buying behaviours, considering what the customer does on a day-to-day basis, 365 days of the year, as well as their social aspirations, value perceptions, interests and hobbies, attitudes, opinions and their self-image. Without this information a brand will not know what content to post on social media, which celebrity to choose for campaigns or the style of aspirational imagery to create.

Having segmented their customers, brands would then put them into groups whose members are homogeneous in their behaviours and type. From these groups the brand will be able to determine that each segment meets the following criteria: the segment is distinguishable from others, substantial enough to be worth focusing on, will be financially viable with a positive return on investment and accessible to ensure engagement with the segment. This will lead the brand to make the decisions on which segments the brand will target.

Customer segmentation versus profiling

There are differences between segmenting consumers and profiling, with segmentation focusing on grouping customers based on common characteristics, such as marital status, age, location and other factors, whereas customer profiling is based on the customer's personality, habits and experiences. Having used the market research and analysis to develop customer segments, the next step would be to dig deeper into understanding the customer by creating detailed customer profiles to offer a better experience, product, or service to the customer who would buy your product.

Creating consumer profiles

A consumer profile is a document that details the characteristics of a specific customer, listing all their interests, lifestyle, pain points, buying behaviours, opinions and values. A fashion brand may compile numerous profiles for different customers, giving each one a detailed description including a name, age and identifiable characteristics and personality traits, as well as their motivations to purchase.

> A consumer profile is a factual model of the customer based on research to ensure the brand develops the right marketing strategy to meet the needs of that customer.

From a marketing perspective, the consumer profile is one of the vital pieces of information that a marketer needs to know (Shaw et al, 2001). There are three approaches to customer profiling based on the consumer's lifestyle and buying patterns, including the psychographic method, typology method and characteristics method (Figure 1.5).

Figure 1.5   Consumer profiling methods

Psychographic method	Characteristics method	Typology method
Lifestyle	Time poor looking for convenience	Impulse consumers
Values		Loyal consumers
Opinions	Personalization driven	
Beliefs		Discount consumers
Aims	Experience driven	Rational consumer
Interests	Review driven	Community inspired
Activities		Innovators

Brands may use one or all three of these methods when assessing the decision-making styles of their consumers. As mentioned above, psychographics relates to the 'lifestyle' of consumers and their activities, interests and opinions. The customer typology approach separates consumers into groups based on their motivations, mindsets and how to engage them. Commence (2020) states that there are four types of consumers: loyal customers, discount customers, impulsive customers and need-based customers. The motivations and changing buying trends mentioned earlier in this chapter would also be incorporated into this approach. The characteristics method considers what traits influence buying decisions, such as some customers being convenience driven due to being time poor, or personalization-driven customers who want unique experiences customized specifically for them (Commence, 2020).

From the research undertaken, a brand should have a considerable amount of data to convert into consumer profiles – the more data they have the easier the process is (see Figure 1.6). Brands need to create detailed written profiles for each ideal customer, considering the details of their life 24 hours a day, every day of the year – identifying and listing their needs; what clothing they wear for work, hobbies or their lifestyle; what other brands they buy; where they spend their disposable income; what magazines, music, celebrities and influencers they like. The brand needs to think about every small detail.

The customer profile must be very detailed, so that the brand team can really envision the person who will buy the product and become a loyal follower of the brand. A more detailed profile will make it easier to develop a marketing strategy, brand storytelling and create content for social media that will connect with this customer. Brands need to be wary of drifting into creating fantasy figures with unrealistic life-

Figure 1.6   Consumer profile example

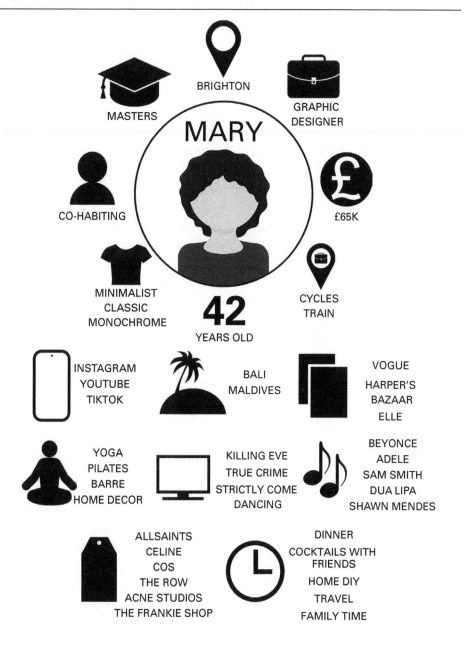

styles, as this will hamper them from reaching authentic customers. The profile must be based on research and hard evidence, as it will inform product design and development, as well as the development of an effective marketing plan.

Building a loyal customer base

It can take considerable time and money to attract a customer, therefore brands need to grow the lifetime value of their customers, rather than be constantly chasing new ones. Connection, engagement and a close relationship with the customer will improve the products that the brand produces, which means they can respond to customer needs, as well as making their marketing and content development more effective. Today's consumers are highly educated and cognisant, aware of poor products, cheap quality, mass production and fake advertising promises. There are many disenchanted consumers looking for more authentic, transparent brands that want to build genuine relationships with their customers. It is strong relationships with the customers that gives a brand a competitive advantage in a saturated market. Good relationships result in lower customer turnover and higher customer satisfaction. In a crowded market-place, brands will have to continually work hard to build affinity with a customer who has endless options and the willingness to gravitate to a brand that they perceive cares more about them. Brands must do more than sell them amazing products, they need to give them a great experience that makes them feel happy, satisfied and loved. Customers who have a great experience and connection with a brand will remain brand loyal, and one happy customer makes another, as this form of word of mouth is the best promotional tool.

Summary

The success of a fashion brand relies on one thing, customers! Great designs and beautiful collections are fantastic, but to make a brand a business the brand must find customers who are willing to pay money for their product. To achieve this, the brand needs to create collections that the customer wants and needs, and this chapter has shown the importance of brands conducting in-depth research to understand every tiny detail of their customer. With this research they can create the correct product but also connect and engage with the consumer in an effective and honest way. Today's customers are more knowledgeable and demanding, and their buying behaviours are changing as they respond to macro- and micro-environmental shifts. This chapter introduced the PACE framework for consumer expectations, which captures their demands under four headings of protection, acceptance, connection and engagement. Brands cannot afford to lose connection with their consumers; they need to constantly research and review their customer's needs, wants and desires, and keep two-way communication channels open to show the customer they care.

Fashion brands must always put the customer first, as it will inform the rest of the development and management of the brand, including product development, sales and marketing, branding and promotion, to ensure they survive in a crowded marketplace where customers can easily shop elsewhere.

Activity

Choose a fashion brand and conduct some provisional secondary research online to analyse who the brand's customer is.

Online resources

PowerPoint presentation with consumer insight trend map and consumer profiling methods.

References

440 Industries (2019) Market segmentation in the fashion industry, *440 Industries*, 440industries.com/market-segmentation-in-the-fashion-industry/ (archived at https://perma.cc/Z3A6-GSS2)

Adam, H and Galinsky, A (2012) Enclothed cognition, *Journal of Experimental Social Psychology*, 48(4), pp 918–25

Afshar, V (n.d.) New rules of customer engagement: key findings from global research, Salesforce.com, www.salesforce.com/resources/articles/customer-engagement/ (archived at https://perma.cc/S7RK-U3N7)

BOF Team (2020) The year ahead: consumers to seek justice in the supply chain, *The Business of Fashion*, www.businessoffashion.com/articles/sustainability/the-year-ahead-sustainable-fashion-consumers-seeking-justice-in-the-supply-chain/ (archived at https://perma.cc/2C8D-QS5S)

Brodzik, C (2020) Win customers with authentically inclusive marketing initiatives, *WSJ*, www.deloitte.wsj.com/articles/win-customers-with-authentically-inclusive-marketing-initiatives-01650302320

Chand, S (n.d.a) Consumer behaviour: meaning/definition and nature of consumer behaviour, *Your Article Library*, www.yourarticlelibrary.com/marketing/market-segmentation/consumer-behaviour-meaningdefinition-and-nature-of-consumer-behaviour/32301 (archived at https://perma.cc/L64F-YR3C)

Chand, S (n.d.b) Classification of buying motives: product buying and patronage buying, *Your Article Library*, www.yourarticlelibrary.com/products/classification-of-buying-motives-product-buying-and-patronage-buying/22154 (archived at https://perma.cc/XQ66-SH6A)

Commence (2020) What are the 3 methods of customer profiling?, *Commence*, www.commence.com/blog/2020/06/16/customer-profiling-methods/ (archived at https://perma.cc/9AP9-S2ND)

Damhorst, M (1990) In search of a common thread: classification of information communicated through dress, *Clothing and Textiles Research Journal*, 8(2), pp 1–12

ETBrandEquity (2021) Consumers want to support brands that represent them and their values: Deloitte report – ET BrandEquity, *ETBrandEquity.com*, www.brandequity.economictimes.indiatimes.com/news/research/consumers-want-to-support-brands-that-represent-them-and-their-values-deloitte-report/87602666?redirect=1 (archived at https://perma.cc/L7SP-RR6Y)

Fashion Revolution (2020) Consumer survey key findings, *Fashion Revolution*, https://issuu.com/fashionrevolution/docs/fashrev_consumersurvey_2020_keyfindings (archived at https://perma.cc/9ZAM-JVAY)

Forbes (2018) How and why does consumer behaviour change?, *Forbes*, www.forbes.com/sites/quora/2018/09/06/how-and-why-does-consumer-behavior-change/?sh=24013a4d86dd (archived at https://perma.cc/9UGM-SYSF)

Gaid, A (2019) Customer engagement: what is it and how to master it, *Oberlo*, www.oberlo.co.uk/blog/customer-engagement (archived at https://perma.cc/2LHJ-G68U)

Kodžoman, D (2019) The psychology of clothing, *Textile & Leather Review*, 2(2), pp 90–103

Lobaugh, K, Stephens, B and Simpson, J (2019) The consumer is changing, but perhaps not how you think, *Deloitte Insights*, www2.deloitte.com/us/en/insights/industry/retail-distribution/the-consumer-is-changing.html (archived at https://perma.cc/SCS4-JLF8)

McKinsey & Company (2022) The state of fashion 2022 – an uneven recovery and new frontiers, *McKinsey*, www.mckinsey.com/industries/retail/our-insights/state-of-fashion?cid=eml-web (archived at https://perma.cc/7MJV-73YY)

Mintel (2022) Global consumer trends, *Mintel*, www.mintel.com/global-consumer-trends (archived at https://perma.cc/P5DU-N8N4)

Positive Psychology (2019) Abraham Maslow, his theory and contribution to psychology, *Positive Psychology*, www.positivepsychology.com/abraham-maslow/ (archived at https://perma.cc/9V7M-XBCK)

Prokopets, E (2021) A consumer research process for your brand strategy, *Latana*, www.latana.com/post/consumer-research-brand-strategy/ (archived at https://perma.cc/A7TY-8GZ7)

PWC (2021) The global consumer: changed for good, *PWC*, www.pwc.com/gx/en/industries/consumer-markets/consumer-insights-survey/archive/consumer-insights-survey-2021.html (archived at https://perma.cc/X9E3-UJFY)

Retail Week (2021) Luxury consumers are changing – here's what you need to know, *Retail Week*, www.retail-week.com/retail-voice/luxury-consumers-are-changing-heres-what-you-need-to-know/7040799.article?authent=1 (archived at https://perma.cc/7P4P-QHE2)

Scott, E (2020) Why is demonstrating authenticity on social media important, *Sendible*, www.sendible.com/insights/authenticity-on-social-media (archived at https://perma.cc/32RG-L6YT)

Shaw, M, Subramaniam, C, Tan, G and Welge, M (2001) Knowledge management and data mining for marketing, *Science Direct*, https://www.researchgate.net/publication/228913141_Knowledge_management_and_data_mining_for_marketing (archived at https://perma.cc/UA3P-A8VD)

Solomon, M (n.d.) Consumer trends – Michael Solomon – consumer behaviour and marketing expert, *Michael Solomon*, www.michaelsolomon.com/consumer-insights/consumer-trends/ (archived at https://perma.cc/9XND-QHKN)

Sprout Social (n.d.) #BrandsGetReal: what consumers want from brands in a divided society, *Sprout Social*, www.sproutsocial.com/insights/data/social-media-connection/#whats-next-for-brands-on-social (archived at https://perma.cc/HCL4-CJVR)

Trend Monitor (2021) Mapping out the future for your brand, *Trend Monitor*, www.trend-monitor.co.uk/mapping-out-the-future-for-your-brand/ (archived at https://perma.cc/G4KP-TPCC)

UKEssays (2018) Consumer behaviour in fashion industry, *UKEssays*, www.ukessays.com/essays/marketing/consumer-behaviour-in-the-fashion-market-marketing-essay.php?vref=1 (archived at https://perma.cc/3VZM-9D9Y)

We Are Zeitgeist (n.d.) What is greenwashing? And how do you identify fashion brands that use it?, *Zeitgeist*, www.wearzeitgeist.com/fashion-sustainability-ethics/what-is-greenwashing#:~:text=In%20fashion%2C%20greenwashing%20refers%20to%20the%20practice%20of,of%20business%20practices%20that%20back%20up%20these%20claims (archived at https://perma.cc/HBG2-YYH8)

WGSN (2022) Future Consumer 2022, *WGSN*, https://www.wgsn.com/assets/marketing/WGSN_Future_Consumer_2022_Executive_Summary.pdf (archived at https://perma.cc/RV6L-G556)

Wicker, A (2020) Does luxury fashion still need wholesale showrooms?, *Vogue Business*, www.voguebusiness.com/consumers/does-luxury-fashion-still-need-wholesale-showrooms-nicholas-k-maggie-marilyn-misha-nonoo (archived at https://perma.cc/RMR4-ENTL)

Competitive advantage

2

LEARNING OBJECTIVES

After reading this chapter you should be able to:

- Explain the concept of competitive advantage
- Understand the difference between threshold and core competences for competitive advantage
- Define the process of competitive analysis
- Explain the processes brands can use to add value for competitive advantage

Introduction

Competitive advantage determines the fate of a fashion business. The fashion industry is a highly competitive, saturated market moving at an incredibly fast pace and fashion brands need to constantly review the environment they are operating in so as to keep ahead of the competition. Understanding the competitive landscape helps distinguish a brand from others who are vying for the same customer, helps them stand out and attract consumers to spend their money with them. Competition can come not only from other similar fashion brands, but from any type of fashion product or any other experience or place that the customer can spend their money. Therefore, brands can take the information and research they have developed about their customer to identify who their actual competitors are.

Brands rarely have a complete understanding of the competitive environment they are operating in, due to lack of continual research and failure to track how competitors and consumers are changing. Or they believe that what they do is so unique that they have no competitors, without the research or evidence to prove that this is true. Emerging brands tend to only identify established mega or heritage brands as their competitors but fail to compare themselves against more direct competitors such as other smaller emerging labels. Researching where potential consumers spend their money and what others in the market are offering them can help a brand identify what is unique about their proposition, as well as discover potential conflicts and threats. A brand cannot effectively compete if they don't know their competitors, and they cannot differentiate themselves if they don't know what other brands are offering. This understanding of the competition, both direct and indirect, helps a brand develop a better strategy and make more accurate decisions about their future.

This chapter will investigate the process of environmental scanning, competitor analysis and identifying potential areas for differentiation to develop a competitive advantage.

What is competitive advantage?

Competitive advantage is the context that puts a fashion brand in a better business position so that it outperforms its competitors. Competitive advantage does not happen by accident, it arises from deliberate, planned strategies to achieve opportunities or identify niche markets for the brand that its competitors do not have (Campbell, Edgar and Stonehouse, 2011). Competitive advantage can take considerable research, time and hard work. It is also very hard to sustain, therefore a brand must invest resources into the process if they seek to gain a sustainable competitive advantage in the industry.

There are various competitive strategy options for fashion labels depending on the brand's master plan. These can include competing based on price or quality, innovation or customer service, design excellence or technology, or a mix of all of these and other strategies. The business community has been discussing strategies for competitive advantage for more than half a century and one of the leading economists in this area, Michael Porter, defines a competitive strategy as an offensive action taken by a company in a specific industry to cope with competitive market forces and, thereby, increase business profitability (Porter, 1980). Porter's generic strategy framework states businesses can position themselves above their competitors in three ways, by offering lower prices through cost leadership, through differentiation and focus (Porter, 2004). A brand choosing a cost leadership strategy would look at being the lowest-cost producer to achieve lower-priced products for their consumers or higher profits; a differentiation strategy focuses on a unique product or service offer that the consumer perceives as superior to the competitors. Having decided on the path of cost leadership or differentiation, then the brand would focus on how to utilize this approach in either a broad or a niche, narrow profile of market segment (Campbell, Edgar and Stonehouse, 2011). Porter stresses that firms must select and implement either a cost leadership or differentiation strategy rather than trying to simultaneously implement them both, as different skills and organizational resources are needed for each element (Porter, 1980). There are risks with the strategies identified by Porter, as cost leadership can involve huge investment and brands that focus too heavily on reducing costs may fail to identify changes in the market or changing consumer trends and needs, whereas the risk in the differentiation strategy for a fashion brand comes from the difficulty of maintaining it over a long period of time, due to the potential of imitation, or inefficiency resulting in a product that is too expensive for the market. Relating this to fashion, the perception is that mass-market brands look more towards a cost leadership strategy, whereas luxury brands will seek to position themselves with a clear differentiation strategy to a focused niche market, with their offer of exclusive luxury products to a small customer base. There is a body of evidence that suggests a successful strategy could be a hybrid strategy of a mixture of differentiation, price and cost control (Campbell, Edgar and Stonehouse, 2011) and this hybrid approach is more prolific in times when the market is volatile, and consumers are more price sensitive.

Core competences for competitive advantage

Another approach to competitive advantage is the resource-based theory propounded by Wernerfelt in 1984, where brands exploit their internal strengths and core competences, including skills and experience, to position their business as different to the competitors and outcompete them (Barney, 1991). This is particularly relevant in the fashion industry with brands whose core competences include the exceptional design talent, knowledge and skills within the brand that make the product and the brand itself unique.

A competence is an attribute, or numerous attributes, that companies have in running their businesses, and these can be separated into threshold competences that every fashion company has, or core competences that are distinctive, or unique competences that a brand has that gives it an above-average performance (Campbell, Edgar and Stonehouse, 2011). An example would be that every fashion brand needs the threshold competences of sourcing, designing and manufacturing a fashion product, but a leading brand may have core competences of exclusive manufacturing relationships, or more refined design skills. A core competence needs to bring the business added advantages such as accessing more markets, having added customer benefits or something that is unique or difficult for its competitors to copy (Ohio University, 2021). Core competences that fashion brands exploit include:

- The customers' perceptions: the reputation of the brand, its history, credibility and products are perceived to be of greater value.
- The uniqueness that the brand offers through its design signature, niche products and services, storytelling, showcasing and brand experience, and the knowledge and experiences that the brand has through its designer or design team.

- Continuous improvement including developments in sustainability, transparency and ethics, as well as the use of new technologies such as the metaverse, digital showcasing and collections, and the use of augmented reality (AR) and artificial intelligence (AI) for improved customer service.

- Collaboration offers a competitive advantage through the unique relationships the brand has with suppliers, customers, other brands as well as celebrity collaborations.

Every brand needs to look at their own organization to determine the competences that are relevant to their business. Figure 2.1 provides an example of building blocks for competitive advantage for a fashion brand.

A successful brand can exploit their core competences to grow the business and profits, but they need to be aware that the market and consumers change, so they cannot be complacent. They need to constantly review and update their competences, as continuous improvement and making the most of tangible resources (such as human and financial) and intangible resources (including the brand name or registered designs) give the brand a competitive advantage.

Fashion brands that achieve competitive advantage have increased brand value, increased profit margins, greater brand awareness, and can ultimately dictate the pricing of their product based on perceived value rather than cost.

Figure 2.1   Building blocks for competitive advantage

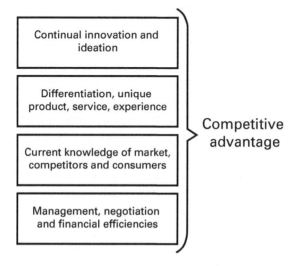

Competitive advantage is not a permanent feature and can be lost if a brand does not constantly review, research and innovate to stay ahead of other brands in the marketplace. The aim for a brand is to create sustainable competitive advantage over the long term and to do this they need to offer their customer a value proposition, the product or service benefits that create value for customers, which they would pay a higher price for. Value propositions can be created through operational effectiveness, which is doing the same as the competitors but doing it better, or by strategic positioning, which is doing things differently to their competitors and offering something new to the customer. Fashion brands must make strategic decisions on how they will work to offer value to the consumer and gain competitive advantage. To develop this strategy they need to conduct thorough research, including assessing the external environment as well as identifying and analysing their direct and indirect competitors.

Research

Research is an essential business function that ensures the brand builds their strategy with a clear understanding of the market, their competitors and where there is a gap in the market for competitive advantage. Many brands lose out on business to competitors they have never even heard of, simply because they have never taken the time to do full competitive research. 'Understanding what your competition is doing will help you position yourself, and your product or service, within the market' (Johnson, n.d.).

Joei Chan, in an article for Linkfluence, talked about an extraordinary statistic from McKinsey research that stated, 'In the last 10 years, all of the profit in the fashion industry has come from only 20 per cent of those companies. Most brands barely break even or actually lose money' (Chan, n.d.). In the same article it stated that when McKinsey looked for key drivers in the fashion industry, what separated the successful 20 per cent from other brands was that they relied heavily on data analytics, especially early in the creative process. These global brands are investing heavily in market research and consumer insights in order to access good, timely consumer data, to which they would react quickly, before a trend dies out (Chan, n.d.).

The research process involves the brand collecting and interpreting information on both external and internal perspectives to understand and determine its competitive position. External research includes the state of the brand's market, identifying new developments and technologies emerging in the market, new needs of consumers, competitor developments and new trends. Internal research includes recognizing the key strengths, weaknesses and competences within the organization, the value of the products or services offered, the quality of service, the companies' resources and cost effectiveness of their operations. Research is a valuable investment in a brand. With the constantly changing, turbulent environment of the fashion industry, brands must consider new perspectives of competitiveness, looking beyond the basic customer and competitors' analysis to take advantage of a wider view, by also considering environmental scanning as a key part of the process. 'While the environment has a profound impact on the organization, the organization has little impact on the environment. The best any organization can do is to continuously scan the environment for opportunities, threats, weaknesses and strengths. An organization's strengths are often used to create value and sustain competitive advantages' (Researchomatic, 2011). The process of environmental scanning is also covered in Chapter 4 (Business foundations for fashion brands), but many of these highly valuable frameworks and theories are also relevant for identifying competitive advantage.

The research process for competitive advantage includes considering what primary and secondary research the brand should take, running an environmental scan to include external and internal factors that will affect the brand and its competitors, as well as identifying indirect and direct competitors and conducting in-depth research of the top ones. By using the various resources, brands will collect pertinent information about their rivals and develop strategies to stay ahead of the curve (Jain, 2020). Brands need to conduct this research before they design or manufacture their first product, to ensure they create a suitable collection for the market.

Primary and secondary research

There are two forms of research, primary and secondary, that brands can use to investigate the market and competition. Most brands do not conduct enough research, either because they think they already know the market, are too keen to jump straight in to launching their products, or because they think they don't have the time or resources for it. It can be costly to conduct research, but it may cost a business much more in the long run if they don't do the research and end up creating the wrong product or cannot connect it with their perceived customer. Larger brands often employ consultants or agencies to conduct market research, but it is possible for brands to conduct research themselves.

Primary research is often called field research and involves the brand conducting research themselves, collecting data through interviews, surveys or practical, observational research such as visiting the competitors' stores. As this research is conducted by the brand, it can be more accurate as it directly answers the brand's questions and enables them to understand first-hand the competitive environment. Research of competitors can easily be conducted by visiting the stores, or online on their website, by signing up to their email newsletters, or through their social media, which will offer information on their current product offerings but also evidence their marketing and branding approach and their engagement with the consumer (Kolb, 2020).

Secondary research involves gathering research that has been conducted by others and can include industry reports, databases, government websites, research journals and media sources. Today most research is available online, so brands do not have to spend hours in a library to find relevant data as the growth of online websites and social media apps makes access to other brands easier than ever before. Secondary research can be used to answer questions on a more global scale about the market as well as consumer data and statistics. The questions investigated through secondary research into the global market include:

- Determining the leading fashion brands in the industry.
- The new products or product categories that have launched in the industry in the past few years.
- Brand comparisons on price, design, prestige, consumer perception.
- Identifying the barriers to market entry in the fashion industry or lack of them.

Primary and secondary research complement each other and if the data gathered is accurate, relevant and gathered from a reputable source then it can provide the brand with all the information it needs to analyse the market, benchmark themselves against competitors and determine the strategy going forward.

Direct and indirect competitors

Every business must fight to win customers and get them to spend their money with them rather than with the competitors. Attracting customers in today's digital world can be extremely challenging, as they can be easily distracted by competitors not only in the fashion industry but also by businesses in the entertainment, beauty, travel and food industries who will all be vying for the disposable income of the same customers (Taylor, 2022). Every business has competitors, so while some brands may consider their product or service unique in the world and think they therefore have no competitors, they will still have to compete with any business where their customers spend their money.

Brands are often too limited in their consideration of the competition, leading to marketing myopia when businesses are short-sighted in their marketing, leading to research blind spots. The term 'marketing myopia' was first coined by Theodor Levitt in a 1960 *Harvard Business Review* marketing paper, which refers to businesses that define their competitors too narrowly, by focusing only on their immediate industry competitors offering a similar product, failing to recognize the threat posed by potential competitors in divergent industries (Beverland, 2018). According to Levitt, businesses need to address the practical aspects of their product in a societal context, rather than just selling product. This has become very relevant to the fashion industry since the Covid-19 pandemic, as customers would rather spend their money on experiences than fashion product. Customer experience has become the thing that increases revenue and business growth and, with too many competitors out there, customers will gladly switch to any business that gives them a great experience (Bulao, 2022).

The starting point of competitor analysis is to identify which brands to analyse. Brands need to consider competitors of different sizes, looking at smaller and start-up brands as well as the more established larger, well-known brands. Kaleigh Moore in a blogpost for Shopify identified three types of competitor: direct competitors, who will sell a similar product to a similar audience, for example Nike and Adidas are primary competitors; indirect competitors that offer a high-end or low-end version of your product to a different audience, such as Victoria's Secret and Walmart; and tertiary competitors, which are related brands that may market to the same audience but don't sell the same products as you or directly compete with you in any way. They may be potential partners or future competitors if they choose to expand their business, for example: Gatorade and Under Armour (Moore, 2021). Competitors do not have to only create a product of a similar style or with similar benefits, they could be a brand that creates any fashion product that would appeal to the customer – it is better to research competitors too widely than too narrowly (Kolb, 2020). To identify indirect competitors, the brand needs to consider the wants and needs of their customers that these businesses are satisfying rather than specific products or services (Granger and Sterling, 2012). Once the brand has created a full list of direct and indirect competitors, then these will be analysed to identify the main competitors that the brand will research in a more detailed, thorough way, but first the brand will need to scan the environment that all these companies sit in.

Scanning the competitive environment

In a highly competitive world, businesses need proper strategies to give them competitive advantage. Brands must create firm foundations for growth, as discussed in Chapter 4 on business structure, and the environmental scan on the competitive environment will feed into that process. For competitive advantage, businesses need to use the environmental scan to keep ahead of their competitors, giving a detailed investigation into internal and external factors. Competitiveness of an organization depends on its business strategy, and to develop an efficient strategy it is necessary to understand what makes the organization more competitive. Therefore, the organization needs to know the environment in which it operates before it develops its competitive strategy (De Lorenzi Cancellier, Blageski Junior and Rossetto, 2014).

The volatile fashion industry with its rapid pace of change in the macro-environment, alongside the growing sophistication of customer needs and the shortening life of the product cycle, means brands need to continually look within and without their organizations, using a range of strategic business tools to determine potential areas of competitive advantage. Brands often make the mistake of heading straight into competitor analysis without analysing the market environment first. To consider the position of a brand in relation to others in the market it is necessary to establish its strength in the market in relation to the environment they are positioned within (Johnson and Scholes, 2006). Environmental scanning and analysis help in the detection of opportunities and threats for the brand and its competitors at an early stage, and identifies opportunities the competitors might take advantage of to create a maximum share of the market, which would then be a threat to the brand. The environmental scanning process can identify the potential in the different levels of the industry to determine the attractiveness of the market size, stability, knowledge, barriers for entry and impact of environmental forces. For example, a fashion brand may review the environment and perceive that the couture level of the fashion industry is too risky for them and decide to develop a strategy around the mass market instead.

Figure 2.2 provides a model for brands to consider the competitive environment and evidences the multi-levels that businesses operate in that can have an impact on their success. This model is used for brands to delve deeply into the competitive environment, looking at their own internal environment before moving outwards to consider the wider micro- and macro-environment within which the business operates. Environmental scanning collects data on various areas that affect the brand alone, or factors that affect all businesses.

Internal environment

Internal environmental components are those that lie within the brand and changes in these components impact the overall performance of the organization. Brands must consider their own infrastructure and working processes and how effective they are, as with poor foundations the brand will not be able to compete successfully. There are various internal environmental components such as human resources, capital and investment, technological resources, organizational structure, value and human resource systems, to name a few. A weak structure, or badly managed internal structure, will affect a brand successfully competing. An internal audit serves as a watchdog over an organization's integrity and accountability, scrutinizing the financial reporting, guarding against fraud, errors and risks, and providing objective assurance that the entity is following the regulations and standards that it should (Scherer, 2020).

Figure 2.2   Competitive environmental scanning

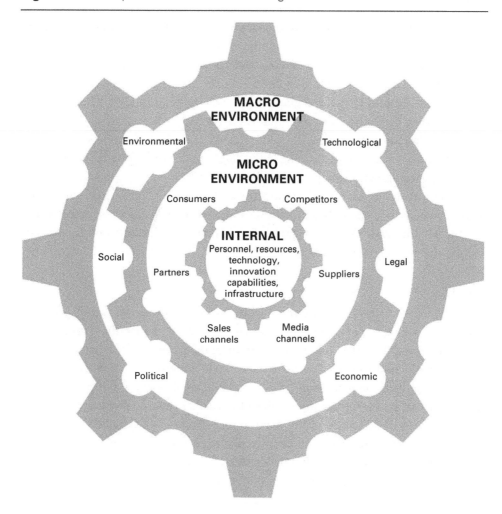

Micro-environment

The micro-environment refers to the nearby environment that has a direct impact on the business and how it operates. It includes factors that affect the brand and can influence its daily proceedings such as competitors, suppliers, consumers, market and industry operations. The brand has some control over the micro-environment factors, and an agile business will anticipate and find solutions to the challenges within their strategy.

Macro-environment

The macro-environment refers to all the factors in the general environment that are part of the larger economy and are commonly known as the PESTLE, which includes the political, economic, social, technological, legal and environmental forces that affect all businesses. A brand has no control over the macro-environment apart from the way they respond to the changing factors. For fashion brands the PESTLE factors need to be carefully understood and researched in order to carry out the business in ethical and environmentally conscious ways, as well as understanding the importance that technology is playing in the development and promotion of fashion, posing a greater threat of competition (Chavan, 2018).

The business tools that are used to identity and understand the micro- and macro-environment include the PESTLE analysis and SWOT analysis. These frameworks are discussed in more detail in Chapter 5, but here is an introduction to them in relation to competitive advantage:

PESTLE

The PESTLE looks to the future to consider the key external factors of political, economic, social, technological, legal and environmental change that can possibly affect a business. The PESTLE analysis considers the potential future challenges of an increasingly turbulent business environment to help a business prepare for change, anticipate what the competition may do in different circumstances and create a competitive advantage. Businesses should consider whether their market is static or in a period of uncertainty, then assess the environmental issues including PESTLE, before moving on to the competitive forces to enable the brand to identify a competitive position (Johnson and Scholes, 2006). The aim of this analysis process is to develop an understanding of the opportunities a brand can act upon, or threats it needs to be wary of when developing its competitive advantage.

SWOT

The SWOT analysis helps a brand develop strategies that will take advantage of strengths and opportunities while limiting the risk of weaknesses and threats. The SWOT is a competitive analysis framework that lists a company's strengths, weaknesses, opportunities and threats. A brand can conduct a SWOT for their own brand but it is also a valuable tool to use for competitors, considering their strengths, weaknesses and how they may respond to opportunities and threats to define competitive advantage. The strengths and weaknesses focus on the present, the elements the brand controls and can change over time, such as reputation, product, design aesthetic, partnerships or intellectual property. The opportunities and threats focus on the future and from the PESTLE analysis can consider the elements that are outside the control of the brand such as economic changes, consumer trends or changing market demand.

Competitive position

The PESTLE and SWOT analysis frameworks analyse the current and future situation, but brands also need to conduct deeper research into the competitive environment to identify their position in the market. A business tool that is often used for this is the Five Forces of Competitive Position Analysis, which was developed by Michael E Porter as a framework for assessing and evaluating the competitive strength and position of a business organization (Porter, 1980). This theory identifies and analyses five competitive forces that shape every industry and determine an industry's strengths and weaknesses, and helps to identify where power lies in a business situation. Porter's framework is useful for understanding the strength of an organization's current competitive position, as well as future potential situations. The five forces under consideration consist of the following: new entrants and barriers to entry, threat of substitutes, bargaining power of suppliers, bargaining power of buyers and rivalry among competitors (Porter, 1985).

Rivalry amongst competitors

The fashion industry is saturated with global brands all competing in the same marketplace vying for the same consumers. With so many brands making and selling very similar products, there is already strong rivalry in the market, but there is also the 'concept of brands, which allow some companies to sell apparel for ridiculous rates' (Bush, 2016). With limited innovation in fashion product the market is becoming saturated with very similar products.

New entrants and barriers to entry

Potential for new entrants is high due to low barriers to entry, which means there can be a constant flow of exciting new brands that could capture the customer who looks for something different. Start-up fashion brands need to consider barriers to entry as this is particularly relevant to how easy or difficult it is to start a business in the market in a particular location. For fashion designers there have always been very low barriers to entry, as it is easy for them to start working from their homes with a sewing machine and a laptop; their success rate, however, is low. The industry favours larger established businesses that can achieve economy of scale through substantial fabric orders and production runs, which results in them being able to secure better unit costs (Burke, 2015).

Buyer power

Buyer power relates to customers having the power to demand lower prices, shop elsewhere from other fashion brands, or choose not to buy fashion at all and choose experiences instead of fashion product.

Supplier power

While traditionally supplier power in the fashion industry is low for larger labels, for small brands or labels looking to make smaller minimum order quantities they can find that the suppliers have the power to demand brands place higher order numbers or charge much higher prices for low order quantities.

Threat of substitution

In fashion there is little to substitute clothes, so this force has been negligible. However, as already mentioned in this chapter, today's customer is happy to buy less fashion product as they seek experiences from other sectors if the fashion brand does not deliver the customer experience they demand.

An environmental scan of the internal and external, micro- and macro-environment and competitor factors will have a strong influence on how successful a brand is. Knowledge of the wider environment that businesses operate in will prepare a brand for the future but also enables it to consider how the changes will impact their competitors and anticipate how these competitor brands will take action to overcome environmental challenges. Analysis of the differential impact of environmental influences and competitive forces, customer value perceptions, and the strength of the competitors in the market segment, assists with examining the competitive position of a brand (Johnson and Scholes, 2006).

In-depth competitor analysis

Having reviewed the wider environment and identified a broad range of potential direct and indirect competitors, a brand would now be ready to select their top competitors and conduct in-depth analysis on them to determine a competitive advantage. A brand should not start with a limited competitor list, as it is necessary to cast a wide research net to make sure that the brand has a good understanding of indirect competitors on a global scale before categorizing them into areas such as product, price or promotion. From this broad list of competitor brands in the industry, they can then refine this list to identify the most direct competitors that the brand will initially position themselves against. Below are some of the basic steps of in-depth competitor analysis:

Identify the top 10 competitor brands

From the list of direct and indirect businesses created through the primary and secondary research, a brand should select the top 10 fashion brands they feel are their nearest direct competitors. These will be the fashion brands that have the same or similar product and service, are targeting the same customer base, within the same pricing structure and at the same level of the industry. This is not an easy process as it can take time to refine the key players vying for the same customer base both locally and globally. Smaller labels often make the mistake of only identifying superbrands as their competitors, but this is unrealistic as the smaller brand doesn't have the brand recognition, history, and manufacturing and sourcing capabilities that this larger brand has. For the smaller label the direct competitors will be brands that are in a similar position, or just a couple of years ahead. It is important to investigate brands in-depth and not make assumptions or believe the hype, as a brand regularly seen at fashion week or featured in well-known fashion magazines might not be doing as well as their promotion indicates. Often the most successful brands are the under the radar ones that are successfully building their business with more direct-to-customer strategies, and these may be better competitors to research. Therefore, in determining the list of top competitors a business must ensure that they are identifying brands that have commercial viability to follow and position themselves against.

Competitor matrix table

It is recommended that as a brand starts to identify the top competitors, they create a competitive matrix as an analysis tool to capture the data and identify opportunities. This matrix can be a simple table to capture each brand's main information, including:

Analysis of competitors' product and price

Analyse the competitors' product and price in detail, including elements such as the quality, uniqueness, design features, signature, finishing, fabrics, embellishments and hardware. It would also include their size ranges, how many different stores carry each product, then finally, analysis of the price of the product and the pricing architecture of the full range. Detail the brand's approach to sustainable or ethical production and management as well as any circular processes that they offer, including recycling, rental, reuse, etc.

Analysis of competitors' customer

Using in-store primary research, or secondary research on the competitors' social media platforms, the brand can analyse the competitors' customer, looking to identify whether they seem to have a particular type of customer, in a particular country, within a consistent demographic, as well as checking to see if some of their customers engage more with the brand than others.

Analysis of marketing, branding and language

A brand should analyse their competitors' key messaging and unique selling proposition as well as the features and benefits they highlight in their sales and marketing materials, and the key words they use to describe their brand and products. The brand should also analyse their experience offer and storytelling as well as how they build community and engagement with their customers.

Analysis of processes and logistics

Consider the logistic, shipping and delivery processes that the competitor brands offer, including free returns, speedy delivery or unique ways of distributing their products to the customer. As consumer demands for immediacy increase, an efficient supply chain and logistics process that is responsive and agile can give a brand a competitive advantage. Brands that have systems in place to provide real-time data to accurately track supply and demand, ensuring a centralized approach that integrates data from across the brand's network to offer the product and experience that the consumer demands, will have a competitive advantage (Londrigan and Jenkins, 2018).

Analysis of resources, investment and partnerships

Identify any advantages the competitor brands have from investment. Analysis should consider whether competitors have well-funded resources including staffing, equipment, technology and innovation, as well as partnerships that give the brand advantages such as with high-profile celebrities or unique manufacturing partnerships.

Analysis of competitor's social media

Through the competitors' social media platforms, the brand can list on the table what their customers are talking about, what they like, what they comment on, how they spend their time, the kind of language they use and what other brands their customers follow. Analysis of social media can also record brand sentiment and perception, analysing brand awareness and influence, using apps that can interpret this such as Hootsuite, BuzzSumo and Brandwatch, which can provide consumer insights on areas such as competitor content and product categories.

A competitor matrix table will capture detailed records about the competences and resources the top 10 competitors have to ensure the brand has taken a strategic approach to identifying the right competitors, in a similar way that consumer profiles help a company know the details of who they are targeting. The key to being successful in any market segment is differentiation, and differentiation requires that a brand

understands themselves and their competitors inside out. That way they can continually offer unique and distinctive products and services, and deliver measurable benefits to their customers. 'A competitive matrix is a powerful tool to reveal all of this,
and thus, a much-needed instrument in the journey to profitable and sustainable
growth' (Mehrotra, n.d.).

Positioning

When the brand has completed the research and competitive analysis, they will be
able to confirm the particular brands they will position themselves against both in
the market but also in the mind of their customer. Positioning refers to the development of a strategy that helps to influence how a consumer segment perceives a brand,
product or service in comparison to the competition. Positioning is all about defining
how the customer thinks of, and associates with, the brand's products in relation to
the competitors' products, such as whether it is less expensive, performs better or fits
better with the customer's lifestyle (Niosi, 2021).

From the detailed research the brand should have a good understanding of how
to occupy a clear, distinctive and desirable place relative to competing products in
the mind of the consumer.

Positioning is a persuasive marketing tool for a business. Good positioning helps a
brand connect with and form a sense of community with a target audience.

Figure 2.3   Positioning maps x 2

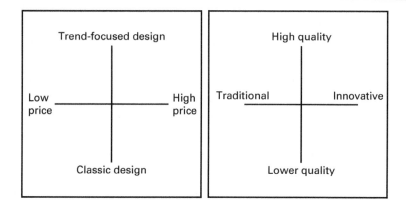

The positioning also determines the brand's messaging, values and overall business strategy, and understanding the competitors' positioning helps the brand separate themselves and build a favourable reputation with the customer.

The examples in Figure 2.3 are just two versions of positioning maps that brands can use to position themselves against the competitors. The axis can be changed according to the way the brand is positioning themselves against their competitors, such as price, storytelling, trend or quality.

'Customers choose products based on their perception of a product's value proposition – how they perceive the merits of the product relative to the alternatives (competing products). Therefore, providing a superior value proposition than the competition is a likely source of competitive advantage – but only if it can be sustained' (Tutor2u, 2021). A successful positioning occurs when the target customers find that the product or brand satisfies their expectations and desires.

Gaining competitive advantage

The end process of all the research into the competitive environment, direct and indirect competitors and positioning of the brand should be the identification of how the brand can gain a competitive advantage. A brand creates competitive advantage by discovering new and better ways to compete in the industry and then delivering the innovation that adds value to the customer, such as new unique products, new activities or engagement, new technologies or an amplified brand image (Goncaloglu, 2015).

The competitive advantage comes from creating a value chain, a focus on developing the maximum value within your product or service for your customer while still maintaining a healthy profit margin. Fashion brands can add value in every stage from concept to sale of their products, therefore need to have a systematic way of examining all the activities they perform, including their product development, sourcing, manufacture, marketing, promotion and sales. A brand can gain competitive advantage by performing these strategically important activities more cheaply or better than its competitors, and competitive advantage can come not just from great products or services, but from anywhere along the value chain, which includes its suppliers, channels and buyers (Goncaloglu, 2015). The concept of the value chain was introduced by Michael E Porter in his book *Competitive Advantage: Creating and sustaining superior performance*, with his framework highlighting the importance of adding value at every stage of an organization's processes. Porter explained that 'Competitive advantage cannot be understood by looking at a firm as a whole [...] It stems from the many discrete activities a firm performs in designing, producing, marketing, delivering and supporting its product' (Porter, 1985). An important element of a value chain is the links between each element, as all the organization's processes should be working together towards adding value, interacting with each other rather than being seen as independent elements.

A simplified version of a value chain for fashion brands is given in Figure 2.4, showing that competitive advantage can come from linking different processes within the organization to achieve an overall value chain for competitive advantage. This model introduces some of the main ways that a fashion brand can add value through unique designs; the purpose, values, ethics and sustainability processes of the brand; the production and supply chain processes and partners; marketing and communication; the sales strategy; as well as the brand's processes towards community and engagement.

Through the value chain a fashion brand can also map and analyse its strategically relevant activities in order to identify existing and potential sources of differentiation, identifying ways to effectively produce goods or services better than its competitors, which ultimately results from higher profit margins for the company and ultimately paves the way for the company to earn a competitive advantage. The value chain is not static and needs to be continually reviewed to ensure that all the links are connected, as well as creating new advantages to add value and remain ahead of the competitors.

Figure 2.4 Value chain

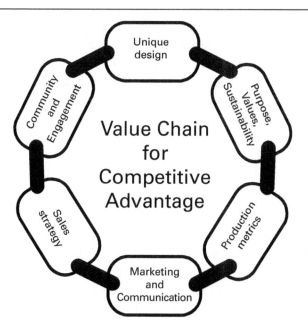

Ongoing research

Research is not just for the start-up stage, a brand needs to continue to do research as it develops because the market, competitors and consumers do not stand still and will all change over time. Undertaking ongoing research will make sure the brand maintains its competitive advantage, therefore processes need to be put in place for continual monitoring. The research needs to include measuring awareness and perception of the brand and its competitors, to understand customer sentiments, behaviours and changing values. Brands need to remember that their competitors will not be standing still, they will also be researching and adapting to customer needs, adding value, adapting to new technologies and innovations, and responding to changes in the macro-environment. Over time, some competitors may no longer be relevant as they pursue new customer groups, but there may also be new competitors who join the market.

As the brand develops, it has to evaluate the relative attractiveness of growth strategies that leverage both existing products and markets versus new ones. A framework was developed by H Igor Ansoff to help management teams plan and evaluate growth initiatives. The Ansoff Matrix is a simple two-by-two framework used to conceptualize the level of risk associated with different product or market growth strategies. The elements of the framework are market penetration, the concept of increasing sales of existing products in the existing market; market development, which focuses on selling existing products into new markets; product development, which introduces new products to an existing market; and diversification, which is the concept of entering a new market with altogether new products (Mishra, 2020). The Ansoff Matrix is often used in conjunction with the other business and industry analysis tools mentioned in this chapter, including the PESTLE, SWOT and Porter's five forces frameworks, to support business growth and competitive advantage.

Summary

This chapter has discussed why having a competitive advantage is essential if a fashion brand is going to survive and thrive in a highly competitive, saturated market. It has explained that understanding the competitive landscape provides the information brands need in order to create a distinctive brand that stands apart from others. With so many companies vying for the same customer, a brand needs to know definitively that their offering is different and that customers will need, want and pay for their product.

A competitive analysis is a comparison of competitors' strategies and helps a business determine potential advantages and barriers within a market around a product or service, and generally helps brands monitor how direct and indirect competitors are executing tactics like marketing, pricing and distribution (Moore, 2021). The research to create competitive advantage is essential, as brands cannot work on assumptions or limit their research as they will lose advantage to competitors who are more astute and attuned to changes in the market, environment and in consumer behaviours. The chapter introduced the research processes that fashion brands use, including environmental scanning, direct and indirect competitor analysis, positioning, and identifying potential areas for differentiation. Having a complete understanding of the competitive environment that they are operating in will assist a fashion brand in developing an effective strategy, identify their value chain and create a position of competitive advantage. They can gain competitive advantage through a host of competences including delivery, design, speed to market or customer experience, as well as improved logistics, collaborations, continuous innovation, greater customer engagement and connection.

Key terms

competitive advantage	indirect competitors	primary research
competitive landscape	internal environment	secondary research
core competences	logistics	SWOT
cost leadership	macro-environment	threshold competences
differentiation	marketing myopia	value chain
direct competitors	micro-environment	value proposition
environmental scan	PESTLE	
focus	positioning	

Activity

Identify five direct competitors that you can observe online and list 10 questions that you will use as a guide to research the brands. For example, in which country does the brand produce its products?

Online resources

Competitive environmental scanning, including PESTLE and SWOT.

References

Barney, J (1991) Firm resources and sustained competitive advantage, *Journal of Management*, 17(1), pp 99–120

Beverland, M (2018) *Brand Management: Co-creating meaningful brands*, SAGE Publications, London

Bulao (2022) 36 astonishing customer experience statistics for 2022, *Techjury*, techjury.net/blog/customer-experience-statistics/#gref (archived at https://perma.cc/T3GD-FLS6)

Burke, S (2015) *Fashion Entrepreneur*, 2nd edn, Burke Publishing, Ringwood

Bush, T (2016) Five forces analysis of the fashion retail industry, *PESTLE Analysis*, www.pestleanalysis.com/five-forces-analysis-of-fashion-retail-industry/ (archived at https://perma.cc/474H-UW8U)

Campbell, D, Edgar, D and Stonehouse, G (2011) *Business Strategy*, Palgrave Macmillan, London

Chan, J (n.d.) Consumer insights for fashion: how top brands keep up with consumer trends, *Linkfluence*, www.linkfluence.com/blog/consumer-insights-for-fashion-industry (archived at https://perma.cc/X4EL-M8AJ)

Chavan, R (2018) Analysis of fashion industry business environment, *Lupine*, www.lupinepublishers.com/fashion-technology-textile-engineering/fulltext/analysis-of-fashion-industry-business-environment.ID.000144.php (archived at https://perma.cc/9864-2PT9)

De Lorenzi Cancellier, É, Blageski Junior, E and Rossetto, C (2014) Environmental scanning, strategic behaviour, organizational characteristics, and performance in small firms, *Journal of Information Systems and Technology Management*, 11(3), pp 611–28

Goncaloglu, B (2015) How to gain a competitive advantage in business, Linkedin, www.linkedin.com/pulse/how-gain-competitive-advantage-business-bugra-goncaloglu (archived at https://perma.cc/VKU2-2NGW)

Granger, M and Sterling, T (2012) *Fashion Entrepreneurship*, Fairchild Books, New York

Jain, A (2020) Why competitive research is important and how to do it right, *Relevance*, www.relevance.com/why-competitive-research-is-important-and-how-to-do-it-right/ (archived at https://perma.cc/MU6D-YS57)

Johnson, G and Scholes, K (2006) *Exploring Corporate Strategy*, FT/Prentice Hall, Harlow

Johnson, J (n.d.) How to conduct competitive research for your business, www.uschamber.com/co (archived at https://perma.cc/LSF2-ED26), www.uschamber.com/co/start/strategy/how-to-conduct-competitive-research (archived at https://perma.cc/8VKL-38YT)

Kolb, B (2020) *Entrepreneurship for the Creative and Cultural Industries*, 2nd edn, Routledge, Abingdon

Londrigan, M and Jenkins, J (2018) *Fashion Supply Chain Management*, Fairchild Books, New York

Mehrotra, M (n.d.) Competitive matrix: a detailed guide with analysis, examples and report templates, *Contify*, www.contify.com/resources/blog/competitive-matrix/ (archived at https://perma.cc/385D-4T7L)

Mishra, A (2020) Ansoff Matrix: explained with examples, *Management Weekly*, www.managementweekly.org/ansoff-matrix-explained/ (archived at https://perma.cc/HQ24-BLBT)

Moore, K (2021) How to do a competitive analysis, *Shopify*, www.shopify.com/blog/competitive-analysis (archived at https://perma.cc/5QBF-URG2)

Niosi, A (2021) *Introduction to Consumer Behaviour*, KPU, British Columbia

Ohio University (2021) Core competencies can lead to competitive advantage, *Ohio University*, www.onlinemasters.ohio.edu/blog/developing-core-competencies-can-lead-to-competitive-advantage/ (archived at https://perma.cc/26ZS-AYQ9)

Porter, M E (1980) *Competitive Strategy: Techniques for analyzing industries and competitors*, The Free Press, New York

Porter, M E (1985) *Competitive Advantage: Creating and sustaining superior performance*, Free Press, New York

Porter, M E (2004) *Competitive Advantage*, Free Press, New York

Researchomatic (2011) Environmental scan, *Researchomatic*, www.researchomatic.com/Environmental-Scan-72846.html (archived at https://perma.cc/5VBL-W3U7)

Scherer, T (2020) 6 benefits of internal auditing, *Reciprocity*, www.reciprocity.com/6-benefits-of-internal-auditing/ (archived at https://perma.cc/RJB7-V8KN)

SIS International (n.d.) Using brand positioning and perceptual maps for competitive advantage, *SIS International Market Research*, www.sisinternational.com/using-brand-positioning-perceptual-maps-for-competitive-advantage/ (archived at https://perma.cc/TEV2-SFHV)

Taylor, R (2022) 7 ways to win your competitors' customers, *Fleximize*, www.fleximize.com/articles/001027/7-steps-to-attracting-customers-away-from-your-competitors (archived at https://perma.cc/NVU8-PVGY)

Tutor2u (2021) Market positioning, *Tutor2u*, www.tutor2u.net/business/reference/market-positioning (archived at https://perma.cc/W4GP-U9AS)

Case study
Bethany Williams

Photo credit: Natalie Hodgson

London-based designer Bethany Williams launched her eponymous gender-neutral label in 2017, with the belief that social and environmental issues go hand in hand, and through exploring the connection between these issues the brand will find innovative design solutions to sustainability. Bethany is recognized as one of our most progressive young designers who works to implement positive change within fashion, both through her own brand, and through working as a consultant with businesses across the world. Bethany hopes to shape the fashion industry towards businesses working with ethical practices, both socially and environmentally, as a standard.

The Bethany Williams brand has an innovative business structure that strives to prove that a socially engaged and thoughtful fashion system can exist within the design and manufacturing of garments. While the brand continues to grow, Bethany Williams stays loyal to the brand's purpose to use organic, recycled and deadstock materials, and each season explores new ideas of transforming waste into garments to treasure. Providing an alternative system for fashion production, Bethany believes fashion has the power to be utilized to create positive change. The brand works with social projects and local manufacturers to produce the collections, for example her bespoke woven textiles have been woven by women from a substance abuse rehabilitation community in San Patrignano, Italy, and non-knitwear pieces assembled as part of a rehabilitation scheme from a women's prison in the UK.

Bethany is renowned for her passion and work to shape the industry towards a more sustainable future and creating change from the inside of the fashion sphere. She has won numerous awards for her work including the Queen Elizabeth II Award in 2019, an LVMH Prize finalist in 2019, she won Emerging Menswear Designer of the year at the 2019 Fashion Awards, was included in the Business of Fashion 500 in 2020, a finalist for the International Woolmark Prize and announced as the recipient of the BFC Vogue Fashion Fund 2021.

www.bethany-williams.com

Purpose, planet, people   3

LEARNING OBJECTIVES

By the end of this chapter, you will be able to:

- Understand the need for ethical working practices in the fashion industry
- Explain the difference between sustainability and transparency
- Understand the needs for fashion businesses to have a purpose
- Explain why fashion brands should embed corporate social responsibility within their organizations

Introduction

It is widely reported that the fashion industry is one of the biggest contributors to global waste and climate change, due to using vast quantities of non-renewable resources including the raw materials and energy inputs, which in turn produce high emission levels. The signs of climate change and environmental damage are increasingly visible, with extreme weather conditions happening more often and temperatures continuously rising. The growing amount of waste from fashion includes plastics in our seas to overflowing landfills, which is threatening the health of our natural ecosystems and the people who live and work in them.

While many fashion brands are declaring moves towards more sustainable fabrics and manufacturing, in reality there is a huge amount of greenwashing, with fashion businesses falsely declaring environmental efforts without evidence of business practices to support their claims.

This chapter will look at why the fashion industry needs to clean up its act, and the steps brands can take towards a future circular fashion ecosystem. It will address the challenges brands face and discuss the approaches being recommended for improvements, looking at the opportunities the industry has to transform to more regenerative models and address the systemic environmental and social challenge in their supply chain. The chapter will review how a fashion brand can build a profitable business with purpose that cares about the planet and its people.

Industry challenges

The vast numbers of facts and figures that are reported about the impact of fashion on our environment and people are terrifying and evidence the critical need for change. The Intergovernmental Panel on Climate Change (IPCC) sent a stark message to the fashion industry in their sixth assessment report, that time is running out to prevent catastrophic climate change, with some experts stating that society has four years to deliver urgent and radical action (IPCC, 2021). The World Textile Forum reported that the fashion and textiles industry is the joint third highest emitter of greenhouse gases globally, accounting for around 5 per cent of global emissions. The industry also consumes 98 million tonnes of non-renewable resources every year and uses 93 billion cubic metres of water annually (World Economic Forum, 2021).

Driving change quickly is really challenging for the fashion industry due to the complexity of its extensive, often opaque, global supply chains. The environmental and social impacts are felt across the globe in terms of carbon emissions, water use, pollution, human rights and gender inequality. Add to this, mountains of unsold inventory that are sent to landfill, incinerated or dumped on distant shores. The industry has to address the issues of overconsumption and overproduction, changing the business models of brands producing large quantities of apparel, months in advance, with no certainty of how well it will sell. Part of this change will be encouraging new consumer buying behaviours, and the industry is facing unprecedented challenges to inspire and clothe consumers around the world while dramatically decarbonizing and reducing the waste arising from its activities (Institute of Positive Fashion, 2021). The Institute of Positive Fashion's Circular Fashion Ecosystem Project identifies three areas of change including reducing the volume of new physical clothing, maximizing utilization through product circularity, and optimizing sorting methods and materials recovery (Institute of Positive Fashion, 2021). These three targets would move the industry towards a circular fashion ecosystem ensuring its long-term viability, resilience and prosperity.

Alongside the drivers to make more sustainable fashion products, the industry has to ensure that it is acting in the interests of all its stakeholders including customers, employees, contractors, investors and wider society. There has been much discussion around the use of sustainable fabrics and manufacturing in the fashion industry, but another challenge the industry needs to address is the needs of the workforce for fair wages and decent working conditions. Over the past few years there have been numerous scandals on the treatment of workers in factories making fast fashion, even in countries with minimum wage laws. Many of the brands involved also had codes of conduct and fair employment policies listed on their websites, but the scandals proved that there was no transparency in how these policies were delivered in practice. The House of Commons Environmental Audit Committee report about fixing fashion discussed how fast-fashion overproduction and overconsumption of clothing is based on the globalization of indifference towards the poverty and pay conditions of garment workers (House of Commons, 2019). Across the industry there are concerns about the use of child labour, prison labour, forced labour and bonded labour in factories and the garment supply chain across the world.

One of the greatest challenges facing the movement towards an industry that improves its impact on society and the environment is the use of language. There has been worldwide misuse and exploitation of the word 'sustainability' and the many other phrases that are used around the subject including green, eco, conscious, recycled and clean fashion. It has now got to the point where the consumer no longer understands what any of these terms mean and if there is any difference between them. All the way back in 2013, Doug King declared that the word sustainable 'has become so corrupted as to not only be meaningless, but to actually obscure the real issues' (King, 2013). With sustainability being such a buzzword, it means businesses are obviously looking at ways to make money out of it, and they are using and abusing sustainability as a good marketing strategy to sell products and increase income. To stop this abuse of language, there may need to be legislation in place to restrict the use and set the criteria for how the words can be used.

The challenge for the future is for the fashion industry to be filled with visionary purpose-driven brands that better serve humanity and the planet, while also making a profit. To achieve this more brands will need to develop a triple bottom line business model, which is a transformation framework based on the 3Ps of people, planet, profit (see Figure 3.1). With this business concept, brands across the sector need to take responsibility for measuring their social and environmental impact as well as financial performance.

Purpose

Purpose relates to the reason something exists, the sense of resolve or determination to achieve a specific goal. Purpose creates meaning and a sense of direction to guide the path or behaviour (Simple Minded Life, 2019). There has been a movement towards more purpose-driven brands, and while for some it is just another buzzword that they have adopted but don't deliver on, other more authentic brands with genuine purpose are witnessing higher market-share gains. Deloitte Insights reported that purpose-driven companies grow three times faster on average than their competitors

Figure 3.1   Purpose, people, prosperity and planet

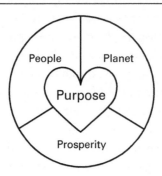

and achieve greater workforce and customer satisfaction (O'Brien et al, 2019). The rise of successful direct-to-consumer and digitally native brands with purpose baked into their DNA has shown that purpose can be a critical factor in attracting customers willing to pay more for a premium or niche product (Shopping Gives, 2022).

Purpose helps brands create deeper connections with their consumers, do more for the communities in which they work, attract and retain talent, and in the process achieve greater results and impact. Customers today will make purchasing decisions based on how the brand behaves towards its people and the planet. There has been a monumental cultural shift following the global pandemic and increasing issues around social, racial and economic inequalities and climate crisis. This is leading consumers to seek brands that better resonate with their values. Shopping Gives reported that business leaders needed to re-examine their values after macro issues such as Covid-19, the growth of the Black Lives Matter (BLM) movement and climate change impacts, and they needed their brands to move beyond empathetic ads, posts and statements, and move towards real action that can be measured and felt (Shopping Gives, 2022).

When a brand authentically leads with purpose, they are more trusted by their consumers, employees and partners. By standing for something bigger, something more than just their own profit, they can connect with consumers on a deeper level. Fashion brands need a purpose that articulates why the business exists, what problems it solves and what it wants to give back to its customer, community and the wider world. Authentic purpose-driven businesses walk the walk by being transparent and accountable for everything they do.

A brand's purpose needs to be relevant to the consumer and align with their values, and if the brand engages with their customer to work towards the purpose then they become active stakeholders who invest their time, money and attention to the brands (O'Brien et al, 2019).

According to Porter Novelli (2020) research, 70 per cent of customers would stop buying products/services if they learnt of a company's irresponsible or deceptive business practices, and consumers are more willing than ever before to hold brands accountable. Deloitte Insights was aligned with this research, believing that brands who fail to identify and articulate their purpose may survive in the short term, but over time, people are likely to demand more (O'Brien et al, 2019).

Purpose is the very heart of a business, it forms the DNA of the brand, which then leads its commitment to the planet and people, ensuring prosperity for everyone along the journey.

Planet

The glamour of the fashion industry often hides the dirty secrets of wasteful consumerism, pollution and ecological crisis. There is an urgent need for the fashion industry to reduce its impact on the planet. Though fashion is not alone in its need to clean up its act, there has been a surge in environmental concerns that has led all kinds of businesses to accelerate their sustainability plans. However, brands working alone will not solve the problems, it will take a collaborative approach across all industries and there has been movement towards this with various international agreements and initiatives.

At the UN Climate Change Conference (COP21) in Paris, it was agreed that as climate change is a global emergency that goes beyond national borders, then it needs international cooperation and coordinated solutions at all levels, and a breakthrough was made with the historic Paris Agreement (United Nations, n.d.). The agreement came into force in 2016 and set long-term goals to:

- Reduce global greenhouse gas emissions to limit the global temperature increase in this century to 2 degrees Celsius while pursuing efforts to limit the increase even further to 1.5 degrees.
- Review countries' commitments every five years.
- Provide financing to developing countries to mitigate climate change, strengthen resilience and enhance abilities to adapt to climate impacts (United Nations, n.d.).

The Paris Agreement covered all business sectors and provided a durable framework to guide the global effort, and marked the beginning of a shift towards a net-zero-emissions world. The Paris Agreement sits alongside the 2030 Agenda for Sustainable Development, which is a plan of action for people, planet and prosperity, which incorporates 17 sustainable development goals for United Nation (UN) member countries to use to influence their policies. The goals aim to end poverty and hunger, ensure healthy lives, achieve greater inclusivity and equality, along with aims to combat climate change, protect oceans, restore ecosystems and aim for responsible consumption.

The fashion industry has started to develop its own agenda for change and at the G7 summit in 2019, led by French president Emmanuel Macron, 32 fashion companies signed a fashion pact to fight the climate crisis and protect biodiversity and the oceans (Butler, 2019). The group included large luxury brands such as Chanel, Ralph Lauren and Prada, as well as fast-fashion brands H&M Group and Zara parent company Inditex. The hope is that through collective action more can be achieved, however the pact has come under criticism for not detailing specific goals.

While there is a slew of policies under consideration globally, the fashion industry is still under-regulated, with most of the large fashion brands still failing to disclose even basic data about their environmental impact (The Business of Fashion, 2022). This leads to a growing demand for legislation to force the industry to take more responsibility.

Sustainability

Sustainability includes various elements from the raw materials, through the production and distribution of garments. It is a multi-pronged issue with several complex factors that consumers struggle to grasp or trust, adding to the growth of greenwashing within the industry (Edited, 2021). Some brands are declaring they are sustainable but on investigation are found to only have one capsule collection, which has a limited percentage of recycled fabric within it. To be sustainable, a brand has to ensure that all elements of their business processes, including design, manufacturing and distribution, are conducted in environmentally friendly ways.

There are huge opportunities for brands to move towards more sustainable business models – to use more sustainable materials and manufacturing processes that are less damaging for the environment. There is also a growing consumer base seeking more authentic, sustainable brands, but the challenge is producing sustainable product at the price they will pay for it.

Below are some of the areas that fashion brands need to address to ensure they produce fashion that is truly sustainable and has less impact on our planet.

Net zero

Net zero refers to the amount of all greenhouse gases (GHGs) including carbon dioxide, methane or sulphur dioxide being removed from the atmosphere being equal to those emitted by human activity, in other words, activities within the value chain of a company result in no net impact on the climate from GHGs (Carbon Trust, n.d.).

Action to reach net zero is happening on a global scale and fashion has an important part to play due to being one of the least environmentally sustainable industries, accounting for approximately 2.1 billion tonnes of CO_2-e emissions per year, or 4 per cent of annual global emissions (Business of Fashion and McKinsey & Company, 2022).

The Business of Fashion reported the COP26 goal is to secure global net-zero emissions by 2050 and keep the 1.5 degrees Celsius warming limit within reach (Business of Fashion and McKinsey & Company, 2022), which is an ambitious race to net zero that will need significant change from all countries to meet the target.

In fashion, the highest emissions come from the production process, with the remainder coming from retail, logistics and consumer use, including washing and drying. To meet net zero, fashion brands can start first of all with planning greater energy efficiencies in their offices, factories, stores and transport fleets, but the biggest challenge comes from the emissions that are created in the supply chain stages that are out of their control. Fashion brands will need to work with their suppliers and manufacturers to help them become more efficient, such as switching to renewable energy sources. Brands that set targets on their use of materials and source more sustainable fabrics with fibres that are recycled, recyclable or regenerative will address a critical component of decarbonization.

No singular change or solution by a fashion brand will be the answer to emissions on its own, it will take wider industry investment and commitment to make a significant impact, but even the small steps that each brand takes will add to the overall chance of net zero.

Water usage and pollution

Fashion is one of the largest users of water, relying on it throughout the supply chain for the irrigation of cotton crops at the start, to the domestic washing of clothes at the end of the chain. Common Objective reported that the fashion industry currently uses around 93 billion cubic metres of water per year, which is 4 per cent of all freshwater extraction globally (Common Objective, n.d.). There are huge parts of the world already experiencing severe water scarcity, so fashion brands and manufacturers all have to take responsibility in minimizing water use in the production process.

The fashion industry creates water pollution through chemicals, dyes and untreated factory waste entering water supplies and ecosystems. Garments produced by fast-fashion brands often require a number of finishing processes, which involve applying harmful chemicals then washing them, which contributes to the 0.5 million tonnes of microfibres being released in the waterways every year (United Nations, n.d.). Synthetic fabrics were once heralded as environmentally friendly as they required less water than cotton and did not require toxic pesticides to grow, but over time understanding has grown of the damaging environmental impact of the heavy emissions it takes to produce and the non-biodegradable waste left behind. With nearly 60 per cent of our clothes now made from polyester, every time this synthetic fabric is washed it causes microfibres, or microscopic pieces of plastic, to be released in the water systems and oceans (Brodde, 2017). This plastic can then enter our food chain when swallowed by fish, or will remain in our oceans for hundreds of years.

It would be impossible to stop using synthetic fibres altogether, but innovative solutions are needed to find new materials or develop more efficient filters for washing machines. The consumption of fabrics could also be addressed by encouraging consumers to buy less and waste less in order to reduce water usage and pollution.

Soil pollution

The fashion industry has been responsible for soil degradation due to overgrazing of land, or the impact of chemicals used in growing cotton crops and factory waste. Soil degradation can have huge environmental impact resulting in landslides and floods, desertification and a decline in global food production.

Carbon insetting

Carbon insetting refers to the implementation of nature-based solutions such as reforestation, agroforestry, renewable energy and regenerative agriculture. It focuses on doing more good rather than doing less bad within a value chain. This means it is about more than simply reducing a brand's carbon footprint, it is about the business investing in the ecosystems their supplier depends on, to increase their resiliency and provide significant, measurable benefits to communities surrounding the value chain (Cooper, 2018). For example, fashion brands are implementing this using tree planting or community water initiatives.

Waste

The rise of the population and consumerism have led to negative environmental impacts, meaning the current 'take–make–waste' economy has to change and the world needs to take a new approach to resources.

The take–make–waste economy (Figure 3.2) is based on constantly extracting raw materials from the planet, acting as though they are an endless source. We are

Figure 3.2 Take–make–waste model

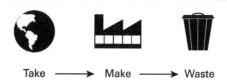

Take ⟶ Make ⟶ Waste

Figure 3.3 Linear product lifecycle

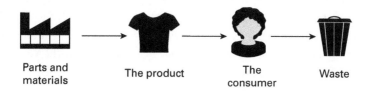

Parts and materials   The product   The consumer   Waste

now seeing the results of this approach with depleting resources, climate change and huge mountains of trash choking our planet. The fashion industry has been working on a linear 'take–make–waste' model (Figure 3.3) using huge amounts of resources to make clothing that is perceived as disposable.

The fashion industry is resource intensive, using significant amounts of water, land, wood and pesticides for the farming of raw materials such as cotton. On top of this, 17.5 cubic metres of textiles, the equivalent of one garbage truck, are either burnt or sent to landfill every second (Business of Fashion and McKinsey & Company, 2022). Waste occurs throughout the product lifecycle including pre-consumer waste, which is any by-product discarded at any point during the making process of the product, to post-consumer waste when they discard products they no longer want. Hundreds of thousands of tonnes of fabric are wasted at the design and production stage – for instance, when garments are cut out from the patterns as much as 15 per cent of the fabric can end up on the cutting-room floor (House of Commons, 2019). At the consumer end of the process, Sustain Your Style reported that a family in the western world throws away an average of 30 kg of clothing each year with only 15 per cent recycled or donated, and the rest goes directly to landfill or is incinerated (Sustain Your Style, n.d.). As many of our fashion products are made from synthetic fibres such as polyester, they are either non-biodegradable or can take hundreds of years to decompose. Fast-fashion retailers in particular have come under fire from environmental campaigners for encouraging a market that sees around 300,000 tonnes of clothes dumped in UK landfills each year (Helmore, 2019).

Overproduction

One of the greatest causes of waste is overproduction, with fashion brands using resources to create products that they are unable to sell. Unsold inventory is a waste of all the resources, energy and labour that were used to make the product and then it is sent to landfill or incinerated, adding to the emissions that are damaging our planet. Brands overproduce due to short fashion-trend cycles, manufacturer demand for higher minimum order quantities, or in order to get a lower cost price as it is cheaper and logistically easier to order more and deal with the excess later.

The management of overproduction is causing a furore, as consumers read news headlines about brands destroying and burning stock. In 2018, the British luxury brand Burberry faced a storm of criticism when it revealed in its Annual Report for 2017/18 that the cost of finished goods physically destroyed in the year was £28.6 million (2017: £26.9 million), including £10.4 million of destruction for beauty inventory (House of Commons, 2019). The brand explained that they had burnt the goods to protect their label and keep their products out of the secondary, discount market; however, they have now developed new business models to eradicate this practice. It is not only luxury brands that dispose of their surplus stock this way, most fast-fashion brands also have unethical ways of disposing of their unwanted stock. Some brands state that rather than send their surplus stock to landfill or incineration, they are offering take-back programmes that will recycle, repurpose or resell clothes, but research shows that these can end up dumped in places like Ghana and Chile, with huge clothing mountains damaging the local environment as well as the local designer/maker economy.

Brands need to adopt new business models to eradicate overproduction, and while small batch production is more expensive it can be worth it if that is the best strategy for meeting customer demand and also saves the brand from worry about excess inventory (Chen, 2021).

Distribution

In all the talk about sustainability of fashion brands, an area that is often missed is distribution, and with a global market and goods being shifted all over the world, logistics also need to be considered within sustainable business models. Logistics include outbound logistics, which is goods being sent out, and reverse logistics for returns. The logistics module of the supply chain encompasses all transportation, packaging, warehousing, inventory management, waste disposal practices, collection and reprocessing of used products (DHL, 2022). The logistics processes all create emissions that contribute to the carbon footprint of a garment, which means brands need to limit the journeys of all the components of their production and seek more green distribution channels. Fashion goods are normally shipped factory to warehouse, warehouse to distribution centre and then on to the customer, but some larger e-commerce brands are now using a factory-direct shipping strategy in order to cut down this process to reduce carbon footprint and shipping costs (Chen, 2021).

Protecting our planet and environment is a priority and, as the importance of sustainability in fashion grows, brands need to develop more circular business models, be more transparent and ensure sustainability is embedded in all the business activities.

Circularity

The fashion industry needs to make a real change to reduce the strain on our planet and brands need to do more than make token efforts. Brands and the industry as a whole need to explore new circularity business models if we are to make significant change to environmental impact. With the fashion industry being responsible for a large share of global greenhouse gas emissions and the environmental impacts of its land and water use and pollution as well as waste, it needs to embrace the circular economy.

To transition to a circular economy requires a change at the heart of the supply chain with innovation across the board including in materials, products, packaging, more sustainable agile production methods, and smarter product return and recycling processes developed. To bring these elements to life, supply chains need to be designed in a circular way, ensuring visibility and close orchestration throughout, and establishing new consumer behaviours (DHL, 2022). Fashion brands need to move away from the take–make–waste model towards a circularity one that encourages the extension of the use phrase and turns waste into valuable inputs going back into the 'produce' phase (DHL, 2022). This means reconsidering production volumes, optimizing material use, extending product lifecycles and new solutions for end-of-life recycling.

Fashion industry circular economy innovation will be centred around new design and manufacturing approaches that will shift the whole economic system from take–make–waste to one that eliminates waste, keeps products and materials in circulation and regenerates nature.

Circular model

The circular fashion model is a mission-led system that places equal emphasis on the inputs, production and end-of-life of fashion products (Figure 3.4). The circular business model incorporates a strategy of design thinking, 'focusing on designing products that can be reimplemented into the economy after use, retaining some value compared to disposing of the product in a waste stream' (Ellen MacArthur Foundation, 2021).

Figure 3.4   Circular product lifecycle

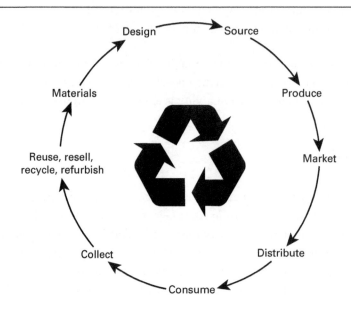

The Ellen MacArthur Foundation advises the circular system has three principles, which are to eliminate waste and pollution, circulate products and materials, and regenerate nature (Ellen MacArthur Foundation, 2021).

Before producing products, brands need their design teams to consider the whole lifecycle perspective of their products, considering the impact of making the product but also impacts resulting from their use, transportation and disposal. They have to consider the product range and size, looking at the potential of a smaller drop model to reduce overproduction, as well as analysing the potential of new material innovations. This includes reviewing the use of different materials in each product and the difficulty this would cause later on for disassembly. The repair and recycling of many products is further complicated by the ways in which certain materials or component parts are held together. Snaps and glues make for easy assembly, but they make disassembly virtually impossible (DHL, 2022).

Brands that focus on just sustainability only tend to look at the business model up to the sale of product, whereas with a circular model the brand takes responsibility of the life of the product post-sale as well. To move to a circular model may sound like a complex challenge for most fashion brands but, in reality, it is quite simple. The starting point is a change of attitude from the linear take–make–waste model to a circular closed loop that considers how instead of throwing something away it gets fed back into the system to be reused.

Circular business models

The Ellen MacArthur Foundation identified three categories of circular business model that brands can incorporate. All these models provide economic benefits to the brand as well as benefits to the greater economy and environment, helping businesses make better product margins, increase their competitiveness and reduce costs (Ellen MacArthur Foundation, 2021). The models are:

- More use per user, creating better-quality products that can be worn more and have a longer life through styling tips or offering repair, remake or customization services.

- More users per product, designing products and creating the systems for products to be passed from user to user such as through resale or rental.

- Beyond physical products, which can mean designing digital products or services that replace physical goods and enhance customer experiences and aspirations.

These models all rely on a careful orchestration of the physical supply loop across different elements but also the development of innovative business models that look at post-sale involvement in the reselling, repairing, refurbishing and recycling of products. To address the three categories of the circular business model identified, brands can take five approaches to circularity, as set out below.

The five Rs of circularity

The five Rs of circularity include reduce, repair, resell, rental and recycle, which provide dimensions through which circularity can be achieved. Brands that work to integrate all the dimensions will lead the way in circular fashion, increasing their competitiveness in the market as well as achieving sustainable goals.

Reduce

Brands need to reduce their impact by cutting overproduction, reducing the size of the range and number of products produced, as well as considering how to reduce the negative impact of resources and materials used in production. There are also opportunities to reduce returns, as well as the number of pieces customers buy through encouraging less consumption and making quality products that last longer and offer multi-wear, styling options.

Repair

Brands should offer options for consumers to fix damaged products by offering a repair service, providing a mending kit with products, or information to help the consumer repair a piece themselves.

Resell

The resell market is growing, not only for luxury brands but fast-fashion labels are also offering the consumer opportunities to resell the product when they no longer need it, either through the brand or a third-party partner, such as eBay or Vinted. Growing numbers of young consumers are turning towards reuse and resale sites such as Depop or The RealReal and the second-hand market is expected to overtake fast fashion in the next few years and be 50 per cent bigger than it currently is by 2028 (Butler, 2019).

Rental

Another growing market is rental, an option for customers who want pieces that they only want to wear once. It also gives some customers access to luxury brands that they may not be able to afford to purchase from. There has been a surge in platforms offering rental opportunities such as My Wardrobe HQ or Hurr, or brands are offering rental through their own stores or online sites. Rental encourages more users per product and enables brands to offer a different option to their consumers, as well as providing a solution for overproduction pieces that haven't sold.

Recycle

At some point, the product may reach the end of its life and no longer be a viable product as a whole, but there can still be value in the materials and parts, which can be fed back into the production cycle through recycling. Second-life garments cause 55–75 per cent less emissions than new items from virgin materials, however there can still be emissions in the recycling materials so brands would need to consider using green energy to reduce the footprint (DHL, 2022). There are still huge challenges around recycling that the fashion industry needs to address, such as garments made from fabric blends that are impossible to recycle.

Brands will need to redesign their supply chains and develop new supply models that incorporate the five Rs as the foundation to build upon. There are still major challenges to overcome, namely in how to engage all partners to be committed to the process, how to capture end-of-life products and unused inventory to reintroduce it into the cycle. Transitioning from a traditional, linear supply chain towards a closed and circular supply loop also needs to consider benefits for all stakeholders and society as a whole. The Ellen MacArthur Foundation advises brands to act in four areas, rethink, design, co-create and scale, to maximize the economic and environmental outcomes of circular business models (Ellen MacArthur Foundation, 2021). These areas relate to brands rethinking their performance indicators and rethinking what incentives and experiences they can offer to customers. They need to design products that are better quality and can be used more for longer. The third area refers to co-creation with brands creating supply networks that are able to circulate products locally and globally, and finally scale the variety of circular business models embracing a range of options including resale, rental, repair and remake as well as continuing to explore and innovate new options.

People

The fashion industry talks a lot about sustainable fashion, although a lot of this talk is greenwashing rather than authentic sustainable business practices, which has led the call for more ethical practices in the industry. Ethical fashion refers to the production of garments from concept to consumer that focuses on reducing harm to people and the planet, ensuring everyone in the supply chain can thrive. Brands should have a code of ethics as part of their brand values, which provides employees and partners with the knowledge of what their business expects in terms of responsibilities and behaviour towards fellow employees, customers and suppliers.

Ethical practices about environmental issues have been addressed above, but brands also need to establish ethical practice in how the people along their supply chain are treated. There have been concerns that although in the industry there are many policies stated on websites, in practice there are often issues around employment and workers' rights, inclusivity and equality, labour safety standards, bribery and anti-corruption, counterfeiting and unfair business practices. Unethical practices have been uncovered in the industry that have revealed the use of forced labour in factories, horrendous work and health conditions of cotton pickers, low wages, exploitation and harassment. The treatment of garment workers was brought to the forefront following the 2013 Rana Plaza garment factory collapse, which killed 1,133 people and critically injured thousands more (Crumbie, 2021). This led to the Accord, a legally binding agreement between brands and trade unions to work towards a safe and healthy garment and textile industry in Bangladesh. Fashion Revolution was also founded following the Rana Plaza collapse and has been campaigning for nearly 10 years for a clean, safe, fair, transparent and accountable fashion industry. It is one of the world's largest activism groups that is campaigning for a fashion industry that 'values people and the planet over profit and growth. We are a truly people-powered movement, working together in communities around the world to create positive and lasting change' (Fashion Revolution, n.d.).

As fashion brands move towards circularity, it was noted in the Chatham House research paper entitled 'Promoting a Just Transition to an Inclusive Circular Economy' that 'Combining circular economy policies with social protection measures will be important in order to ensure that the burden of efforts to promote circularity will not fall on the poor through worsening working conditions and health impacts, reduced livelihoods, or job losses' (Institute of Positive Fashion, 2021).

Equality, diversity and inclusion

Greater equality, diversity and inclusion is called for in the global fashion industry. In the first BFC and MBS Group Report on Diversity and Inclusion 2022, chief executive Caroline Rush stated, 'The fashion industry is historically an inherently exclusive industry, which presents barriers to entry that deter social and geographical mobility' (Shoaib, 2022). The report, which captured industry-wide data on leadership diversity from more than 100 top brands, found that 42 per cent of the brands do not collect data on diversity, only 51 per cent of the companies have a coordinated strategy, and few have specific targets for representation of underprivileged groups or specific budgets allocated to diversity and inclusion efforts (Shoaib, 2022).

Corporate social responsibility

Fashion brands that are working to be more sustainable and taking action to have great positive impact on people and planet may develop a corporate social responsibility (CSR) policy. This will detail the guiding principles for selection, implementation and monitoring of all the business activities that help them be more socially accountable to their employees, partners and the wider community.

For many fashion brands a CSR strategy is becoming a mainstream operation and these are expected to be implemented with honesty and transparency by companies with an aim to give back to society (Tewson, 2017).

As noted in Figure 3.5, the core drivers of CSR are authenticity and transparency, and creating benefits across the brand's community including its customers, workforce, partners, the environment and society as a whole.

Prosperity

While fashion brands need to address sustainable and ethical issues, working to reduce their impact on the environment, they still need to make a profit. The primary

Figure 3.5   Corporate social responsibility

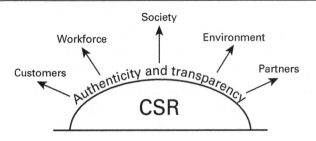

goal of any company is to make profit and stay in business and they would not be able to do good if their businesses failed due to poor financial management. Making a profit and doing good are not exclusive approaches, the two elements can and should work together. In the mid-1990s, John Elkington coined the idea of the triple bottom line (Elsey, 2021), a concept that businesses can build prosperity centred on 'people, planet and profit'. This approach evidenced the value that can be assigned to doing good, as well as looking at profit margins.

Fashion brands of the future should be building prosperity into their operations as prosperity relates to the condition of thriving or economic wellbeing, which should be embedded in their approach to everyone in their supply chain.

Authenticity and transparency

Fashion brands have no alternative but to make a commitment to develop strategies that will address the impact they have on the environment and society. The first step in the process is to be authentic and transparent in all their activities and be prepared to disclose information about their business practices rather than hide it or use greenwashing. Brands that are open and accountable build stronger relationships with consumers who share their values, and authenticity is rewarded with customer loyalty. While there has been some improvement in this area, the majority of brands are still disclosing very little information about their own sourcing and making practices, as well as failing to disclose the working practices of their suppliers.

A lack of authenticity and transparency will eventually start to affect the brand's bottom line, as consumers will start to seek out brands that they can see are being more honest and transparent, which increases their trust in them.

Summary

This chapter has addressed the challenges that the fashion industry faces as one of the biggest contributors to waste and climate change. It has looked at how the industry is using vast quantities of non-renewable resources including the raw materials and energy inputs, which are causing high emission levels that will lead to monumental climate crisis if not quickly addressed.

The industry has no alternative but to move away from the linear take–make–waste model and explore and develop new circular business models across the supply chain and by taking responsibility post-sale to offer new dimensions including reselling, repairing, refurbishing and recycling of products.

Fashion brands have an opportunity to transform to more regenerative models and address the systemic environmental and social challenge in their supply chain, building profitable businesses that have purpose at their heart to ensure greater responsibility to the planet, people, and prosperity for all.

Key terms

carbon insetting	greenwashing	reduce
circularity	linear supply chain	rental
corporate social responsibility	net zero	repair
	overproduction	resell
emissions	prosperity	sustainability
ethics	purpose	transparency
greenhouse gases	recycle	waste

Activity

Visit the Ellen MacArthur Foundation website to discover more about the processes of building a circular economy.

Online resources

Circular product lifestyle model.

References

Brodde, K (2017) What are microfibres and why are our clothes polluting the oceans?, *Greenpeace International*, www.greenpeace.org/international/story/6956/what-are-microfibers-and-why-are-our-clothes-polluting-the-oceans/ (archived at https://perma.cc/FH4D-MUJW)

Business of Fashion and McKinsey & Company (2022) The State of Fashion 2022

Butler, S (2019) G7 and fashion houses join forces to make clothes more sustainable, *The Guardian*, www.theguardian.com/world/2019/aug/21/fashion-g7-summit-sustainability-kering-inditex-macron (archived at https://perma.cc/GM24-SRUR)

Carbon Trust (n.d.) Net zero, *The Carbon Trust*, www.carbontrust.com/what-we-do/net-zero (archived at https://perma.cc/N2HC-M6F3)

Chen, C (2021) How fashion can tackle its supply chain crisis, *The Business of Fashion*, www.businessoffashion.com/articles/retail/how-fashion-can-tackle-its-supply-chain-crisis/ (archived at https://perma.cc/Z8KP-A4AH)

Common Objective (n.d.) The issues: water, *Common Objective*, www.commonobjective.co/article/the-issues-water (archived at https://perma.cc/J7KG-ZM8H)

Cooper (2018) Carbon insetting: what it is and how it works, *Native Energy*, native.eco/2018/01/carbon-insetting-what-it-is-how-it-works/ (archived at https://perma.cc/BQX2-RRXQ)

Crumbie, A (2021) Workers' rights in the clothing industry and what consumers can do, *Ethical Consumer*, www.ethicalconsumer.org/fashion-clothing/workers-rights-clothing-industry-what-consumers-can-do (archived at https://perma.cc/34DU-TV23)

DHL (2022) Delivering on Circularity, DHL White Paper

Edited (2021) The sustainability EDIT 2021 retail analysis, *Edited*, blog.edited.com/blog/resources/the-sustainability-edit-retail-analysis (archived at https://perma.cc/3GSC-B7QD)

Ellen MacArthur Foundation (2021) Circular business models in the fashion industry, *Ellen Macarthur Foundation*, ellenmacarthurfoundation.org/news/circular-business-models-in-the-fashion-industry (archived at https://perma.cc/NW4D-P3HP)

Elsey, W (2021) Council post: how sustainability can be profitable for your business, *Forbes*, www.forbes.com/sites/forbesbusinessdevelopmentcouncil/2021/10/04/how-sustainability-can-be-profitable-for-your-business/?sh=26900a2592a2 (archived at https://perma.cc/K8UN-2KTS)

Fashion Revolution (n.d.) Our impact, *Fashion Revolution*, www.fashionrevolution.org/impact/ (archived at https://perma.cc/U7LG-S9XJ)

Helmore, E (2019) Can fashion keep its cool … and help save the planet?, *The Guardian*, www.theguardian.com/fashion/2019/aug/31/can-fashion-keep-its-cool-and-help-save-the-planet (archived at https://perma.cc/A3XR-B4NP)

House of Commons (2019) Fixing fashion: clothing consumption and sustainability, *House of Commons Environment Audit Committee*, publications.parliament.uk/pa/cm201719/cmselect/cmenvaud/1952/1952.pdf

Institute of Positive Fashion (2021) The circular fashion ecosystem: a blueprint for the future, *The British Fashion Council*, instituteofpositivefashion.com/uploads/files/1/CFE/Circular_Fashion_Ecosytem_Report.pdf (archived at https://perma.cc/HJB3-UE9V)

IPCC (2021) Sixth assessment report, *IPCC*, www.ipcc.ch/assessment-report/ar6/ (archived at https://perma.cc/332L-BK7K)

King, D (2013) Why the word 'sustainability' should be banned, *The Guardian*, www.theguardian.com/environment/blog/2013/aug/29/meaningless-word-sustainability-banned (archived at https://perma.cc/UA3F-YFUD)

O'Brien, D, Main, A, Kounkel, S and Stephan, A (2019) Purpose is everything, *Deloitte Insights*, www2.deloitte.com/us/en/insights/topics/marketing-and-sales-operations/global-marketing-trends/2020/purpose-driven-companies.html (archived at https://perma.cc/HX44-R7HK)

Porter Novelli (2020) Purpose driven data, *Porternovelli*, www.porternovelli.com/wp-content/uploads/2020/04/COVID-19_Tracker_WaveII_Infographic_V4.pdf (archived at https://perma.cc/M89P-F334)

Shoaib, M (2022) British Fashion Council calls for 'braver approach to hiring' amid lack of diversity, *Vogue Business*, www.voguebusiness.com/fashion/british-fashion-council-calls-for-braver-approach-to-hiring-amid-lack-of-diversity?uID=c3f9f40646d5511ecf991a0757a713a5f2179c9953c544ca6cf2da3ef904a7bb&utm_campaign=newsletter_weekly&utm_source=newsletter&utm_brand=vb&utm_mailing=VB_NEWS_FRIDAY_010722&utm_medium=email&utm_term=VB_VogueBusiness (archived at https://perma.cc/6AQS-ZC2L)

Shopping Gives (2022) Social impact is driving shifts in consumer behaviour and ecommerce marketing, *Shopping Gives*, www.shoppinggives.com/brand-values-report/ (archived at https://perma.cc/ZZ3T-HG6A)

Simple Minded Life (2019) What does it mean to have purpose?, *Simple Minded*, www.simpleminded.life/what-having-purpose-means/ (archived at https://perma.cc/NL2T-2VMH)

Sustain Your Style (n.d.) Fashion and environment, *Sustain Your Style*, www.sustainyourstyle.org/en/whats-wrong-with-the-fashion-industry#:~:text=The%20fashion%20industry%20plays%20a%20major%20part%20in,about%20it%3F%20Choose%20fibers%20friendly%20to%20the%20soil (archived at https://perma.cc/2EVN-V7LX)

Tewson, S (2017) Positive impact: the power of fashion and CSR, *Front Row*, www.frontrowedit.co.uk/posi tive-impact-power-fashion-csr/ (archived at https://perma.cc/S6Z6-JAA6)

The Business of Fashion (2022) Fashion's sustainability secrets, *The Business of Fashion*, www.businessoffashion.com/articles/sustainability/fashion-transparency-index-revolution-traceability/ (archived at https://perma.cc/F3WE-92SW)

United Nations (n.d.) The Paris Agreement, *United Nations*, www.un.org/en/climatechange/paris-agreement (archived at https://perma.cc/46VD-V8ZP)

World Economic Forum (2021) Net-zero challenge: the supply chain opportunity, *World Economic Forum*, www.weforum.org/reports/net-zero-challenge-the-supply-chain-opportunity (archived at https://perma.cc/UNJ8-MBA4)

Case study
Charli Cohen

A passionate and driven entrepreneur who started her first fashion brand at 15 years old, eight years later Charli Cohen launched her eponymous, technical fashion label, which combines a sustainable ethos with high-performance fabrics and high-fashion design. Cohen describes her label as being born out of a need for evolved clothing and progression within the fashion industry. 'We make NEXTWEAR: looking to the future of fashion, aesthetically, in terms of technology and in terms of sustainability.'

The brand produces limited, exclusive collections made from premium, responsibly produced technical textiles, also upcycling military surplus and tactical wear, as well as creating one-off unique upcycled pieces. Charli Cohen has sustainability embedded in the foundations of the business, only working with certified and regularly audited factories that offer fair pay and good working conditions to all their workers. The brand aims for 70 per cent of their fabrics to be created using recycled ocean plastics, as well as working with mills that proactively innovate to minimize their carbon footprint. In addition, Cohen is dedicated to building a healthier, more inclusive creative industry and launched a mental health awareness initiative Shades of Blue. This uncensored community platform offers the opportunity to openly discuss, highlight and act to change endemic issues and abuse within the creative industries that contribute to poor mental health.

Cohen has been a leader in digital fashion and the metaverse, exploring augmented reality (AR) and virtual reality (VR) immersive technologies very early on. The brand now creates digital counterparts of physical fashion pieces, which can then be experienced in games, AR, VR and across the metaverse. Working on a collaborative project with Pokémon, Yahoo Ryot Lab and Selfridges London, Cohen created a virtual city and retail platform. Electric/City offered consumers a chance to immerse themselves in a new reality where they could explore different zones, purchase digital and physical designs, or create a customizable avatar to use across 300 other virtual platforms.

Cohen believes that digital fashion will continue to evolve, and the brand's mission is to give people a way to express identity freely and fluidly everywhere.

www.charli-cohen.com

Business foundations for fashion brands

4

LEARNING OBJECTIVES

After reading this chapter you should be able to:

- Identify the main fashion market segments
- Understand the business models and analysis tools used to develop a business strategy
- Understand how to create a business plan
- Explain the different types of business structure for fashion brands
- Understand the initial legal responsibilities and intellectual property considerations of a fashion brand

Introduction

This chapter explores the fashion market segments, the purpose of a strategy and the necessity to use the strategy to build a solid infrastructure for a fashion brand. The chapter will investigate a range of business models used to understand and develop a brand's purpose and competitive advantage. The business models and tools covered will look at internal analysis to develop an understanding of the organization's competences and added value processes, as well as external analysis to determine how the macro-environment can affect the brand in the future.

Developing a concept for a fashion brand is easy but making it a reality is the hard part. This chapter will advise on the need for a business to conduct thorough research into the market and the consumer to ensure the brand is not built on vague assumptions. The chapter presents the view that business modelling helps a brand develop the concept into a feasible strategy, using the visual one-page templates to capture all the key elements of the brand, before developing a more comprehensive business plan.

It is not the end of the process when a brand has determined its strategic capabilities and competitive advantage, as the fashion industry is a dynamic and volatile market that is constantly changing. The chapter considers the need to develop evaluation, monitoring and review processes to ensure that the business models and plans are living documents. Strategic planning ensures that the business has a systematic process to testing the vision, setting clear goals, monitoring the external environment and achieving success. The strategic planning process must be continual to ensure the brand remains relevant, viable and agile to adapt to changing market conditions.

Following the business planning processes, the chapter introduces some of the initial legal and intellectual property issues that support long-term growth and success for a fashion brand.

Market segments

Brands need to ascertain at which level they will position their label in the market, as this will then determine their strategy and how they will build value to meet customer expectations. The main market categories of haute couture, ready-to-wear and mass-market segment brands by price, value, quality and creativity. There has been significant movement of brands between these main market segments over the past two decades due to economic and commercial need, resulting in some sub-segments to offer price and product variations, with bridge or diffusion and value segments now recognized as main segments as well.

Haute couture

Haute couture describes brands offering exclusive, luxury, bespoke pieces that are hand-created with a high level of craftsmanship. The term 'haute couture' is a legally protected term that only brands accredited by the Chambre Syndicale de la Couture can use. If brands have not been accredited, then they should use the term couture. Haute couture brands include Christian Dior, Chanel, Schiaparelli and Givenchy. Many of the haute couture brands also have a ready-to-wear line, but the couture line is for a very limited few customers who can afford to have an individual piece made, whereas ready-to-wear is available to a wider customer base.

Ready-to-wear

Ready-to-wear or prêt-à-porter brands produce collections that are available to buy in a range of standardized sizes, but still have limited production numbers and a high level of creativity, quality and finish. Ready-to-wear brands include Gucci, Balenciaga, Chanel and Dior. A sub-segment of ready-to-wear are diffusion lines.

Bridge/diffusion

Bridge or diffusion are brands, or sub-brands, that create ranges that bridge the gap between the high-end ready-to-wear and mass market. There are brands that only position themselves in this segment such as Diesel, Coach and Kate Spade, whereas some diffusion brands are created by luxury labels to increase market share and gain a greater customer base by offering lower or midpoint price products. Luxury brands must be careful in the positioning of their diffusion lines in order to avoid compromising the aspirational identity of their main lines, something that some brands have struggled with, which has led them to close the lower-point lines. Bridge or diffusion brands include Marc by Marc Jacobs, See by Chloe, Armani Exchange.

Mass market

Mass-market fashion brands offer affordable fashion that is easily available on the high street and online to the masses. In this segment, products are mass produced in high volumes, in standard sizes with many examples of the same or similar designs available through various retailers. Mass-market fashion brands include Zara, H&M, M&S and Uniqlo. A sub-segment of the mass market is the value fashion market.

Value fashion

The value fashion market segment includes brands that rely on huge sales of cheap, lower quality, fashionable product that is perceived to be easily replaceable. Value fashion market brands include Primark, BooHoo and Shein.

Business modelling

Fashion brands often focus purely on their product offer, and emerging labels can be obsessive about their designs rather than considering consumer need, market and competitor analysis, which is detrimental to their future success. They rely instead on conjecture of the market or the customer, making vague unfounded assumptions or relying on hearsay. Management consultant Peter Drucker developed his theory of business to suggest that companies make assumptions in three areas: about the environment of the business, the mission and the core competences the organization needs. He noted that these assumptions often did not fit with reality, that there was no connection between the different parts, that the assumptions might not be known or shared across the company, and finally that the organization had not set up the processes to continually monitor and test the relevance of the assumptions over time (Drucker, 1994).

A brand cannot survive without in-depth research into all areas of the business. All brands need to constantly scan the macro-environment to assess the scenario within which the business is operating, as well as monitor competition and changing consumer behaviour to ensure they can create, deliver and capture value. External factors such as unstable market conditions, new consumer and cultural trends, wars and trade policies can have a huge impact on any company and influence its performance and success. In an ever-changing industry, the brands that shun constant monitoring of the political and macro-economic changes around them as part of their strategic planning could fail or lose market share to their more astute competitors. The State of Fashion 2022 discusses how the fashion industry 'faces a complex mix of challenges and opportunities, in which there is little room for missteps', therefore more complex strategic planning is essential for all fashion brands (Amed and Berg, 2022).

In developing a long-term business strategy, the starting point is business modelling, a process of using valuable business analysis tools to gather research, test concepts and develop the most effective path for the business. Business models are important for both new and established brands in identifying the company's journey to satisfying customer need and making a profit. There are as many different business analysis models as there are types of brands, but in its simplest form, a holistic business model should capture how the brand can create and offer value to the customer, the organization and the planet. Given below are some of the main models and analysis tools used by fashion brands to build their strategy.

Brand value business model

This model was created specifically for fashion brands to offer a simplistic model to guide the strategic direction by mapping out the who, what, how and why of the business. This simple model (Figure 4.1) was devised to assist brands that knew it was important to have a strategy but struggled with how to start to write it. This straightforward template captures the key elements that will form the baseline strategy of the brand. The 'what' is about the mission and goals that the organization will achieve; the 'why' is the vision, purpose and impact that the company will create; the 'who' is for whom and with whom the brand will create value; and the 'how' is the process that the business will take to achieve its aims, produce the product and add value to the customer.

The golden circle

Simon Sinek's 'golden circle' is a highly credited model that was designed for use in leadership, but works equally well for businesses, as it was based on the understanding that people do not buy what you do, or how you do it, they buy *why* you do it.

Figure 4.1   Brand value business model

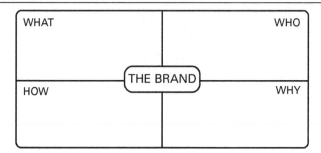

Sinek's model of three concentric circles can be used to analyse not only what product you create and how you do it, but to dig deeper to the middle circle to consider
why you even exist (Sinek, 2011).

Porter's five forces framework

This framework was designed by American academic Michael Porter who has developed numerous business strategy theories including this framework for businesses to
analyse the competition of business. This framework considers the competitive position
of a business by drawing out the influences of suppliers and buyers, the threat of substitutes, barriers to entry and the rivalry amongst existing competitors (Porter, 1980).

Porter's Diamond Theory of National Advantage

This is another theory designed by Michael Porter for businesses to analyse why
there are specific advantages for some industries in certain locations. These advantages are based on the set of interrelated elements of firm strategy, structure and rivalry; factor conditions; demand conditions; and related and supporting industries
(Porter, 1990).

Location advantage model

This analysis tool is a simple model (Figure 4.2) designed specifically for fashion
brands to provide a framework to review the benefits of basing a brand in a particular
country or even city. Using the framework, a brand can take into account the potential advantages from the local economy of the area, including how buoyant the market is, employment and wages, disposable income, investment opportunities, interest
rates and taxes. The framework asks the business to reflect on how the local culture
impacts employees, customers' values and priorities, dress codes, local practices, work
ethos and communication protocols. Accessibility considerations questions the ease

Figure 4.2   Location advantage model

Figure 4.3   PESTLE analysis

POLITICAL	ECONOMIC	SOCIAL + CULTURAL	TECHNOLOGICAL	LEGAL	ENVIRONMENTAL
Government policy	Economic recession	Demographic	Innovation	Laws:	Weather
Political instability	Inflation rates	Cultural	R + D	Employment	Climate
Foreign trade policy	Exchange rates	Religious	Automation	Consumer	Sustainability
Labour laws	Unemployment rates	Attitudes and beliefs	AI, AR and VR	Health and safety	Circular models
Environmental laws	Disposable income	Health and welfare	Data analysis	Copyright	Global impact
		Social trends	Communication channels	Intellectual property	

of import and export, access to resources, sourcing and manufacturing as well as digital technologies and innovation in their territory. Finally, community is important for fashion brands as there are competitive advantages of being part of a vibrant creative community. Fashion brands need access to a wide range of related creative businesses for idea generation and to deliver their creative outputs, as well as advantages in building a strong community with the local consumer market.

PESTLE analysis

PESTLE is the most recognized tool for assessing the macro-environment, the conditions that exist in the global economy that are outside of the control of the business but could affect it in the future. This theoretical concept has been credited to Francis J Aguilar, who described the need for 'scanning for information about events and relationships in a company's outside environment, the knowledge of which would assist top management in its task of charting the company's future course of action' (Aguilar, 1967). He developed the original acronym as ETPS but over time it has been adapted to its current PESTLE form (Figure 4.3). This framework should be used regularly by the business, with the template being made available to everyone in the organization to add information gained from industry publications, networking, international news channels or more formal research. Subjects written on the framework can be marked according to importance or risk to the brand, strategic decisions made, and actions taken to avoid the risk or take competitive advantage.

SWOT analysis

SWOT is a framework used by most brands to evaluate the strengths, weaknesses, opportunities and threats of a business idea, brand development and position in the market (Figure 4.4). While a popular business tool, it is often used incorrectly as a quick scan of the brand without connecting it to the overall environmental scanning. Using this internal view only could mean that the brand misses market opportunities or fails to identify threats from a changing market. Mullins (2013) states that 'SWOT analysis is essential for effective strategic management and evaluating the relationship between the organization and its environment'. The SWOT analysis therefore should always be conducted after the PESTLE analysis to ensure the business has an external as well as internal view on the brand and the macro-environment. The opportunities and threats section of the SWOT will take the future-facing information from the PESTLE analysis.

The business model canvas

The business model canvas was invented by Dr Alexander Osterwalder and defines the key activities, relationships and revenue streams for the business through the nine building blocks of customer segments, value proposition, channels, customer relationships, revenue streams, key resources, key activities, key partnerships and cost structure (Osterwalder and Pigneur, 2010). Fashion brands like this framework as it offers a way of capturing an overview of the business in a one-page, visual document.

The lean canvas

Adapted from the business model canvas by Ash Maurya, this model is for lean start-ups. The canvas investigates the problem rather than making assumptions with the solution or jumping straight to the product. The nine elements include problem, solution,

Figure 4.4　SWOT analysis

	CONSTRUCTIVE	NEGATIVE
INTERNAL	STRENGTHS	WEAKNESSES
EXTERNAL	OPPORTUNITIES	THREATS

key metrics, unique value proposition, unfair advantage, channels, customer segments, cost structure and revenue streams (Maurya, 2012).

Value proposition canvas

Another canvas created by Dr Alexander Osterwalder, which focuses on selling solutions not just products, ensuring that there is total alignment between the emotional and physical needs of the customer with the features and benefits of the products and services (Osterwalder et al, 2015).

Iterative fashion brand development model

This model (Figure 4.5) is another one developed specifically for the fashion industry to map the iterative process needed for brands to ensure they continually practise reviewing, reflecting and refining their business and their product. This process ensures a brand stays relevant to the customer and agile in a changing and competitive market environment. The framework is based on the need for brands to constantly refine and improve their processes and products as they develop their business.

Set across three different stages, the business should first 'discover and define' the customer need, their vision and values, their competitors and areas of differentiation, constantly reviewing and reflecting on these steps to ensure customer need is met and the brand has a competitive advantage. The second stage 'test' takes the brand through

Figure 4.5   Iterative fashion brand development model

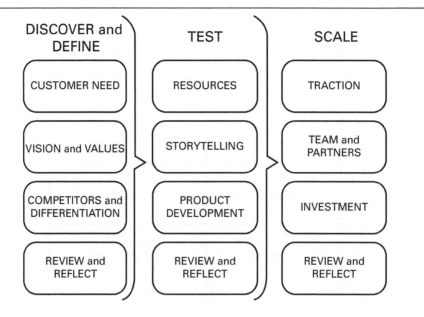

the process of gathering their resources, building their brand story, developing their product, and reviewing and reflecting that these steps meet the needs and vision determined in stage one. The third stage prepares the brand to 'scale' through increased market traction, building the internal team and external partnerships, and securing investment for future growth. This final stage also needs reflection and review to ensure that in the process of scaling the business has not moved away from its initial aims.

Circular business models

Circular business models have been developed to respond to the huge global environmental impact created by the fashion industry. All brands must focus on learning more about and building new circular business models that offer both revenue and cost benefits. Circular business models ensure products are designed to keep a high value state and remain in use over a longer period to ensure the maximum value is made, while minimizing ecological and social costs. A leader in the development and education of circular business models for the fashion industry is the Ellen MacArthur Foundation, who list the four main circular business models as rental, resale, repair and remaking (Ellen MacArthur Foundation, 2021). Circular business models are discussed in more detail in later chapters when looking at product design, development and production.

A brand can use some or all of these business analysis models in the development of their business and strategy. It is advisable that they use as many as possible as this would give a greater understanding of their organization's environment. Working through these different models, a brand will identify areas for competitive differentiation and advantage, and potential to develop a unique selling proposition. The frameworks can act as a means to capture information and identify areas for improved business performance and growth, and are a resource to use when moving on to write a full business plan.

The business plan

The business plan is a detailed written document that encapsulates how the business is structured, the product and service offer, the market, how the brand plans to meet its aims and achieve its strategic and financial objectives. The purpose of a business plan is to determine whether the concept is viable, detail every facet of a business, and is a tool to provide potential partners, investors and stakeholders with a thorough overview of the business to demonstrate it is a good investment. The business plan should be a living document that is used as a roadmap for the growth of a brand, which is reviewed annually to ensure it meets the challenges of a changing environment. The lack of a business plan, or failure to update it, can result in a business losing direction, missing opportunities or failing to meet the goals set. A business plan is an asset to the brand owners and business team to acknowledge successes as well as helping them avoid disaster.

Working on the business modelling and analysis tools, as well as the more in-depth market, competitor and consumer research needed for the business plan, may take considerable time, but will ensure that the brand has built the firm foundations that it needs for future growth.

Business plan format

There is no golden formula for writing a business plan as each business is different and the plan should reflect the uniqueness of the brand, but there are certain elements that need to be included and it needs to have a simple structure to be a useful tool for the future.

- **The executive summary:** This maps out an overview of the plan, including a description of the brand, what it does and what competitive advantage it has. It is beneficial to include an 'elevator pitch' or statement of the brand's unique proposition and should quickly address the opportunities for the business. The executive summary is always written last so that it can include the financial requirements needed to meet the goals.

- **Company overview:** The overview details the purpose and background to the brand in depth: what it is, what it does, what the competitive advantage is, how it will stand out, why people will buy the product and what position in the market the brand has already achieved.

- **The market, customer and competitor analysis:** This is the section for all the research into the market opportunity including market size, detailed description of the target customer, review of direct and indirect competitors and what makes the brand different to them. This section will need to be very detailed to evidence that the market and consumer base chosen is viable for the brand.

- **Organization and management:** Within this section the brand's organizational structure will be outlined and include details of the directors or owners, staff and any mentors, professional partners and advisers including lawyers and accountants. The experience and education of the founders would be included to evidence a skilled leadership team. This section can also detail all administrative tasks, legal status of the company, registered business and trading address, and intellectual property protection including trademark and design rights.

- **Product and service offer:** A detailed description of the product and service offer is included in this section, which could include a range plan, fabric and trim sourcing, manufacturing, stock levels and pricing. The detail should include what makes the brand's product and service offer unique such as the design aesthetic, brand signature and brand experience.

- **Sales strategy:** This section details each sales channel the business will use, including business-to-business, wholesale, marketplace and direct-to-consumer strategies, and detailed descriptions of e-commerce and retail sales strategies.

- **Marketing strategy:** This section will detail the development and communication plan of the unique selling proposition (USP) of the brand. It will include the value proposition, tangible and intangible customer benefits, communication strategies and brand storytelling. The marketing plan can include the 10 Ps – product, price, place, promotion, process, packaging, proof, pictures, personality and physical environment, which will make the unique market position for the brand.

- **Implementation plan:** This plan will define the specific goals, objectives, key performance indicators (KPIs) and actions that will be taken within a particular timeframe, including a critical path analysis.

- **Financial projections:** The financial elements would include a detailed cost analysis for the brand's products, sales projections for a three-year period, as well as a cash flow forecast, balance sheets and profit and loss.

The business plan needs to include clear strategic aims and objectives that can be easily measured and monitored, detailing the milestones the brand needs to work towards to grow and be successful. As author Alan Lakein (1974) said, 'Planning is bringing the future into the present so that you can do something about it now'. The business plan is setting the future for the brand, clarifying all the elements, goals and objectives to achieve success. Writing the business plan is not the end of the process, it needs to be constantly reviewed and evaluated to see if the brand has achieved the goals set and is still on target to meet the original purpose. When evaluating the plan, the brand may have had to pivot and adapt to changing markets or situations, so a regular review process will allow reflection and consideration of whether to embrace change or strategize how to get back on track. Ann Gatty (2022) advises: 'the business climate is always changing, so it can be expected that you will need to adjust or pivot directions as you continue the business journey. Successful companies will pivot from Plan A to Plan B or Plans C, D and E, if necessary, to stay competitive.'

The business structure

The business structure refers to the legal organization of the brand, which influences every element of the organization from personal liability to day-to-day operations, taxes and accountancy procedures. Choosing the right business structure from the start ensures the business has the firm foundations needed to grow without future restrictions or legal implications. Financial journalist Nick Green (2022) advises brands to consider that: 'the way in which your business grows, pays tax, takes big decisions and deals with liabilities will depend on its legal structure'. Depending on the country of origin, the brand will need to register, obtain licences, and consider local rules and regulations. There are some common business structures for fashion brands, which vary slightly in name and nature in different countries, but the main types are listed below.

Social proprietor/sole trader

A sole proprietor structure is a brand owned and operated by an individual. Often also referred to as self-employed or freelancer, it is a popular structure for a start-up as there is limited bureaucracy and paperwork and more control of decisions. The disadvantages include more exposure to personal risk as business and personal finances are not separated, limited access to finance and difficult to scale the business in the future.

Partnership

This structure is a legal agreement between two or more people who agree to share the profits and liabilities. Like the sole trader structure, each partner is registered as self-employed and submits separate tax returns. The advantages of this structure are simplicity and flexibility with the bonus of support from partners. The disadvantages are the need for a very clear legal agreement between the partners, challenges of decision making, and that partners are equally responsible for the other partner's debts. It can also be challenging to scale a partnership business.

Limited liability partnership

A limited liability partnership is a more formal version of the partnership mentioned above, with liability limited to the amount of money the partners have invested into the brand and to any personal guarantees given when raising finance. This option is sometimes chosen by a brand that has a silent partner who has invested but is not involved in the day-to-day running of the business.

Limited company/limited liability

This structure involves registering the brand as a legal entity, whose shareholders and directors can change over time, but the company continues to exist as a separate entity. The main advantages of a limited company are the finances are separate from the individual's, which reduces the personal risk, it offers increased credibility, the company name is protected by registration and there will be more opportunities to scale the business in the future. The disadvantages include a lot more administration and the need to file annual accounts and subsequent accountancy costs.

Social enterprise

This is a structure for a brand created to meet a social objective rather than just being profit-focused, with any profits being invested back into the business to meet the organization's goal. It is recommended that a social enterprise seeks advice from a business lawyer as it is a more complex structure to set up and, if not done correctly, it can affect the business's ability to raise money, eligibility for tax concessions or the reporting requirements.

It is important for a fashion brand to choose their business structure wisely as it is one of the most important decisions they will make for the success of their business and will influence their liability, tax and earning potential in the future. Registering a company is a simple process and will add more credibility to the business, making it easier to build relationships with suppliers and raise money in the future. Mark Hayes (2022) at Shopify advises: 'Incorporating your business makes it official in the eyes of the government. You'll protect your personal assets, build credit and history for your company, and even enjoy lower taxes in some cases. But the best benefits of business incorporation are perhaps intangible. Incorporation transforms your idea into a real, official business – the rest is up to you.'

Legal and intellectual property considerations for businesses

There are some important legal considerations that every business needs to adhere to, from ensuring they have a robust business structure for future growth, to matters around insurance, health and safety, data protection, contract law, legal obligations to employees and intellectual property protection. A brand needs to consider the legal framework they are operating in and plan how they will ensure they uphold their obligations and what professional legal support they will need. Below are some of the main business and legal considerations that fashion brands need to address.

It's all in the brand name

A great fashion brand needs a great name, and a name should be for life, as businesses can find it very difficult to change their name or rebrand later. The brand name really matters as it is part of the communication process, it differentiates a brand from competitors, and communicates the brand value and essence. A consumer will assume various brand values, associations, image and quality after encountering the name of the brand – and a strong brand name will stick in their mind.

A business needs to carefully reflect on various elements when choosing a brand name to make sure that it is available, works in various languages, is easy to say, has no negative connotations and evokes a positive emotion or memory. It is advised to check for all the meanings of a brand name or associated words in different languages and test the name to make sure it works on an international scale, as some words and names are much harder to say, understand or remember in different cultures and languages. A brand also needs to question the emotional value of a name, what it will mean to the customer, and whether it reflects the brand values and matches the types of products and service the brand delivers. A luxury label would need to consider whether the brand name reflects the luxury image that the business wants to portray.

There are legal implications in deciding a brand name, with time needed to fully investigate the availability of the name in all the forms and territories and confirm there are no conflicts or similarities with other brands. This means that brands need to research the availability of their chosen name across various channels including company name, trademark, domain name and social platforms.

> Registration of a company as a legal entity prevents others from registering a business with an identical name, but it does not prevent others using the name on the web, social media or from selling products under an identical or a similar name. A great misconception is that company registration automatically provides trademark protection and exclusivity, or the right to an associated domain name – it does not!

A business will need to register a domain name for the brand and secure the social media channels, and it is important to have a consistent name across all channels to ensure a smoother customer journey. If a domain or social media account name is not available, then a brand should be very wary of choosing something that is only similar not exactly the same, as this can badly affect e-commerce sales. Customers need to find a brand's social channels, website and e-commerce shop quickly and easily. Jose Palomino, president of Value Prop Interactive, says businesses selling directly to consumers should try harder and perhaps spend a bit more on matching domain to brand. 'You can get away with some disparity between company or product name and domain name with business to business, because it usually has a direct-sales component,' says Palomino. 'It's not so good for business to consumer, because consumers will not spend as much time trying to find you' (Klein, 2012).

Once a brand is satisfied that the name is secured on all the channels they will use, then the next step would be to protect it with a trademark, which prevents another business from using a name that is the same or like the registered mark. The subject of trademarking is covered in more detail below in the section on intellectual property protection.

Deciding and securing a brand name on all channels can occasionally be an easy task, but often in today's saturated market the process can be long-winded, difficult and take much more effort than anticipated. 'While it may seem that finding the right brand name requires significant investment (and it does), you will definitely get your money back. Just think about the ROI in terms of extra sales, talent attraction, and brand loyalty – there's no denying that a good brand name will be worth the investment in the long term' (Polachek, 2022).

Logo

Alongside the name, fashion brands need a logo that makes their brand stand out, reflects their personality and acts as an emblem for the label. Alexander Westgarth (2022) discussed the importance of having the right logo, 'The right logo says everything without saying a word. It connotes feelings of honour, trust, pride, excellence and integrity. It conveys a series of virtues and a set of values without pages of copy and a team of copywriters. It evokes a sense of connection between a brand and consumers. It establishes a bond between a company and its community of fans, friends, critics, allies and champions.'

The logos of the most successful fashion brands are unique, simple and mostly typographic, but the creation of a motif, a recurring narrative element with symbolic significance, can be the element that stands the test of time. Fashion brands that have motifs as part of their logos include Nike with the swoosh motif and Louis Vuitton with the damier motif. Many luxury brands have a monogram motif, which over time becomes the key identifier for their products.

Brands need logos that have longevity and enduring value for consumers. A Business of Fashion article reviewed what logos are worth as brands evolve. Rati Sahi Levesque, chief merchant at The RealReal luxury recommerce site, revealed the value of the logo in the resale of Chanel quilted handbags: 'We've found that the demand for logo product is more than 20 per cent higher than similar, non-logo product from the same brand. Chanel's Timeless flap bag, with its iconic CC logo, retains 30 per cent more of its resale value versus the 2.55 flap bag, which is the original flap bag design, sans logo' (Amed, 2022). Once a unique logo or motif has been created, then this will also need to be registered as a trademark to give the brand ownership and make it easier to enforce trademark rights and prevent infringement.

Intellectual property protection

The fashion industry has always had prolific issues with copying and brand infringements. The risk of copying is growing as access to brand collection imagery is now more readily available through the internet and social media. Also, with squeezed design departments needing to constantly produce more ideas and more products faster and more often, it is not surprising that designers and mass-market brands are constantly on the lookout for the latest ideas, designs and product concepts that are being produced by others in the market. Intellectual property breaches often go unchallenged due to difficulties in making claims and the vast amount of time and resources it takes when brands get locked into legal battles. Smaller fashion brands may not understand the processes of intellectual property protection or are unable to fund the registration process or the litigation. In an article in Drapers discussing fashion's intellectual property crisis, Laurian Davies, international business manager at the UK Fashion and Textile Association, said: '[Smaller brands] sort out their VAT and get a reasonable accountant, but they don't do enough in most cases to protect the most vital ingredients in the success of their company: their trading name and their designs. In the excitement of getting their designs out to market, they don't think to register them' (McGregor, 2022).

Intellectual property protection for fashion brands can include trademarks, copyright, patents and design rights. To give you a quick understanding of the different elements, the trademark can refer to the brand name, such as 'Chanel'; copyright protects the two-dimensional figures, drawings or prints; the design right may protect the appearance and shape of a garment, for example 'the Chanel style jacket'; and finally, a patent, would cover an innovative function, construction or operation of a product, or a new type of material.

Registering a trademark

Registering a trademark is one of the most effective ways to protect a brand's name and work. A trademark is a vital asset to the brand's reputation and image and can be used to generate income through selling or licensing it in the future. A trademark is a symbol used to distinguish the goods and services from competitors. A trademark can be any word, phrase, symbol or design that identifies the brand's goods or services. The process of registering a trademark includes conducting a full clearance search to make sure no one else has registered it, before considering the registration territory (or countries) that the brand needs protection in. A brand will need to file separate applications for each of the territories it wishes to trade in, and global trademark registration is prohibitively expensive; therefore, brands must often prioritize the territories they apply for a trademark in according to their budget and where there is most risk. Having a trademark in one territory or country does not protect a brand from someone using their brand name in another country that they have not covered.

Trademark is also determined by 'class', which is the industry grouping that the trademark will come under. In the UK there are 45 classes listed by number and covering certain products and service such as watches and jewellery or clothing, footwear and headwear. A brand can be classified under more than one class.

Trademarks typically take three to six months to process for each territory and are covered for 10 years initially, allowing the brand to use the registered trademark symbol, the circled 'R' (®). The trademark can last forever if renewal fees are paid, and the mark continues to be used for the products and services covered by the registration. During the registration process, a brand can use the symbol TM (™) to provide notice of a claim of common-law rights. A TM is usually used in connection with an unregistered mark, to inform potential infringers that a term, slogan, logo or other indicator is being claimed as a trademark. Use of the TM (™) symbol does not guarantee that the owner's mark will be protected under trademark laws.

Copyright

Copyright relates to two-dimensional work and in the UK a brand does not need to register a copyright as there is automatic protection, however in some other countries a brand can, or may need to, formally register a copyright for their work. In the UK, copyright will arise automatically as soon as pen is put to paper. For a fashion brand copyright can apply to images, website and content, patterns, drawings and unique prints. For the copyright to be granted, the work must be original. A copyright lasts for 70 years after the death of the designer in the UK, however if the work is put into production through an industrial process (such as manufacturing) then the copyright only lasts 25 years from the end of the year that the piece was first marketed.

For a brand to claim copyright infringement, they must be able to prove they did the work first, with evidence such as proof of origin, date of creation, where they were working at the time. To prove copyright, brands need to keep clear records so that they can quickly prove ownership. The process of declaring copyright on all two-dimensional works is to apply the copyright symbol © with name and year of creation.

Patent

Brands can apply for a patent if they have invented a totally new type of product, an innovative construction process, fastening or a unique fabric. A patent gives inventors a monopoly on their products for up to 20 years by giving them the right to stop anyone else from making it or using it without their permission. The patent will establish the invention as belonging to the brand, which means they can sell, rent or license it to others.

Design rights

In the UK a designer has an automatic 'design right' that protects their design for 10 years after it was first sold or 15 years after it was created, whichever is the earliest. A brand can use their automatic design right to stop someone copying a design if they can provide evidence of the earliest date when they created it or produced it. To evidence this, the brand will usually need to show examples such as signed and dated copies of drawings, patterns, specification sheets and agreements with suppliers and manufacturers to prove the case.

The design right can apply to the shape, structure, look and design of a fashion piece such as clothing, shoes, handbag or accessory. The design right can apply to the whole or part of the product, such as the design of a dress or a unique collar detail can be covered by design protection.

It is also possible to register a design for better protection, provided it meets the eligibility criteria. The application to register a design can be made at any time in the first 12 months of the design first being shown. As the process is very expensive, registered design rights are usually only sought for a core product that has longevity, a product that a brand will produce many times in future seasons, such as the Chanel-style jacket, rather than a one-season trend piece.

Confidentiality and non-disclosure agreements

An additional way of protecting a brand's ideas and designs is to use confidentiality or non-disclosure agreements before revealing details of any proposed business, brand or design. These agreements should clearly state that any information the brand discloses will be kept confidential and not shared with any third party or used for any other purpose than in the discussion between the two parties. It is recommended that a brand uses non-disclosures with all suppliers, manufacturers, freelancers and staff before any detailed conversations are started or designs shared. If the other party will not sign the agreement, then this may be an indicator that they do not value the brand's intellectual property.

In fashion, all the different intellectual property protections can cross over and co-exist, so that a brand can seek protection with copyright, trademark and design rights. The fashion design industry is based on the reinterpretation of styles and concepts, so there is always the potential for copying. For smaller brands who struggle to finance litigation against bigger brands who steal their designs, the only option is to ensure they protect themselves as much as possible by keeping detailed records of all work, but more importantly use their agility to stay ahead by constantly innovating and creating new work.

GDPR – data protection

In May 2018, the General Data Protection Regulation (GDPR) was enforced across Europe, including the UK. The law aims to give citizens more control over their data and create a uniformity of enforcement rules across the Continent. The law insists that brands set up systems to protect data, as well as gain consent from individuals to hold their personal data in the first place. GDPR defines 'personal data' as any information relating to an identified or identifiable natural person (data subject). In other words, any information that obviously relates to a particular person and can be used to identify them (Irwin, 2022).

Brands need to respect all data collected on their website through cookies, subscription and contact forms, and must include a cookies policy and privacy notice on the website. They need to obtain explicit consent from website visitors or contacts that signifies their agreement to their data being processed. Consent is specific to the type of communication in question, so if an individual opts into cookie tracking, they have only given their consent for cookie tracking, whereas if they have given consent to be communicated over email, they have only given their consent for email communication. Brands now need to get consent for each element of their marketing activity and keep an audit trail to prove consent. Individuals have the right to request information on how their personal data is being processed, including where and for what purpose, as well as the right to request the deletion or removal of their personal data at any time.

Insurance

There are inherent risks in running a business and, in an ever-growing litigious world, businesses need insurance to protect themselves, as well as meet the legal requirements of the countries they trade in. If a brand fails to have the legally required cover, then it can lead to fines, civil or criminal penalties, and exclusion from some business and public contracts. Therefore, businesses need to consider risk management strategies to ensure they have a wide range of protection in case of disaster or claim. There is no one-size-fits-all system to insurance, therefore fashion brands will need a unique package of protection that fits their business. This can include protection and cover for product, property, computers and stock from fire, theft and water damage, as well as business interruption insurance to cover themselves in case they ever must stop trading due to a disaster of some kind. There are legal requirements to take out employer liability insurance, and it is recommended – although there is no legal requirement for it – to take out public liability to cover the brand against claims from third parties. Public liability insurance is required for events or pop-up shops, or when hiring venues. Additional insurance can be taken to cover legal claims or tax investigations, and there are policies available to protect a brand's intellectual property or protect themselves in case they were accused of infringing another brand's intellectual property. With the growing increase in litigation trends in the fashion industry, a brand needs to understand insurance in order to maximize successful recovery of their business in worse-case scenarios.

Health and safety

Health and safety laws apply to all businesses and different laws apply around the world, but all businesses have duties to assess risks in the workplace for both their staff and the public. This involves the business conducting thorough risk assessments, keeping appropriate records, implementing health and safety processes, and ensuring the processes are communicated and adopted by all staff.

Employment laws

Employment law refers to legislation that is designed to protect employees from exploitation. Around the world the laws about employment can change, but in the fashion industry there is a growing focus on ensuring that all employee rights are protected. Employment laws include fair recruitment processes, minimum wage laws, fair working conditions including diversity, inclusion and equality, as well as the business's responsibility to provide safe working conditions. A breach of statutory rights would give rise to legal action but also lead to negative press, which would damage the brand's reputation.

Brand advisers, mentors and consultants

The steps to build a firm foundation mentioned in this chapter can be complicated and time consuming, and not every business will have a person or team with all the skills to develop and manage the strategic development of a fashion label. Every good entrepreneur, business founder or manager knows that a brand needs advice in order to grow and thrive, whether an established label or a start-up. Help and advice for building a business, and developing the strategy, can come from mentors, consultants or an advisory board and more brands are starting to see the value in surrounding themselves with experts from different fields.

In an article on Forbes, David Chen wrote about why advisory boards are important for growing businesses, 'Members of an advisory board focus directly on certain aspects within the company and use their expertise in ways the company may be limited, whether it be due to time, money, formalities or approvals. This advice provides a third-party perspective – an important point of view that combats emotional decision making. By having an advisory board, C-level executives illustrate their responsibility and willingness to include multiple perspectives' (Chen, 2022).

Designers who set up fashion brands alone often struggle with all the business aspects of running their own label, so need to find people who will advise and help them set up the structures and processes that will keep the business on its path to success. In the early stages, it will be unlikely that they can afford to hire and pay a permanent team of consultants and advisers, but they may need to pay for some professional services such as legal and accounting. If they do struggle with the business processes, the smaller brands need to be wary of rushing into taking on staff as this can be a huge cost pressure on the business, instead they can buy in freelancers or consultants on a needs basis.

An extensive network of mentors and advisers can be instrumental in making any business a success, as they bring in a wealth of knowledge, contacts, connections and industry experience that it could take the brand years to build. This network is invaluable to creating the infrastructure that will enable a brand not only to survive but to thrive and scale. There is a well-known proverb that says it takes a village to raise a child, and that community approach is appropriate for businesses too, though it might take a city to build a fashion brand!

Summary

This chapter has emphasized how important it is for a fashion brand to build a solid infrastructure and develop their business based on in-depth research rather than assumptions. Every year, hundreds of fashion brands around the world fail due to lack of planning and understanding of the market. Many more, and this includes well-known, established brands, have failed because they have ignored the need to continually review and revise their plans and were therefore left behind as the world changed and the industry transitioned. The business tools and frameworks discussed in this chapter are an invaluable resource for a fashion brand to use to take and scale their idea from concept to reality, with a planned and effective strategy.

A brand needs to work hard on developing a well-planned strategy and going through the business modelling, planning and developing. The legal infrastructure mentioned in this chapter can be a daunting process, particularly for smaller brands who only have solo entrepreneurs or small teams. Even larger brands can struggle with managing business development strategies and conducting the research needed to build the brand on clear facts rather than assumptions. Developing a business strategy is a complex process, and with the current state of the market and an ever-evolving fashion industry, the leaders of fashion brands are having to deal with multifarious issues on a daily basis. They need to determine a clear direction for the brand to have an advantage to succeed in a saturated and competitive market.

Key terms

advisory board	GDPR	non-disclosure agreement
brand value model	haute couture	patent
bridge/diffusion line	intellectual property protection	PESTLE
business model		ready-to-wear
business plan	iterative fashion brand model	social enterprise
business strategy		sole proprietor
business structure	limited liability	SWOT
circular fashion model	location advantage model	trademark
copyright	market segments	value fashion
design right	mass market	

Chapter review questions

- Why is it important for a fashion brand to use business models and plans?
- How can assumptions damage a brand's strategy and future success?
- Can you explain the different business structures and the advantages of each one for a fashion brand?
- What type of intellectual property protection can a brand use to protect their designs?

Activity

Conduct a PESTLE and SWOT analysis on a fashion brand of your choice.

Online resources

- Business plan template
- Iterative fashion brand model template
- Brand value model template

References

Aguilar, F (1967) *Scanning the Business Environment*, Macmillan, New York

Amed, I and Berg, A (2022) The State of Fashion 2022, Business of Fashion and Mckinsey & Company, www.businessoffashion.com/events/luxury/state-of-fashion-2022-professional-live/ (archived at https://perma.cc/23GR-UQ3X)

Amed, O (2022) As branding evolves, what's a logo Worth?, *The Business of Fashion*, www. businessoffashion.com/articles/news-analysis/as-branding-evolves-whats-a-logo-worth/ (archived at https://perma.cc/WFR5-ET7V)

Chen, D (2022) Council post: why advisory boards are important for growing businesses, *Forbes*, www.forbes.com/sites/theyec/2019/07/23/why-advisory-boards-are-important-for-growing-businesses/?sh=37b4e38f2ba0 (archived at https://perma.cc/9PJF-N8TD)

Drucker, P (1994) *Theory of the Business*, Harvard University Press, Boston, MA

Ellen MacArthur Foundation (2021) Circular business models in the fashion industry, *Ellen MacArthur Foundation*, ellenmacarthurfoundation.org/news/circular-business-models-in-the-fashion-industry (archived at https://perma.cc/9FZQ-KUZ3)

Gatty, A (2022) When is it time to pivot with your business plan?, *Strategic People Solutions*, www.strategicpeoplesolutions.com/posts/when-is-it-time-to-pivot-with-your-business-plan/ (archived at https://perma.cc/3GMG-6AQL)

Green, N (2022) Choosing a business structure, *Unbiased*, www.unbiased.co.uk/life/small-business/business-structure (archived at https://perma.cc/CFD4-UT7Y)

Hayes, M (2022) Types of businesses: which legal structure is right for your new venture?, *Shopify*, www.shopify.com/blog/business-types (archived at https://perma.cc/QA7E-LFTV)

Irwin, L (2022) The GDPR: What exactly is personal data?, *IT Governance*, www.itgovernance.eu/blog/en/the-gdpr-what-exactly-is-personal-data (archived at https://perma.cc/Z7AA-HLFD)

Klein, K (2012) When should domain names match company names, https://www.zinzin.com/press/articles/when-should-domain-names-match-company-names/ (archived at https://perma.cc/PQA4-YKGA)

Lakein, A (1974) *How To Get Control of Your Time and Your Life*, Signet, New York

Maurya, A (2012) *Running Lean*, 2nd edn, O'Reilly Media, Inc (n.p.)

McGregor, K (2022) The imitation game: fashion's intellectual property crisis, *Drapers*, www.drapersonline.com/companies/the-imitation-game-fashions-intellectual-property-crisis (archived at https://perma.cc/E2D7-ZU4P)

Mullins, L (2013) *Management & Organizational Behaviour*, Pearson Education, Harlow

Osterwalder, A and Pigneur, Y, (2010) *Business Model Generation*, Wiley, Hoboken, NJ

Osterwalder, A, Pigneur, Y Bernarda, G, Smith, A and Papadakos, T (2015) *Value Proposition Design*, Wiley, New York

Polachek, G (2022) 4 reasons your brand name matters, *Business 2 Community*, www. business2community.com/branding/4-reasons-your-brand-name-matters-02326332 (archived at https://perma.cc/C56Z-YRBZ)

Porter, M (1980) *Competitive Strategy: Techniques for analysing industries and competitors*, Free Press, New York

Porter, M (1990) Competitive advantage of nations, *Competitive Intelligence Review*, 1(1), p 14

Sinek, S (2011) *Start With Why*, Portfolio Penguin, London

Westgarth, A (2022) The importance of having the right logo, *Forbes*, www.forbes.com/sites/theyec/2018/11/30/the-importance-of-having-the-right-logo/?sh=47e711d71ccb (archived at https://perma.cc/DJ2G-WBXY)

Case study
Ecoalf

Ecoalf has been a pioneer in sustainable fashion since 2009 and was the first Spanish fashion brand to become a certified B-Corp in 2018. A purpose-driven company with a mission to create the first generation of recycled products with the same attention to quality, design and technical properties as the best non-recycled products on the market. Javier Goyeneche founded Ecoalf in response to his frustrations with the excessive use of the world's natural resources and the amount of waste produced by industrialized countries. The fundamental drivers of Ecoalf are innovation and technology, sustainability and design.

After years of sourcing fabrics, Goyeneche found that most recycled fabrics only contained about 20 per cent recycled materials, so he formed partnerships with factories throughout the world in order to develop their own innovative, recycled fabrics, linings and trims. The company continues to invest in new research and development to remain industry leaders in the field. Where other people see discarded fishing nets, used plastic bottles, old tyres and coffee grounds as trash, Goyeneche sees high-quality raw materials, and continues to find innovative ways to recycle discarded materials.

Ecoalf is proactive in taking action to improve sustainability in the industry by forming the Ecoalf Foundation in 2015, a non-profit organization whose main objective is to promote the selective recovery of waste in order to recycle it and avoid its harmful effects on the environment. The foundation has embarked on ambitious projects such as 'Upcycling the Oceans' with the aim of cleaning up the Mediterranean by 2025. The project works directly with fishing personnel who separate rubbish they collect in their nets into containers provided by Ecoalf Foundation, which is then classified and recycled. Ecoalf will keep the plastic bottles collected from the bottom of the ocean and turn them into high-quality ocean yarn (recycled polyester) to develop their 'Ocean Waste Footwear' outerwear and accessories.

The brand has grown steadily into offering a full lifestyle collection of innovative sustainable staples including outerwear, swimwear, casual apparel, shoes and accessories. The brand distributes their products through prestigious department stores around the world and in its integrated Ecoalf sustainable concept store and head offices in Madrid.

www.ecoalf.com

Product design and development 5

LEARNING OBJECTIVES

After reading this chapter you should be able to:

- Explain why fashion brands need to research the consumer before they design the collection
- Understand the concept of the fashion cycle
- Describe how adding elements from the product star can add value for the consumer
- Review a brand's collection to identify their design signature
- Explain how fashion and consumer buying trends impact the production of fashion apparel

Introduction

This chapter will discuss the elements of the design process that increase the likelihood of a brand being successful and selling their designs. This chapter will not attempt to teach practical fashion design and making skills, instead it will focus on the business aspects of design rather than technical drawing or construction processes.

Many fashion labels are started by designers who have graduated from a fashion school, and they struggle to build successful brands due to a lack of commercial awareness. Fashion design courses often lack detailed business training, resulting in the 'critical problem that fledgling designers lack the imperative business skills needed', meaning they do not consider the commercial aspects of consumer need when designing collections (Dhillon, 2016). Therefore, this chapter will delve into the commercial aspects, as all fashion brands need to design commercially viable collections and avoid creating pieces that are either unwearable or do not appeal to the brand's perceived customers. For the collection to sell, either by wholesale or direct to customer, their range must be cohesive, have a recognizable signature and meet the needs of an identified customer.

The fashion industry is famously fickle, biased and often trend-driven, 'You are only as good as your last collection' is something we often hear in the industry, so it is vital to know how to design a commercially strong fashion collection that is cohesive and makes sense to the buyers (Tsolova, 2022).

The chapter will discuss the areas of development in the design process from developing the brand's design DNA and signature through the collection development process including ideation; inspiration; development of trends, colour, shape, silhouettes and textures; and creating a range plan to satisfy the customer need. The chapter uses the terms 'collection' and 'range', which are used in the industry to describe a group of fashion apparel items that are presented together to the buying public at a set period of time (Davis Burns, Mullet and Bryant, 2011). Another term used is 'apparel line', which refers to multiple collections and all the clothing a fashion brand produces within a certain category, such as a sports line or a shirt line. This chapter will look at design, product development and functionality, with the areas of the patterns and tech pack development covered in Chapter 6 on Supply chain management. It will also introduce the need to consider how the brand's sales and marketing strategy impacts the collection they develop.

Research

Too many brands enter the market with the perception that they can find their feet, refine their design process and discover their design signature over time. This approach is not viable in a fast-paced fashion industry that gives brands only one opportunity to get it right. The fashion industry is an oversaturated market with thousands of labels competing worldwide, all fighting to break in and maintain a viable market position. Brands have to develop a unique proposition and brand DNA through their product signature and collections as well as through their branding right from the start. Fashion brands must use market research to start the design and development of their collections, taking a 'systematic and objective approach to the development and provision of information for the marketing management design-making processes (Kinnear and Taylor, 1996). The research would need to investigate the wider market and competitive environments before in-depth research into the potential consumer and their needs for fashion product. Research is an integral part of the design system that supports the design process from conceptualization to the product development, involving the initial hunt for ideas, market and client study, fabric and resources, production and execution, finding out vendors prior to design until the stage where it gets final feedback from the experts and the users (Sonika Soni Khar et al, 2018).

Figure 5.1 shows steps taken in the design to production process with each step related to the others and completed in order, so that the end result would be a fashion collection of products that are suitable for an identified market. The mistake that many brands make is rushing into later steps without the concept development and research needed to make the collection and the brand a success.

Figure 5.1 details sequential steps in the process from design to production, but another approach is design thinking. This is a non-linear, iterative process that brands can use to understand users, challenge assumptions, redefine problems and create innovative solutions to prototype and test. Design thinking is a consumer-facing process in the production of designs that was first mentioned by cognitive scientist Herbert A Simon and involves five phases of empathize, define, ideate, prototype and test (Interaction Design Foundation, 2021). Design thinking relates to the fashion design process with *empathize* referring to understanding the potential customers; *define* relates to accurately profiling consumers and identifying their need; *ideation* is using the first two research phases to generate ideas; *prototype* is the experimental phase of creating samples to test design solutions and product ideas; and *test* relates to getting feedback, refining the designs, or, as it is an iterative process, going back to the start to identify other ideas or solutions. The design thinking model can be used throughout a fashion brand's processes, including design, sourcing, making, selling and marketing. The iterative process should continue through the lifecycle of the brand, as the company should always be looking to identify and test new ideas to meet consumer need. As the brand grows, the pressure to design and create more collections at faster speeds will increase, therefore, brands need to embed design thinking in their processes to ensure they continually innovate and adapt to changing need and demand without compromising the brand's design aesthetic and signature.

Figure 5.1   Design to production process

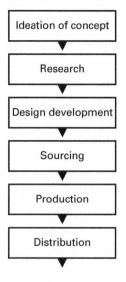

The customer

As identified in Chapter 1, the customer always comes first. Many designers and brands dive straight into designing, and even produce their collection, without thinking about their customer. In any other sector, a business would always identify the customer and what they want first, and then create the product for them. Fashion brands, however, often only consider their customer once they have already designed and made their products. The customer should be at the very core of a brand, as a label without customers is not a business, it is a hobby. To achieve success in the fashion industry the brand needs to know the target market and provide the merchandise assortment that the customer wants and needs (Davis Burns, Mullet and Bryant, 2011). There has historically been a perception in fashion that if you create an amazing collection then the customer will automatically come, but that is rarely the reality. Fashion is a consumer-driven market, and a brand stands more chance of success if they have clearly identified and researched the customer.

> The simple truth is that no matter how amazing the designs, if the customer doesn't need it, want it or understand it, they won't buy it.

Fashion is a very personal purchase and the customers' needs can be very different. By putting the customer at the front of the process, a brand can be sure that the product they are creating will be suitable and will meet the customer needs.

The market

Fashion designers and brands need to understand the market environment and its challenges to ensure their collections are relevant to the consumer and meet their needs. Changes in the macro-environment – including political, economic, social, technological, environmental or legal changes – can impact on how and what consumers purchase and what they need. Designers need to consider these factors prior to designing products or collections, for example Trend Hunter states that during times of political unrest consumers often turn to military chic looks, but chaotic and unpredictable economic times drive other trends such as over-the-top accessories, i.e. extremely oversized jewellery (Trend Hunter, 2008). Changes in the macro-environment can also create challenges that affect access to fabrics, materials or manufacturing in certain countries, so the brand would need to consider other options in their design process. By researching the market, the designer should be able to predict future trends that will appeal to their customer and also identify opportunities for new markets.

The competitors

Prior to starting the design process, brands should have a great understanding of the competitive environment and have detailed analysis on their direct competitor's product, design signature, branding and storytelling to ensure the product they create has a point of difference. The market is facing a glut of brands that all seem to offer the same product and competitor analysis is a good starting point for identifying niches of untapped value (440 Industries, 2018). The competitor research aims to specify the points that set the brand apart from their competition, enabling it to create competitive advantage in the product design, which will help the brand stand out and capture more market share (Mann-co, 2020).

Developing the design DNA

The brand DNA is the essence of the brand, a complex mix of components including the visual elements that make the brand instantly stand out. The DNA includes the product, logo, brand colours and marketing, as well as all the principles that the brand lives by. The development of the brand's DNA in relation to the design of the product and signature aesthetic across the collections ensures the unique product or aesthetic tells the story of the brand's values and principles. Developing a unique stylistic language that differentiates the brand from the competition, helps fashion brands stand out in a crowded marketplace. There are many complaints today of fashion brands all appearing the same, and one of the reasons for this is because newer ones actively try to copy other successful and established brands, rather than develop their own unique DNA or design aesthetic (Mann-co, 2020).

Creating a brand DNA is key to establishing a successful business, as companies with a strong DNA appear to be more trustworthy, create better long-term customer relations and have more impact on society (Helmke, 2018). Even though fashion businesses may follow trends or create different collections, they need to uphold a certain individual characteristic to maintain brand recognizability. For fashion businesses, stylistic identity is the heart of each product and their branding system (Designers Studio, 2015). The brand's DNA could be a signature design or product that the label produces in every collection that becomes recognizable and synonymous with the brand. The brand signature can be an iconic product that appears in every collection such as the Burberry trench coat, or the signature is featured on every piece such as the Louboutin red sole. Although iconic products are more significant for luxury brands, most brands now work to establish a unique iconic or hero product that is recognizable to their label, as these items are easier to sell (Designers Studio, 2015).

Sustainable and purpose-driven design

Fashion brands have to carefully plan and manage their design process to ensure they meet their business objectives and deliver value to their customers. There are an increasing number of customers who seek brands that offer sustainable products and transparency in how products are made. Today's customer is much more knowledgeable about sustainable fabrics, ethical working conditions and the impact of fashion and overproduction on the environment.

> Fashion brands need to embed their values within the design process, to ensure that in the process of designing and making their product they do not lose sight of their original aims, purpose and values including sustainability, ethics and transparency.

This impacts what products and collections the brand designs and when, how big the collections will be and how they will be made. Sustainability should be embedded in the business model and be part of the brand DNA, providing transparency in the design process of the product from concept to consumer. The design process can use strategies and techniques that offer more ethical and sustainable practices including:

- **Zero waste:** Zero waste is a design process that plans to eliminate fabric waste at the design stage. Zero waste can also be achieved by designing elements that will use surplus fabric such as button covers, pockets, trims, edging, accessories and smaller goods.

- **Upcycling:** Upcycling includes transforming materials or waste products into something new. Brands can design styles that use upcycled materials, dead stock fabrics, or repurpose fabric and clothing to make new ones. Emily Chan wrote in British *Vogue* about the huge increase in luxury brands upcycling, such as Balenciaga and Miu Miu launching upcycled collections and products, which shows a significant shift in the industry (Chan, 2020). This shift has occurred due to consumers being more environmentally conscious and knowledgeable and they will no longer tolerate the shocking practice of brands incinerating or throwing away products due to overproduction.

- **Multi-functional:** This approach involves creating garments that are multi-functional, reversible or can be transformed into a different piece, making it wearable in more ways, so that the consumer can buy fewer pieces.

- **Timeless design:** Timeless designs or 'slow fashion' refers to the design of classic pieces, ones that are not trend-focused, instead designed for longevity. Consumers looking to buy slow fashion garments seek to buy timeless pieces that with care would last for years and be pieces that they would in time either repair, resell, update, recycle or upcycle.

- **Circular fashion:** Incorporating circular fashion into the brand DNA involves a more considered model of designing, sourcing and making garments with the intention that they will be used for as long as possible and then returned safely to the biosphere when they no longer have human use. 'Circular fashion is a holistic design approach [...] that aims to "design out waste" by reducing the number of natural resources used to make our clothing and diverting products from landfills' (Sustainable Fashion Forum, n.d.). A brand would need to consider designing pieces that have longevity and are created from sustainable fabrics and trims that could be repaired, redesigned, swapped, rented or, at the final stage, returned to the earth without creating damage to the planet.

Authenticity and transparency

Authenticity and transparency have become increasingly relevant as the conversations around brands profiting from greenwashing, workforce abuses and cultural appropriation have increased. Today the customer and the industry demand greater authenticity and transparency from brands about how their products are designed and made.

Authenticity has become a popular metric to gauge the artistic merit of modern fashion designs, and fashion designers strive to create authentic garments and accessories that resonate with the consumers of today by refashioning traditional cultural expressions that are design elements embedded in traditional works of art (Mittal, 2020). Numerous fashion brands have been called out for cultural appropriation within their designs that marginalize indigenous people, profiting from traditional cultures and perpetuating inaccurate stereotypes. According to Miuccia Prada in an interview for *Vestoj*, 'all our culture derives from other cultures, but authenticity is when you can add something of your own (to something already in existence) and push things forward' (Cronberg, n.d.). Brands need to be open, honest, with transparent values and opinions that connect with the customer, using authentic storytelling around their culture and heritage. Values matter and, as customers start to feel more uneasy about the processes involved in creating fashion product, brands will need to work a lot harder to build trust with the consumer.

Signature design

The fashion market is full of product from thousands of brands creating the same or similar product with very little to differentiate it other than price. A signature helps the brand stand out and increases brand awareness, as generic product will offer very limited chance of success. Great examples of strong brand signatures can be found at luxury brands, such as the Chanel jacket or the discrete stitches used by Maison Margiela. For emerging brands, the signature must be more than the brand name or logo, as at this stage there is no brand value until the brand becomes more well known. The signature can be an element that features on every piece, or a statement piece that the brand will repeat in each collection until it becomes an iconic signature product in the future.

Developing a collection or product line based on a market niche is important for success and brands need to ensure that they have developed a style or type of product that connects with their consumer and is easily recognized by them (Davis Burns, Mullet and Bryant, 2011). A loyal customer chooses products they are familiar with and easily recognize. Sudden or constant changes in design styles or product will alienate them. Differentiation has always been important for brands, but today it is more important than ever due to younger demographics expecting high levels of uniqueness. Brands that want to succeed and capture more market share need to get with the programme and start differentiating before they are swallowed up in the sea of clones and lose their voice (Mann-co, 2020).

Seasonal collections

Part of the brand's design DNA will be the business model they use for the design and delivery of collections on a seasonal, trans-seasonal or drop-model basis. Global economic, environmental and social changes have affected how and when fashion is, or should be, produced. Many in the industry now question the purpose and viability of seasonal collections, as the traditional seasonal models of spring/summer and autumn/winter are no longer relevant to many consumers and brands. For decades, the traditional seasonal calendar has served the industry well, with brands publicly showcasing their collections six months before they drop in-store. However, as the reality of the climate emergency sets in, designers no longer want to create under these same strict boundaries, moving away from trends in favour of putting timeless pieces on the catwalk that play into the consumer's new desire for clothing that will serve them well for years to come (De Clerk, 2020). Brands are becoming more entrepreneurial to adapt their business models to meet consumer demand, and these models are discussed below in more detail:

Seasonless and smaller collections

Many brands have moved away from the traditional fashion calendar and are adapting their business models to be more responsive to consumer need. This has included moving from seasonal collections to concentrate on creating smaller capsule collections that are more niche. The benefits of this business model include the chance to test products before greater financial investment is needed for larger production runs, or the brand can maintain customer interest through regular drops of product in-store. Another benefit is that with no seasonal date on the collection, there is no need to have a 'sale' or discount the product at the end of a set period of time as the product can be sold on an ongoing basis. There is one final bonus of moving away from the old seasonal model, when collections were shown at fashion weeks six months before the product appeared in-store – and that relates to protecting a brand's intellectual property. With this old seasonal model, fast-fashion brands could take ideas from the catwalk and quickly flood the market with copies. If brands use the 'see-now buy-now' model, or the drop model discussed below, there is no opportunity to copy, as the brand instantly has their product available. While seasonal collections were always necessary for wholesale store buyers, this is changing too as Selfridges womenswear buyer Rebecca Tinker told *Harper's Bazaar*: 'Collections are more seasonless than ever, as brands take more of a considered approach to the longevity of a collection. We have seen more classic silhouettes and less reliability on prints dominating the market. This is strongly resonating with our customers who seek pieces that they can keep in their wardrobe longer than a season' (De Clerk, 2020).

Drop model

The drop model refers to frequent small production runs or capsule collections that are dropped on a more regular basis such as monthly. This model has been heralded as a huge success for brands such as Supreme. The benefits of the drop model are that small production runs avoid overproduction and can also help cash flow through not needing to finance full collection production in one go. Regular drops of new product encourage the consumer to regularly visit the brand to see new product and incentivizes them to buy now before it goes.

Digital design and collections

The digitalization of fashion has seen the progression of new systems of design including 3D fashion, virtual model creation and a huge move in the industry towards the metaverse. Digital fashion design and 2D–3D creation tools are growing rapidly through fashion companies and designers who are willing to reduce their environmental impact, and to make fashion design a more straightforward process (De La Garza, 2021). Creating designs in virtual software platforms is the first step in the process, but the development of innovative technologies is also leading to creating digital products for sale, and digital content for presentations and marketing.

> The rise of digital fashion and augmented reality (AR) clothing has increased the opportunity to offer immersive brand experiences for digitally savvy consumers.

Digitally savvy consumers have embraced the move towards collectable fashion NFTs (non-fungible tokens), investing in digital, authenticated garments that they can use on their avatars and in their virtual spaces in the metaverse.

From the brand's perspective, 3D digital clothing development can eliminate unnecessary physical sampling and waste generated by pattern cutting or fittings. Shortening production and lead times are some of the benefits of virtual garments, also correcting design inaccuracies on the go (De La Garza, 2021). For the consumer, digitalization offers hyper-personalization to give them more tailored products, services and experiences. Mobile games have already proved that customers are willing to spend money on digital assets (McDowell, 2019). According to the Business of Fashion and McKinsey (2022) report 'The State of Fashion: Technology', the fashion industry will see the biggest technological progress in the next decade, with greater advancements in the entire process – from design to multi-channel shopping – solving challenges such as returns, fit and sizing.

The development of digital collections is discussed in more detail in Chapter 8 on innovation and technology, but it would be remiss not to introduce this element in the consideration of product design and development too. While there are obvious opportunities for fashion brands, there are significant barriers to entry. Designers are traditionally unschooled in 3D modelling; sample patterns cannot be easily converted to 3D models and automated technologies are nascent (McDowell, 2019). Therefore, the skills gap will need to be addressed so that designers can access, understand and use new digital design software and tools available (Black, Edwards and Miller, 2015). However, the opportunities are endless, and many designers are excited about the opportunities to take advantage of innovative design software and technologies in the creation of product, but also to use it in their engagement with suppliers, manufacturers and consumers. The anticipation is that the future of design will be a hybrid approach of both physical and digital collections, as many brands are already starting to take this path in 2022.

Collection development

Having decided on the main DNA elements of the brand's design aesthetic and processes, these elements need to be carried forward and considered in the collection development. The designer or design team will use market research and trend analysis to determine each range of products that they will create to meet their customer needs. The designers will interpret the research and translate it into appropriate designs for their customers, while maintaining the brand's signature design aesthetic. This section of the chapter will detail the different elements of developing a collection of products or range that is appropriate to the market, as shown in Figure 5.2.

Ideation

Ideation comes from the design-thinking business model and relates to the process of generating ideas. Design thinking is an iterative process with activities including empathize, define, ideate, prototype and test. The ideation phase represents a key transitional step, taking the knowledge gained through the research and identification of problems and needs discovered in the empathize and define stage, to coming up with solutions, inspirations and design ideas. If carried out properly, an ideation session is where innovation thrives and should help the brand find the groundbreaking solution that the customers have been demanding (Stevens, 2021).

Figure 5.2   Developing a range

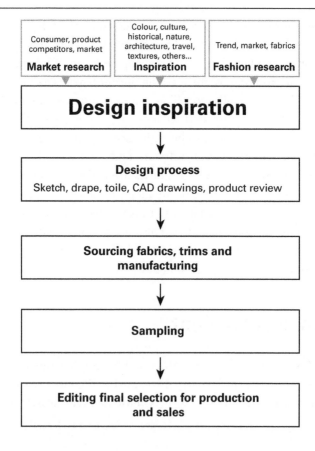

In the ideation phase, the designer or design team will explore and come up with as many ideas as possible. Some of these ideas will go on to be potential solutions to the design brief, whereas some will end up on the reject pile. At this stage, the focus is on quantity of ideas rather than quality. The main aim of an ideation session is to uncover and explore new angles and avenues, to think outside the box. For the sake of innovation and creativity, it is essential that the ideation phase be a 'judgement-free zone' (Stevens, 2021). Many critical decisions are made in the early phase of ideation or the conceptual design phase (Howard, Culley and Dekoninck, 2008). In this initial stage, using various inspiration sources designers are able to move vague ideas towards refining final concepts.

Inspiration and conceptualization

Inspiration is widely known to be the springboard to creativity and, for fashion brands seeking originality, sources of inspiration play a powerful role throughout the creative stage of design process, and also in the early stages of fashion research and strategic collection planning (Mete, 2006). Designers' inspiration for a new collection can come from many sources as well as from their research into the customer and the market. For some designers the starting point can be their research into trend forecasting and their imagination has been triggered by the fabrics and colours they discovered. For others they will find inspiration from history, previous fashion generations, the current populism or arts, nature or music. Inspiration can come from very random sources, but inspiration does not always come easily. Many designers actively seek inspiration through travel destinations, local cultures and traditional crafts, or invest time in studying literature, technology or the arts in order to find new concepts. It must also be noted that some brands, particularly in the mass market, do not need their design teams to be inspired by anything other than the successful ideas, products or collections of other brands.

From the inspiration, the designer or design team will develop a concept for a collection and successful designers will be able to interpret their design inspirations appropriately for their target customer (Davis Burns, Mullet and Bryant, 2011). It is essential that the design team develop a concept that is consistent with the brand design signature, product offer and customer need. It is easy for designers to get excited by particular inspirations and forget that their concepts need to connect with their customer and fit with the brand's product offer, as radical changes in design and product can alienate customers. Conceptualizing the collection should also involve identifying the target definition of the brand's line, such as the season or timing when the product will be sold; the customer profile including gender, lifestyle, income; sustainability considerations around fabric, materials and manufacture; the practical outcomes such as the type of product or size of the range; as well as financial considerations of costs and price points to meet market need. This conceptualization will be realized in a mood board, which helps the design team to visualize the theme for the range and can include trends, colours, fabric, construction, trim, graphics, art and prints. The inspirational mood board draws the final theme together to help refine the concept and ideas, before starting to sketch the shapes and silhouettes of the specific pieces.

Trend forecasting

The fashion industry has historically been based on trends. Whether it is the latest checked cape, the white ankle boot or the velour tracksuit, suddenly the product is everywhere, compelling the consumer to buy it, and people from outside the industry may wonder how all the brands suddenly have the same idea at the same time. The reason for this comes from brands following the same structured fashion timetable and using the same research sources, which means they are all exposed to the same influences or seek inspiration at the same time. Influences can come from numerous sources including films, art, exhibitions, the runway, street style, celebrities and influencers, history, cultural changes, previous trends or archive collections. With the speed the fashion industry now works at, many brands do not have the time or resources to do their own research, relying heavily instead on subscription-based fashion trend-forecasting platforms, such as WGSN or Trendstop. Fashion forecasting predicts the buying habits and moods of the consumers, predicting colours, fabrics, textures and various other styles that are going to be presented on the runway and in the stores for the upcoming seasons (Omotoso, 2018). They provide information on trends for two-plus years ahead, helping brands to enhance their planning and sourcing, and ensuring they create relevant and profitable collections.

The leading fashion trend-forecasting agencies are major powerhouses, heavily leading the trends in the fashion industry. Brands buy into their services and follow their trends because they are scared that by following a different path, they will risk having a collection that will not be on-trend, commercially viable or press-worthy. Fear factor is a big driver in the brands all following the same trends, because if the forecasting agency tells you 'this blue' is the blue of the season, then you know that you will be making pieces in the right trend colour. You will also be safe in the knowledge that these agencies have shared the same information with your competitors, fashion editors, store buyers and more, guaranteeing the trend will occur perhaps more than predicting it.

The industry has recognized that there is a problem with so many brands using the same big trend-forecasting agencies, as they all end up creating the same or similar product. This is counterintuitive, as the brands then have no point of difference and cannot meet the consumer need for fashion pieces that are new and different.

Brands that develop their own unique design aesthetic will avoid following the trends or creating seasonal collections, choosing instead to set the trends by being leaders not followers. Disruptive brands are shaking up the industry by innovating the way they create or market their products, such as Supreme, Balenciaga and Charli Cohen. These brands feel confident enough about their product to go with their feelings and rely on validation from their customer base (Omotoso, 2018). Even if a brand does not use major trend-forecasting agencies, they do still need to understand what is popular, what new opportunities and innovations are going to come on the market and what is coming next.

Fashion trends are cyclical, going through various stages of popularity, and can be classified as fads, trends and classics depending on how long they are popular (see Figure 5.3). Fads tend to be more extreme, short-term trends that will come and quickly go such as leg warmers, onesies or bell-bottom trousers. Trend fashion refers to the pieces that occur within a set time period, such as floral jumpsuits or oversized blazers. Trend fashion can remain popular over a period of time from approximately two to seven years, with small tweaks to designs each season but maintaining the same inspiration throughout the time. Classics refer to those fashion items that are wardrobe staples that change very little over time in their style, shape or construction, such as the trench coat, a white button-up shirt or a Breton-striped t-shirt.

The fashion cycle is a model that captures the period of time or lifespan during which fashion exists, showing how a trend can change through the five stages from introduction through acceptance to mainstream popularity then over time declines until it reaches the obsolescence stage. Each stage in the cycle will attract different customers:

- The introduction stage will attract innovators, bold leaders in fashion who look for something before anyone else gets it and are not scared to challenge perceptions of what is in fashion.

Figure 5.3 Fashion cycle

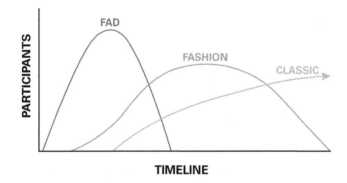

- Acceptance stage will attract an early adopter, someone who buys into a trend early, having had some knowledge about it. This person can be influential in helping the trend spread further.

- The peak or mainstream popularity stage is where the early majority customer will buy into the trend as it starts to appear all along the high street and everywhere in the media.

- The decline stage will attract the late majority, someone who does not buy into the newest trends and fashion and takes their time to accept new ideas.

- The obsolescence stage will be where a laggard will purchase the trend piece, this is someone who would say they don't buy into trends at all.

As a brand you have to determine how trend-focused your customers are in order to know when in the fashion cycle to introduce the trend, as introducing it too early could scare your customers, but if you introduce it too late, they will have purchased it already elsewhere.

It can be very difficult for smaller brands to compete with the high-street names introducing new trends, as they now work months behind the mass-market ones. As trends can be very risky for emerging brands, it is recommended that they are cautious and only introduce elements of a trend rather than fully engaging with it. This can be done by adding spots of the trend colour or only creating a small percentage of trend pieces within the collection. The brand will then have a larger percentage of classic or core design pieces to sell if they have mistimed it. Many start-up brands now create really strong classic or core ranges within their collections as these prove to be the strongest sellers, which the brand has no time pressure to sell, so could still be selling them for years to come.

The changing demands of the fashion consumer is also having an impact on trend-focused fashion, as there is a growing movement towards more conscious consumers who look for sustainable, timeless product rather than fast throwaway fashion. This customer will not buy into trends that could quickly look dated, instead opting for more quality, timeless, classic styles that will be worn for years to come.

Signature style

All brands need a signature design aesthetic to give the label a point of difference from the competition. Designers need to weave the signature into the story for each collection; examples of this would be how Missoni integrates the stripes, or Bottega Veneta using their distinctive intrecciato technique, 'How you use these signature elements in the process of telling a story through a product is what creates your design aesthetic (Tsolova, 2022). Fashion brands may try to create a bit of everything in an attempt to satisfy the needs of lots of different customers, but this strategy usually fails as the conflicting designs just detract from the brand's signature. Greater success can come from developing a small capsule collection with a strong signature that is instantly identifiable.

Developing the collection to match the sales strategy

Brands need to consider their sales strategy when creating a collection as this can have an impact on the type and size of collection that they need to create. If the brand has a wholesale strategy, they need to research the stores they wish to supply in order to understand the type and style of product they carry, how they merchandise products, who their customer is and the price points they offer. The brand also needs to consider whether they will be able to deliver orders to the wholesale buyers' terms, who may want collections on a consignment or sale-or-return basis rather than actually buying it. This means that the brand has to cover all the costs of buying their fabrics and trims, paying their manufacturers, and shipping the goods to the store then waiting for sales to be made before they get any money back. Brands may create collections with a smaller number of options that they will offer to the store, as well as having limited trend pieces in order to avoid being stuck with out-of-season stock if the store cannot sell it. Brands can also offer exclusive options in their range plan to incentivize a store that is looking for products their competitors are not selling.

When developing a direct-to-consumer range, there are also considerations on the type of product to create that will increase sales and manage costs. With this sales strategy, brands need to have enough inventory to sell through their own website, stores or pop-up shops and need the financial backing to produce this. A direct-to-consumer strategy for many brands will involve designing smaller collections to offer regular product drops to test designs and give the customers new products more often to keep their offer fresh.

The collection and product

Developing a collection takes careful planning to make the most of resources and ensure money is not wasted. This process is referred to as range planning, which involves creating a document that details each design. A collection is a cohesive 'range' of garments that work both as standalone pieces but also as a collection with a consistent approach in colour, shape, pattern and silhouette. At the luxury end of the market, a collection can be based around a statement or central piece, with a common thread that ties all the pieces together, or there is a main design influence, inspiration, theme or material that holds the collection together (Tsolova, 2022). Emerging designers can get carried away, creating lots of different types of pieces with no cohesive thread drawing them together, but designing a commercially viable collection is not a melee of all the things that an individual would like to wear (Tsolova, 2022). Brands have to decide on the type and number of pieces they will develop in their collections, dependent on their sales strategy, budget and the consumer need. A collection can be any size from six pieces for smaller brands to over 100 looks from the larger brands. A great collection does not have to be a large one with lots of different options, it is better to focus on creating six amazing looks that have a strong signature and point of difference, than just creating a huge amount of product that might not even sell. There are new brands that create one amazing distinctive piece and build their business on that, with a few options in colour or size as a starting point. Other brands create a 6–12 look collection that they release in a series of drops over several months. Smaller collections and regular drops can help an emerging brand manage their cashflow, as they don't have to put a whole collection into manufacture in one go. For the larger fast-fashion brands the statistics are eyewatering, with brands like Zara dropping 500 new designs a week, resulting in them producing roughly 450 million clothes every year (Martin Roll, 2021).

When a brand starts to plan the designs that will form the collection, they need to consider how the final range will look in store, on the website or on a rail. The collection needs to be easily merchandized, with the products looking cohesive and exciting to entice the customer to buy. When drawing out the range plan, the brand should ensure that the collection tells a story through consistent use of colour, shape, fabric or print elements across the collection. For example, to tie a collection together a print fabric could be used in a full piece, as well as a trim, pocket or belt on a block colour item. This makes the product easier to merchandize, makes it look more cohesive, as well as appealing, with the added bonus of it offering a way to work towards zero waste, as surplus fabrics can be used as trims or to create smaller pieces. The range plan should be planned and drawn out before any fabrics are purchased or pieces made, to ensure that the collection is cohesive, the brand signature is easily identifiable, that fabrics have been used efficiently and the collection can be beautifully merchandized. The range plan, as in the example in Figure 5.4, will detail the design, fabrics, colour and sizing options.

While designing a collection is a creative process, range planning needs to rationalize conflicting managerial and creative processes to ensure the collection meets the company's profit goals as well as customer need (440 Industries, 2019). Well-developed collections can have numerous designs with many colour, size and material options for each design. Brands may also need to meet high production minimums required by suppliers and manufacturers, which means the finances required to bankroll a large collection can become eyewatering, resulting in business disaster if not carefully handled (Tsolova, 2022).

Figure 5.4   Range plan

Product development can easily become complicated and very costly, it is therefore important that brands plan each product carefully to be sure that they fit with the collection and are an economically viable option before patterns and samples are made or sent off to production. The design team needs to be clear on how they want each final product to look, as well as know what the quality, style and functionality requirements are for each piece in the collection. Every product needs to be reviewed to ensure it meets the targeted customers' requirements of fabric, colour, cut, style and design details. Many designers create a full collection, or detailed range plans, without thinking of each product as an individual item on its own; however, the customer is likely to only buy one product at a time, therefore each product needs to offer the customer a unique experience and value, whether it is a simple top or a statement coat. During the design process, the designer should be looking at ways to increase the perceived value of every single piece in the collection, thinking about what they can do to add to the line that increases the perceived value (Tsolova, 2022). The theory of customer-perceived value states that brands need to understand the value of products and services from the customer perspective in order to gain competitive advantage (Bai, Li and Niu, 2016). While value is not decided by the brand but is perceived and decided by customers, designers need to consider the elements that they can include within the design and making of the products that will add value for the customer. Perceived value is the difference between the amount the customers are willing to pay for products and the actual price of it. This perception is not dictated just by the value of the materials used in the products, there are countless intangible factors that help convince customers to pay more for a given product because to them those extra factors are worth paying for to have that product. Customer perceived value can be classified in the three dimensions of functional value, service value and social value. Customers can perceive functional value by areas such as price, quality, shopping ease or multi-use pieces; service value can refer to elements such as the customer experience in-store or on the website, efficient shopping processes such as returns as well as prompt delivery terms; social value includes the consumer's sense of social value and belonging, credibility and self-esteem (Bai, Li and Niu, 2016). Examples of these values can be seen in Figure 5.5.

Brands need to make their products outstanding; Figure 5.5 details some of the ways brands can make each product a 'star' of the collection, making it outshine the competitors' products. Extra benefits and values can be added in the development of a product through design, quality, special features such as embellishments or unique fabrics or prints, and through the manufacturing process if the product is sustainably made with ethical considerations to the workforce. Added values can also come through offering aftercare such as cleaning, repairs or repurposing. The packaging and delivery processes have become increasingly important areas where value can be added as more customers purchase on-line, as the 'unboxing' experience is almost as important to customers as the joy of the product itself, which is why unboxing videos go viral on Instagram and YouTube (Brafman, 2021). Packaging has become particularly important for luxury brands who have to consider how they can replicate the experience they would offer in-store in their online sales. The brand story can add value as customers seek brands that make them feel good about themselves, feel proud and connected, therefore brands that tell great stories have greater

Figure 5.5   Product star

perceived value for customers. Brands may have to make some changes during the range-planning process and drop favourite pieces from the collection, due to availability and lead times of production, minimum order quantity requirements or the high cost of some materials.

Collection review prior to sampling and production

To create a cohesive and realistic collection, a brand needs to use a range plan template. This template will include each of the styles with fabric, colour options and estimated price points. A well-constructed range plan document gives the brand an opportunity to review the collection to make sure it meets the requirements of the brand in terms of signature style, cohesiveness, efficient and effective use of fabrics and styles, as well as meeting quantitative business decisions that relate to pricing and stock levels (440 Industries, 2019). Utilizing the range plan document, the brand can anticipate how cohesive the collection will look on the rail, making sure that all the pieces make sense, the colours and prints work well together and the range can be easily merchandized, as one weak piece or conflicting colour garment can throw off the whole rail, making it look cheap, incoherent or detract from the brand signature. The range plan review would also ensure the brand has made efficient decisions about the width and depth of the range. The width of a collection refers to the number of different styles offered, and the depth of the collection refers to the variations on offer, such as one style offered in different colours, prints or fabrics. While larger brands are able to offer great depth and width within their ranges, emerging brands need to be wary of offering too many variations, as this can cause the collection to lose cohesiveness and be a financial disaster due to overproduction of pieces. Brands will also use the range plan to confirm that they have a realistic pricing architecture, with a balance between lower- and higher-price pieces to offer choices to their customer, and to consider the sizing options they will offer that will meet their customer needs.

Luxury brands will use the range plan to ensure they have a balance between editorial and commercial pieces, as they need to have statement 'WOW' pieces that attract press, buyers and customers and get people talking about the brand (Tsolova, 2022). While the statement piece draws the customer in, they are likely to buy the commercial pieces that have a flavour of the editorial piece but in a more wearable and saleable form. Fast-fashion brands will ensure they include their hero products within a range plan, which are the well-known instantly identifiable best-selling pieces that frequently draw the customer back to the brand, such as a blazer or black jeans.

Summary

Designing a fashion collection is a business competency that needs careful management to meet the design aesthetic, commercial and consumer needs. This chapter has
detailed the different elements that need to be considered in the design process of
fashion product and the development of a collection from detailed research through
the development of the brand's design DNA and market niche to finalizing the range
plan prior to production. It has covered how brands need to design commercially viable collections that meet consumer needs in order to sell. In a fickle, trend-focused
industry, brands need to design cohesive collections that showcase their unique design
signature to make it stand out from the competition. While the creative considerations of design usually have the highest focus and attention, it is equally the business
management of the collection that will make it a success.

Key terms

aesthetic	fashion cycle	range plan
authenticity	ideation	seasonal
brand DNA	iterative process	signature
collection	line	timeless
commercially viable	multi-functional	transparency
digital design	product star	trend
drop model	purpose	zero waste

Activity

Identify five current trends in women's wear or men's wear that are in-store at the
moment, taking into consideration colour, fabric and styles.

Online resources

Downloadable product star template.

References

440 Industries (2018) Fashion firm competitor analysis criteria, *440 Industries*, www.440industries.com/fashion-competitor-analysis-criteria/ (archived at https://perma.cc/7F94-F7E5)

440 Industries (2019) Collection development in the fashion industry, *440 Industries*, www.440industries.com/collection-development-in-the-fashion-industry/ (archived at https://perma.cc/DU2W-ZM59)

Bai, Y, Li, C and Niu, J (2016) Study on customer-perceived value of online clothing brands, *American Journal of Industrial and Business Management*, 06(08), pp 914–21

Black, S, Edwards, M and Miller, G (2015) What's digital about fashion design, *Ualresearchonline*, ualresearchonline.arts.ac.uk/id/eprint/9790/1/WHAT'S%20DIGITAL%20ABOUT%20FASHION%20DESIGN.pdf

Brafman, M (2021) Why packaging is so important for your brand, *Packlane*, www.packlane.com/blog/why-packaging-is-important (archived at https://perma.cc/B7WC-BN7A)

Business of Fashion and McKinsey (2022) The State of Fashion: Technology, *McKinsey*, www.businessoffashion.com/reports/news-analysis/the-state-of-fashion-technology-industry-report-bof-mckinsey/ (archived at https://perma.cc/FQ8R-SNCY)

Chan, E (2020) Upcycling is the biggest trend in fashion right now, *British Vogue*, www.vogue.co.uk/fashion/article/upcycling-trend-ss21 (archived at https://perma.cc/942C-N4D8)

Cronberg, A A (n.d.) Branding Authenticity, *Vestoj*, vestoj.com/branding-anarchy (archived at https://perma.cc/A6LP-XPLM)

Davis Burns, L, Mullet, K and Bryant, N (2011) *The Business of Fashion*, 4th edn, Fairchild Books, New York

De Clerk, A (2020) Are we seeing the end of seasonality in fashion?, *Harper's Bazaar*, www.harpersbazaar.com/uk/fashion/a31255947/end-of-fashion-seasons/ (archived at https://perma.cc/5RVA-FZTZ)

De La Garza, F (2021) Digital fashion designer: 3D disruption in fashion and the design of the Future, *Elle*, www.elle.education/business/digital-fashion-designer-3d-disruption-in-fashion-and-the-design-of-the-future/ (archived at https://perma.cc/HK6P-ASVY)

Designers Studio (2015) Stylistic identity, *The Designers Studio*

Dhillon, K (2016) Is fashion education failing young designers?, *Not Just a Label*, www.notjustalabel.com/editorial/fashion-education-failing-young-designers (archived at https://perma.cc/8LUE-SVXR)

Helmke, S (2018) Build your brand DNA, *Slow Fashion World*, slowfashionworld.com/brand-dna/ (archived at https://perma.cc/X7Z7-VF5W)

Howard, T, Culley, S and Dekoninck, E (2008) Describing the creative design process by the integration of engineering design and cognitive psychology literature, *Design Studies*, 29(2), pp 160–80

Interaction Design Foundation (2021) What is design thinking?, *The Interaction Design Foundation*, www.interaction-design.org/literature/topics/design-thinking (archived at https://perma.cc/4NUA-ZEF8)

Kinnear, T and Taylor, J (1996) *Marketing Research: An applied approach*, McGraw-Hill, London

Mann-co (2020) Why so many brands seem exactly the same, *Mann-co*, www.mann-co.com/why-so-many-brands-seem-exactly-the-same/ (archived at https://perma.cc/AQX4-ZU2J)

Martin Roll (2021) The secret of Zara's success: a culture of customer co-creation, *Martin Roll*, www.martinroll.com/resources/articles/strategy/the-secret-of-zaras-success-a-culture-of-customer-co-creation/ (archived at https://perma.cc/NT8W-SUNF)

McDowell, M (2019) Is digital clothing the next fashion frontier?, *Vogue Business*, www.voguebusiness.com/technology/digital-fashion-virtual-clothing-3d-design (archived at https://perma.cc/27VP-JUSW)

Mete, F (2006) The creative role of sources of inspiration in clothing design, *Emerald Insight*, www.emerald.com/insight/content/doi/10.1108/09556220610668509/full/html (archived at https://perma.cc/Y9L8-ZKG2)

Mittal, H (2020) Tackling cultural appropriation in the fashion industry, *Data Driven Investor*, www.datadriveninvestor.com/2020/07/06/tackling-cultural-appropriation-in-the-fashion-industry/# (archived at https://perma.cc/8TZ8-DJZG)

Omotoso, M (2018) What are fashion trend forecasting agencies?, *Fashion Insiders*, www.fashioninsiders.co/features/fashion-tech/fashion-trend-forecasting-agencies/ (archived at https://perma.cc/CPN9-7P3X)

Sonika Soni Khar et al (2018) Research methods in fashion design, it's compilation and importance in design process, *Academia*, www.academia.edu/38100438/RESEARCH_METHODS_IN_FASHION_DESIGN_ITS_COMPILATION_AND_IMPORTANCE_IN_DESIGN_PROCESS (archived at https://perma.cc/7XDC-E794)

Stevens, E (2021) What is ideation? A guide to the design thinking phase, *Career Foundry*, www.careerfoundry.com/en/blog/ux-design/what-is-ideation-in-design-thinking/ (archived at https://perma.cc/K5MU-76SK)

Sustainable Fashion Forum (n.d.) What is circular fashion?, *The Sustainable Fashion Forum*, www.thesustainablefashionforum.com/pages/what-is-circular-fashion (archived at https://perma.cc/EMX9-FLJU)

Trend Hunter (2008) Recession fashion, *Trend Hunter*, www.trendhunter.com/trends/tough-economic-times-influence-fashion-style (archived at https://perma.cc/R9UE-5QSL)

Tsolova, D (2022) How to design a commercially strong fashion collection, *Fashion Insiders*, www.fashioninsiders.co/toolkit/how-to/design-commercially-strong-fashion-collection/ (archived at https://perma.cc/KK9X-2L8E)

Case study
Ellen MacArthur Foundation

Photo credit: Ron Lach

The Ellen MacArthur Foundation was established in 2010 with the aim of accelerating the transition to the circular economy. The foundation was formed by inspirational sailor Dame Ellen MacArthur, the fastest solo sailor to sail around the world, in 2005. It was during her solo voyage when, confronted by the awesome power and dazzling beauty of nature, Ellen began to ponder the fragility of the systems we have built and to realize that our global economy relies completely on the finite resources we extract, use and then dispose of. When she returned, she began a new journey creating the Ellen MacArthur Foundation, which has emerged as a global thought leader, establishing circular economy on the agenda of decision makers across business, government and academia. The charity's work focuses on four interlinking areas: education, business and government, insight and analysis and communications.

The foundation is committed to creating a circular economy, which is designed to eliminate waste and pollution, circulate products and materials (at their highest value) and regenerate nature. It is an economic system that delivers better outcomes for people and the environment. To achieve the transition to a circular economy, the foundation works with businesses, international institutions, governments, cities, universities, non-governmental organizations, innovators and many others. The foundation believes that businesses play a crucial role in shifting the system, recognizing that currently many businesses are part of the problem, but that given their capacity to innovate and ability to drive change quickly and at scale in global markets they also need to be part of the solution. Underpinned by their independent charity governance, the foundation creates new collaborations and challenges organizations they work with to raise their ambition levels, set ambitious goals supported by evidence-based analysis, and stimulate new and better solutions at scale and speed.

The foundation creates evidence-based original research on the benefits of a circular economy, and how it can contribute to solving global challenges like climate change and biodiversity loss. It also supports organizations and individuals with formal learning opportunities through their circular economy courses, and creates resources for teachers and academics.

www.ellenmacarthurfoundation.org

Supply chain management

6

LEARNING OBJECTIVES

After reading this chapter you should be able to:

- Discuss the challenges the fashion industry is facing in the global supply chain
- Understand the processes and considerations in the supply chain needed to produce fashion products, including concerns around sustainability, transparency and ethics
- Explain the sourcing and manufacturing processes that a brand uses to convert designs into the final fashion product
- Describe the elements included in a tech pack

Introduction

The supply chain for the fashion industry is a unique, global, challenging concept that constantly has to adapt to the erratic nature of economic and political conditions, social norms and consumer demands. For fashion brands, the supply chain involves a complex management process of developing relationships with suppliers and manufacturers to produce fashion products in a timely and efficient way that meets consumer and commercial needs. The supply chain function needs well-integrated operations from design to suppliers through to customers, with decisions on cost, inventory and customer service made holistically throughout as one whole process rather than by each function in isolation (McKinsey, 2017).

The supply chain has so many different functions to manage that there are inherent risks throughout the system. Brands of all sizes and maturity struggle with continuous supply chain challenges that can affect their reputations and bottom line. Consumers have been calling out fashion brands on their environmental impact, overproduction and unethical working practices including slavery, child labour and horrendous working conditions. The fashion industry is therefore compelled to address the supply chain crisis. Sourcing manufacturers and suppliers is a problem for all fashion brands, yet the challenges often take brands by surprise, and they find sourcing a much more difficult task than they had anticipated. Brands that do not pay careful attention to their supply chain, and do not manage their production processes carefully, leave themselves open to considerable risk. Efficient supply chain management ensures reduced costs and better profits for the brand, effective inventory management, improved quality and products that meet customer requirements (Figure 6.1).

This chapter will discuss the challenges fashion brands need to address in their supply chain and the considerations they need to make to their production process. This will include the process of finding and building relationships with suppliers and manufacturers to efficiently and sustainably produce fashion that meets the brand's quality standards and consumer expectations. The chapter will also explain the importance of accurate specification sheets and tech packs to develop saleable product.

Global factors affecting the supply chain

The global fashion industry is facing increasing disruption from market forces such as rising e-commerce, competition, digitalization, changing consumer demand as well as global political and economic instability. Fashion supply chain professionals are grappling with how to meet these demands, improve speed of production and distribution while meeting sustainability, transparency and ethical standards: 'No one can escape the supply chain crisis unscathed' (Chen, 2021).

In tough times brands have to find creative solutions and explore new business models that offer greater flexibility and more agile working systems rather than the rigid systems of the past.

Solutions need to be found that address the global issues of demand and production volatility, international logistic challenges of costs and lead time, unreliable suppliers, short product lifecycles and issues with sustainability and transparency. The volatile market means that it can be very difficult to forecast demand and it is easy to make mistakes, for example if a brand purchases a substantial inventory of the latest fashion trend, but by the time the stock arrives the world has moved on, then

Figure 6.1   What is the supply chain

Sourcing	**Manufacturing**	**Fulfilment**
Selecting all the components for your product	How the components will be put together to make the product	Shipping of products to customers

the brand is left having to pay for inventory that they either cannot sell or must sell at a reduced price (Serai, 2021).

Production volatility came to the forefront during the Covid-19 pandemic with brands affected by supplier shortages and factory closures. This led brands to consider nearshoring for back-up options instead of relying totally on overseas markets. International partners can often be unreliable, not delivering on time or quality, there can be shipping delays, and language differences can make it difficult for the brand to build a relationship with them to improve performance. In the fast-fashion sector, product lifecycles are incredibly short and can now often be measured in days rather than weeks and months (Serai, 2021). Brands have to work out whether it is more efficient for them to produce their products locally or globally. Manufacturing more locally in some countries such as within Europe can result in considerably higher costs, making the product too expensive for the market. While global can be considered cheaper, it does not always work out that way due to increasing transportation costs, taxes and duties, which add to overseas production costs. When looking for cost-effective production, brands have to consider the total cost not just the cost per unit to see if the product can still meet the market price for the goods.

On top of all these challenges is the environmental impact of producing fashion, with overproduction leading to waste products going to landfill or being burnt. The lack of transparency and sustainability across the supply chain is also concerning, with products being made in factories with poor working conditions. Brands need to take greater responsibility to ensure their suppliers meet regulatory and ethical expectations. Their strategy needs to address how they can efficiently and effectively monitor and audit where and how their products are made (Serai, 2021).

Sourcing strategy

Before the brand starts looking for suppliers and manufacturers, they need to develop a sourcing strategy to ensure they are looking for the right partners and suppliers. Without a clear strategy the brand could waste time and money talking to the wrong supplier or end up with the wrong product in the wrong place at the wrong time, resulting in lost sales and overproduction.

While the supply chain can appear linear, it has many moving parts that impact its efficiency. Some brands simplify their management by dividing the supply chain in two parts: upstream (supply) and downstream (demand) supply chain activities (Figure 6.2). Upstream supply chain relates to the activities with suppliers including raw materials and manufacturing, whereas the downstream supply chain refers to activities post-manufacturing, which includes distributing the product to the final customer. Supply chain managers seek to balance demand and supply to make sure that there are no lost sales, inventory shortages or overordering.

Figure 6.2   Simplified supply chain streams

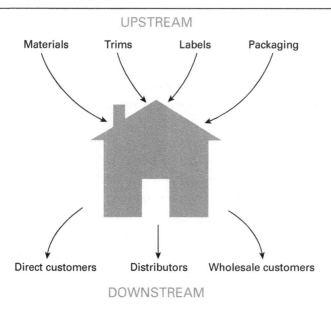

The strategy should start with the brand's goals and market they are targeting and then will analyse the internal and external factors (Fibre2Fashion, 2019). The internal factors, which include budget and quality standards, and the external factors that consider suppliers' locations, flexibility and performance, are listed below:

- **Budget:** Brands have to set the budget needed to get their products to market. They must remember that they need significant budget for marketing and selling, and therefore have to limit how much money is spent on making the collection.

- **Product:** The strategy will detail the product offer and where it will sit in the market such as in the luxury, middle or fast-fashion markets. The brand needs to detail the quality standards for materials, sewing and finishings, particularly for more luxury brands that need to meet high-quality standards.

- **Timeframe:** The strategy will include a critical path timeline that includes all the steps from design through sourcing and manufacturing to sales. The critical path keeps the brand and its partners on track to produce the goods efficiently.

- **Suppliers:** The strategy will detail how the brand will find and build the relationships with reliable, high-quality suppliers that fit the requirements of the brand such as budget, personality, location, skills and minimum order quantity. It also needs to include flexibility in building multiple supplier partnerships to give the brand more agility in a volatile market.

- **Sustainability, ethics and transparency:** The strategy will include the brand's policies on sustainability and ethics to meet the purpose of the brand and how they will track their processes to offer transparency to the customer.

- **Logistics:** The strategy will detail the logistics processes of ordering and distributing the brand's materials and finished goods around the world. This can include detailed processes for tracking purchase orders, management processes for customs clearing, quota numbers and shipping containers.

- **Finances:** The sourcing strategy will explain the brand's approach to financing the development of collections, including payment terms, cashflow management and credit terms.

With many global brands all looking for the best suppliers and manufacturers, a brand needs to take a very planned strategic approach to their supply chain management to give them an advantage over their competitors. The competition is even greater post Covid-19, with many brands exploring new factory options and looking to spread their production through multiple facilities as they plan to mitigate the risk if one factory is suddenly unable to meet production deadlines (Chen, 2021).

Sustainability and transparency

The fashion industry has to address the complex challenges of sustainability, ethics and lack of visibility that are inherent in the supply chain. Consumers are becoming more demanding about the information they want on the products they buy, and expect brands to gather sustainability data and know everything about their products and materials so that they can share this with their consumers. Fashion companies face a daunting task not only in their need to meet new supply chain regulations but also in their efforts to streamline supply chains to support better business outcomes and customer experiences (Raghavan, 2022). This will require brands to track the processes across their complex, intricate supply chains, including everything from dyes and yarns to fabrics and finished goods. Traceability is critical (Raghavan, 2022). The customer is demanding provenance on all the brand's materials, the impact of the brand's fabric and production on the environment, as well as the ethical employment and fair working practices used in making fashion.

The McKinsey Report, Fashion on Climate, reported that over 70 per cent of greenhouse gas emission comes from upstream production, or the suppliers of fabric and manufacturing (McKinsey & Company, 2020). Fashion brands are often not fully aware of how the raw materials they source are produced and managed, so they are unable to offer transparency or qualify the environmental and social sustainability of their products. Sarah Ditty, global policy director at Fashion Revolution, says the start of the supply chain for raw materials such as cotton, leather and wool is the hardest to trace, and is typically where workers are most vulnerable to exploitation. It is also where processes can be most detrimental to the environment, with cotton cultivation using lots of chemicals, and dyes containing pollutants and hazardous chemicals (Fish, 2022). The fashion industry's complex, fragmented and opaque supply chain is renowned for hiding human rights and environmental abuses.

There have been limited regulations and controls in the past, which has enabled brands to plead ignorance or pass the responsibility along the process, but this is no longer acceptable behaviour. There are new legal systems being introduced such as the European Commission's Product Environmental Footprint (PEF) programme, which will require brands to calculate and disclose the environmental impact of their products by tracing their origins through supply chains (Raghavan, 2022). This programme joins a slew of others worldwide, including California's Transparency in Supply Chains Act and Germany's Supply Chain Due Diligence Act, which compels brands to manage their supply chains more effectively. All of these changes, though, will require new technology solutions, such as blockchain, for supply chain traceability, as well as new ways of thinking about sustainability (Raghavan, 2022).

Brands that precisely trace products and materials through their supply chain will be able to address many challenges facing the fashion industry, including proving authenticity and product provenance for consumers. They will also be able to meet new regulatory requirements and monitor greater efficiency in their supply chain. Brands should also meet corporate social responsibility outcomes, ensuring improvements in the quality of life and working conditions of people in the fashion and textiles industry as well as their families, the community they reside within and society at large (Londrigan and Jenkins, 2018).

Blockchain

Blockchain is a technological process that can trace both physical and digital products throughout their lifecycle. This transparency system in the supply chain tracking process offers producers insights into their value chain, giving them the satisfaction of a proper third-party goods handover and final product labelling (Jain, 2021).

Blockchain will transform the fashion supply chain by offering a type of track-and-trace management system, where the origin of each item can be tracked including easily tracing raw materials from their origin to the production factory and finally on to the customer.

The blockchain system creates a link or a serial number like a digital passport, which records every time the product changes hands, enabling the customer to fully trust where their garments come from and how ethically they were made, rather than rely on a brand's vague 'sustainable' statements. An added bonus of blockchain is that brands will be able to protect their intellectual property better, and the system should reduce counterfeits, as the customer will be able to trace the authenticity of a product.

Materials, fabrics and trims

Researching and finding the right suppliers a brand wants to work with is an essential part of the sourcing process and can take significantly longer than often predicted. Larger brands may use in-house teams or international sourcing agents, whereas the smaller brands will need to find and build relationships with suppliers themselves at trade fairs or by visiting the suppliers direct in their mills and factories (Burke, 2015).

A brand needs reliable suppliers who will deliver good-quality materials in the quantity and timeframe they need. Sourcing materials, fabrics and trims can be overwhelming and time consuming but finding the right ones can improve the profitability and reputation of the brand. Most suppliers have minimum order quantities and they set these as servicing, shipping and selling small quantities is less profitable to the suppliers (Gehlhar, 2008). Each supplier sets their own minimum order quantity (MOQ), which can vary greatly – for example from 20 metres to 2,000 metres. As well as MOQs, other considerations when choosing suppliers include understanding the tiered pricing according to the quantity purchased; additional costs for shipping, taxes and import duties; the lead time, including making and shipping; fabric width, as this can vary greatly with no standard widths from some suppliers; and if the supplier always carries a stock of the material for repeat orders.

The challenges

Sourcing materials and fabrics can be a challenge due to high minimum order quantities that suppliers demand, with many imposing quantities that run into hundreds if not thousands. While this may not be a problem for larger and mass-production brands, emerging and luxury labels can struggle to get the elements they need for production in the smaller quantities they want. Brands do not want to sit on large quantities of excess fabric that they cannot use, as this dead stock would tie up money that could be better used elsewhere. Astute brands will plan their collections to use fewer, more quality fabrics, which means they get economies of scale as they can then meet the minimum order quantities (Burke, 2015). Others are being creative by working with end-of-line fabrics or dead stock to produce small limited-edition collections, or upcycling and repurposing fabrics. The difference between upcycling and recycling is that upcycled clothes have been made using waste clothes to turn them into something new; whereas recycling means the fabric is broken down first before it can be used. Some brands will source their own fabrics to upcycle, others will use a production business that takes leftover or used fabrics and turns them into new ones.

Finding suppliers

Finding the suppliers takes time and brands need to manage their sourcing efficiently, particularly small brands with limited resources who may find it difficult to get suppliers to work with them. Most suppliers would rather work with larger brands who place significant orders, so often ignore emails or requests from smaller labels. There are several ways that brands can find suppliers:

Trade fairs

Textile and fabric fairs take place all over the world, where mills, manufacturers and wholesalers come together to showcase their goods, including every type of material, fabric, trim and packaging. There are also specialist fairs for suppliers to the accessories, footwear and jewellery industries. Trade fairs are a great place to easily and efficiently meet numerous suppliers in one go, see the quality, find out about their terms, and start to build the relationship with them. Some wholesalers sell 'stocked' fabrics, such as silks, lace, or cottons in standard colours that they always keep in stock, meaning a brand can place an initial small quantity order but return for additional quantities of the same product again later. If working with 'stocked' suppliers, brands need to ensure they are a reputable company and can be trusted to have the product again in the future, but it is also worth remembering that dye numbers may not be the same across new rolls of fabric, so even with stocked fabrics there can be slight variations.

Mills

Mills are the manufacturers that specialize in certain types of fabric and they control the flow from the beginning yarn through each of the weaving, dyeing and finishing processes (Gehlhar, 2008). Brands can work directly with mills if they are seeking high minimum order quantities and are able to plan around the long lead time it will take to produce the fabric. Smaller brands can work with mills if they offer limited quantity, end-of-run lines or overproduction, but not all mills offer this facility.

Agents

There are numerous agents working in the supply chain around the world, who have relationships with mills, manufacturers and suppliers. Working on a combination of consultancy fee and commission, agents can source the different materials needed. Larger brands will usually work with several agents in different countries to source their materials, but there are obviously additional costs to this that then need to be added to the final product cost.

Converters

A converter is a secondary source that processes unfinished fabric or greige goods (grey loom state woven or unprocessed knitted fabrics) from mills and finish the material themselves by printing, treating or dyeing it for resale (Gehlhar, 2008). Converters will normally have lower minimum order quantities than mills and can offer a wide range of products.

Jobbers

Jobbers is the industry term for people in the secondary market who buy leftover, unwanted or overproduced finished goods at greatly reduced costs to sell on to brands. This is a potentially good place for brands that want smaller minimum order quantities of unique fabrics, such as start-up or luxury brands who make smaller production runs.

Online

Brands can search for suppliers online but will need to be careful to find reliable ones that they can trust to deliver the quantity and quality they order at the right time. Purchasing from companies that they have no knowledge or experience of is a risky strategy. There are online platforms such as the Sustainable Angle, Let's Make it Here, Foursource, Sqetch and Makers Row, to name a few, where brands can search for suppliers.

Material options

Brands should select materials that relate to their brand ethos, storytelling and customer need. Fabrics are an intrinsic part of the brand's quality and storytelling, as well as having an effect on the customer's perceived value of the pieces. For purpose-driven brands they need to ensure that every element in their product production meets the brand mission, and be transparent in the sourcing process to meet their consumers' demand for information on the origin and manufacturing process.

Fabrics are selected on suitability of fibres, colours, weight of the material, price and sustainability, as well as the need to be fit for the purpose and functionality of the design. Brands increasingly focus on the environmental impact of the materials used in their products, as the production and processing of textiles are polluting water, air and soil, wasting energy and natural resources, and impact upon human health as a result of being in contact with toxic substances (The Sustainable Angle, n.d.). There are a growing number of new sustainable fabrics that are created with consideration of minimizing damage, including environmental damage from water, land and air pollution, or ethical damage from human rights violations (Forest Digital, 2021). The most sustainable fabrics include recycled cotton, organic hemp, linen, Tencel and modal, and there are lots of new innovative textiles on the market including Crailar flax fibre; Recyclon, a recycled nylon; Pinatex vegan leather, Qmonos synthetic spider silk; and Econyl recycled nylon.

With more consumers demanding fashion that is ethically produced, a brand moving towards sustainable production will need to understand the different fibres and their environmental impact, as well as possibilities for circular fashion models.

Manufacturing options and challenges

The sourcing process involves finding the production suppliers a brand needs to manufacture the collections. Brands have to decide the production methods and options they will use as early as possible, as it takes time to find the right partners, build the relationship and plan the production calendar. Working with manufacturers is risky and it doesn't matter if the brand is a major high-street label or a start-up brand, the one thing that is guaranteed in the fashion industry is that they will always find the manufacturing process challenging. There are different options for producing fashion products, as shown in Figure 6.3 and detailed below.

Figure 6.3   Manufacturing options

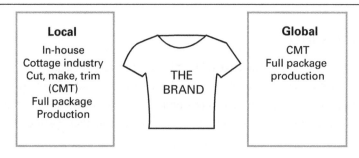

In-house/atelier

Some brands will avoid the challenges of working with external manufacturers by producing their collections in-house. They will employ their own team of pattern cutters, seamstresses and tailors to make their garments. The benefits of this are that the brand has more control, can guarantee quality and finish, and also produce the number of garments they need. A growing number of luxury brands are turning to producing in-house as the atelier model has an added advantage of giving the customer greater personalization and added value from the unique experience of attending appointments with the designer. The downside can be that the brand cannot justify paying a full-time team when the in-house staff are not working at full capacity.

Cut, make, trim (CMT)

Cut, make, trim (CMT) factories rely on the brand providing them with all the elements, so that they can then cut, make and trim the designs into fully produced products. Some brands and designers can make their own patterns and samples, but many are aware of their time and technical limitations and outsource when necessary to specialists including pattern cutting, sample machinists and manufacturing units (Burke, 2015). CMT factories work to different size orders, from making a sample or one piece, up to 100+ pieces. A benefit of CMT for the brand is having control over the sourcing to ensure the fabrics and trims meet the brand's quality standards, which is hugely important for start-up and luxury labels. The brand will keep the intellectual property ownership of the patterns they create, with the added benefit of the pattern offering the right fit for their customer, rather than to just make the production process easier. The downside is that the brand has to supply the factory with all the specifications, tech packs, fabrics and trims, patterns and stitching requirements before production. The brand may also need to find different CMT factories for different jobs and different size orders, which can be challenging for small brands with a limited team, as well as challenging to build and maintain relationships with numerous suppliers.

Full production package (FPP)

Full production package (FPP) manufacturers offer a full-package solution, from initial consultation through creating patterns, sourcing fabrics and trims, making samples, to final garment completion. The benefits of this model come from economies of scale when it comes to fabric and trim sourcing, as the manufacturer can buy in higher MOQs but this can mean the brand competing in the market with the same fabric as the other labels working with that factory (Sewport, 2022a). This option is usually not suitable for start-up fashion brands, as the FPP factories work to high minimum order quantities, but also because there is a chance that the quality would not be as high as needed. There are also concerns that the factory will create a pattern that makes manufacturing easier and cheaper, rather than creating the patterns to ensure the best fit for the customer. They could also use the same patterns for other brands, as they own the rights to patterns that they make.

Local versus global

In developing the production strategy, the brand has to consider whether to work with local suppliers and manufacturers in their own country or source global partners. There are pros and cons with both options, and the decision will depend on which option meets the brand's resources, time and purpose, as well as the availability of suppliers in the local area. Brands that focus on developing conscious collections may seek suppliers and manufacturers in their local market or will offset the carbon footprint of global sourcing by investing in the local community where their manufacturing or main material sourcing originates (Tsolova, 2020). Working with local suppliers can be more expensive but can add value to the brand's storytelling, which would help justify the higher price. Other benefits of local suppliers include reduced shipping and production times. With local suppliers and manufacturers, the brand can easily check on their working conditions, communication is easier in the same language, and regular visits are possible to ensure the production process stays on schedule. The downside of local, as well as the higher cost, is that the factories may be much smaller and therefore it can be difficult to find companies to work with, as the good suppliers may have limited capacity.

Global manufacturing can offer larger production facilities and there are hundreds of international manufacturers who are seeking fashion brands to work with in countries like China, India, Vietnam, Cambodia, Turkey and Morocco. The main advantage of global sourcing is the cost-saving aspect, with many foreign manufacturers offering their services at a very competitive price, especially in regions where typically products are made at low cost (Alibaba, 2020). The downside is these cost savings are usually dependent on high minimum order quantities, which can lead to overproduction issues. For more luxury or conscious fashion brands, overseas manufacturers often produce lower-quality products, may not offer sustainability or ethical working conditions, and with language differences and working at a distance it can be difficult to track production to offer transparency to the consumer. One of the biggest challenges of a global supply chain is communication, with brands losing the ability to track their production. These disadvantages mean that the initial lower cost may not be an advantage. It may end up being costlier if the result is a poor-quality product, or the brand has to employ a production manager to work with the manufacturer to sort out issues.

Manufacturing challenges

Many challenges have already been mentioned but brands of all sizes acknowledge the following challenges in making their fashion product:

- Having to source new or different manufacturers to find better prices, different order quantities or better quality.

- Meeting the minimum order quantities set by suppliers.

- Overproduction owing to having to meet the minimum order quantity demanded by the factory, which means more product than they need or can sell.

- Protecting the brand's designs during the manufacturing stage to ensure they are not stolen or copied.

- The difficulty of managing a global supply chain to ensure the product is produced on time and at the right quality.

- Difficulties in tracking the global supply chain process to offer the customer transparency in how, and by whom, the brand's pieces are made.

- Subcontracting, where the factory they have selected to work with subcontracts their job to another factory without their knowledge or agreement. The subcontracted manufacturers may have unethical working practices.

Finding and selecting manufacturers

Having decided what type of factory the brand wants to work with and where, they then have the challenge of contacting them, in the hope they will be taking on new orders. Factories are selective in the brands they work with, looking for brands that can prove their credibility, have a good business history, a clear idea of what they are seeking to produce as well as the finances to pay in a timely manner (Gehlhar, 2008). Brands often start with only one or two options that they would like to work with, but the likelihood is that they will need to contact many before they get to the point of finding ones that are suitable and available. It can be difficult to get a supplier to even reply, which means brands may make the mistake of jumping at the first factory that makes an offer. This makes poor business sense, as the brand may get a better deal elsewhere, or find a factory with whom they can have a better relationship.

There are online platforms to help brands searching for manufacturers such as Let's Make it Here, Makers Row and Foursource, among others, which list a full range of suppliers and factories. These sites do not endorse the companies listed, which means the brand will still have to research how appropriate and trustworthy they are. Tradeshows are a great resource and an easy way to meet several factories in one place at one time. There are tradeshows all over the world, from big international ones to local trade fairs that promote local manufacturers.

Once the brand has a list of potential factories, they need to contact them to see if they can make the style of garment needed, at the right minimum order quantity and price. Production focuses on making product to the acquired quality in an efficient way (Burke, 2015), therefore the quality of production is as important as price when seeking a manufacturer. The brand will need to be very clear in communicating their expectations to the manufacturer and what services they need from the factory, such as cutting, sewing or full production management. This helps the factory determine if they have the right facilities and skills to make the brand's collection at the minimum order quantity they want.

A brand should never send a manufacturer examples of their designs at the initial conversation stage, as they need to protect their intellectual property and should only send designs once the supplier has signed a non-disclosure agreement (NDA).

Once the brand has selected a range of potential factories, then it is essential they visit each one to decide if they can build an effective relationship with them, as well as assess their production capabilities, physical and working conditions. It is important that brands visit manufacturers, as the best way to know what is going on in the supply chain is to actually witness it (Fish, 2022). By visiting the factory, the brand will have more than a name and address, they will be able to gather information to ensure traceability and offer transparency to their consumers. During the visit the brand can also ascertain what other brands they work with, their specialist skills, the working conditions and procedures. Brands need to look out for how organized and efficient the manufacturer is, as a dirty or disorganized factory could lose or damage the materials, and old machinery and equipment can affect quality, such as oil spots on fabrics, poor stitch tension or skipped stitches. It is essential that brands get all agreements in writing, including MOQs, costs and delivery dates. Contracts are not widely used in the fashion industry, but a brand should push to have one, as a written agreement helps should there be any dispute at a later date.

Booking production space

Once the brand has a confirmed agreement and contract with the manufacturer, they need to book their production space. If using a full production package supplier, the brand just needs to supply the design ideas by the agreed time, but for CMT factories the booking of the production slot will depend on how long it takes the brand to gather all patterns, materials and tech packs. A good factory will get booked up quickly, so smaller brands often have to book their production slots six months in advance and may still be slotted in between the factory's larger orders. Brands need to be sure that they can gather every element of their production and deliver it to the factory by a set date, or risk losing their slot.

Patterns

Pattern making and cutting is a skill that takes years of practice to perfect, and many designers are not proficient pattern cutters, so they have to employ one or outsource. The pattern is considered to be the most critical part of the pre-production process, as the whole product depends on it. A good pattern cutter will pinpoint problems in the design, construction or materials (Gehlhar, 2008) whereas a poor pattern will result in a poor product.

Patterns can be created in the traditional paper way, or digitally using specialist software and computer-aided design (CAD) programmes. Technology is making it easier to produce accurate designs that speed up the production process. Designers using CAD can transform their basic illustrations and sketches into digitized images, which are then printed via garment plotters. CAD can be used in both small and large-scale pattern making and grading, and helps to bring harmony in numerous ways across the manufacturing process, increasing efficiency and productivity (Sewport, 2022b). Many brands create a pattern block – a custom-measured, basic pattern from which lots of different styles are created. The pattern cutter can also provide the brand with pattern grading, which is the scaling of other sizes from the master pattern.

Most factories offer pattern cutting, but brands need to be wary of this. Firstly, there is the intellectual property issue around who owns the pattern if the factory creates it using the brand's designs. A brand needs to make sure a manufacturer cannot use the pattern again or sell it to other clients. Secondly, the factory may make a pattern that focuses on easier production, rather than creating a pattern that offers excellent fit for the brand's consumer. A great design needs a great pattern to make it a good seller. Bad fit is one of the biggest reasons fashion products don't sell, so a good pattern is essential.

Samples

Once the patterns are cut, a sample is made to test it to make sure the design works, and also enables the manufacturer to give a more accurate estimate of production lead time and cost (Gehlhar, 2008). The sample is essential to ensure the factory can produce the garment to the brand's specifications and ensure that the product will be a great fit and good quality. The sample is an opportunity to make the final small changes to fine-tune the garment and fix any problems before putting it into production. Brands must be perfectionists when dealing with sampling to make sure each product fits impeccably and this is done by testing it on a fit model to ensure the product also has the movement and functionality needed to be wearable and keep the customer happy. The final sample needs to be an exact version of the final garment, with all labels, trims and the quality of finishing that meets the brand's quality standards. As factories may rush the first sample, which leads to mistakes, it is important to make sure the brand has checked the sample thoroughly and checked the fit on a model, or the mistakes will be carried through on to the production run. A brand should never sign off a sample until it is 100 per cent accurate – and needs to make sure any amendments are made on the pattern and tech pack to ensure the production run matches the sample.

Tech pack and specification sheets

The tech pack is the crucial business tool for relaying the brand's ideas to the manufacturer to make sure the products meet the requirements of the label. The tech pack is a globally standardized form of communication between a brand and their manufacturer, which includes a comprehensive packet of design details. This set of documents allows a fashion designer to maintain quality control over their idea as it is developed into a pattern and final product (Sewport, n.d.). The tech pack acts as a blueprint for the factory with detailed flat sketches, bill of materials, fabrics, trims, colourways, measurements and size gradings, among other things to minimize the risk of information being lost in communication. The more detail that a brand puts into the tech pack the better, as that way there is less chance of mistakes.

Specification sheet

Within the tech pack will be specification sheets (Figure 6.4) that contain the technical drawing of a design with details of all the construction and styling details, measurements, label positions, stitching details, special requirements such as the positioning of print or embroidery, and views of the front and back of the piece (Burke, 2015).

Production docket

The production docket (Figure 6.5) will be the order to the factory that tells them exactly what to make, including the style, how many of the style to make in which sizes and colours, the different materials and trims to use, the factory price based on the sample and delivery dates agreed.

Figure 6.4   Specification sheet example

Brand Name	Date
Garment description	Garment name or style number

Fabric swatch   Colourways   Front   Back

Colour code:

Fabric 1	
Fabric 1	
Trim 1	
Trim 2	
Zip	
Button	
Thread type and colour	
Interfacing	
Shoulder pad	
Binding	
Brand label	
Care label	
Seam type	
Seam allowances	
Key measurement 1	
Key measurement 2	
Key measurement 3	
Key measurement 4	

Figure 6.5   Production docket for factory

Style Name	Colour	Sizes					Total	Target Make Cost ex VAT	Total Cost
		XS	S	M	L	XL			
Style 1	Colourway 1		1	2	4	2	1	10	£50.00	£500.00
	Colourway 2		1	2	4	2	1	10	£50.00	£500.00
Style 2	Colourway 1		0	5	5	5	0	15	£45.00	£675.00
	Colourway 2		0	5	5	5	0	15	£45.00	£675.00
Style 3	Colourway 1		0	5	5	5	0	15	£60.00	£900.00
	Colourway 2		0	5	5	5	0	15	£60.00	£900.00
								80		£4,150.00

Bill of materials

The bill of materials includes a list of all the components, fabrics, labels, fastenings and trims being used in production of the designs and where they will be used or placed on the designs (Figure 6.6).

If the brand gets the tech pack right and communicates clearly and concisely with their manufacturers, then there is less chance of mistakes. Inaccurate tech packs can increase production costs, result in additional samples having to be made, can affect the quality and fit of the garment, as well as delay the delivery schedule.

Figure 6.6   Bill of materials

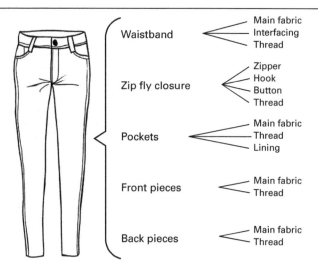

Image	Description	Consumption	Placement	Cost	Supplier	Light	Medium	Dark
	Denim care label	110 pcs	Inwards between right pocket and waistband	£0.50	Supplier 1			
	Denim	310mt	Overall	£3.00	Supplier 2			
	Jeans Rivets	250pcs	Both pockets	£0.35	Supplier 2	Brass	Brass	Antique
	Fabric	90mt	All outer except for waistband	£2.00	Supplier 1	White	Ecru	Black
	Pocketing	40mt		£0.75	Supplier 1			
	PU label	110 pcs	Back right on waistband	£1.00	Supplier 1			
	Tack button	350 pcs		£0.35	Supplier 1			
	Zipper	110 pcs		£5.00	Supplier 1	Brass	Brass	Antique

Production management

Production management is the process that brings together the work of the design studio, pattern cutting, sampling and manufacturing departments, ensuring the collection meets the brand's style, quality standards, price points, delivery dates and points of sale. For every collection, the brand must create a detailed production plan and put the management processes in place to cover every step of the development, from ordering materials to receiving the finished goods. Production management is a juggling act for brands as they have to constantly manage and negotiate orders, delivery and costs to make sure everything comes together at the right time at the right price. There are many different elements to consider – from ordering fabrics, tracking supplies, negotiating prices and minimum order quantities to booking production slots. If a brand does not have good management systems in place, then things can start to go wrong very quickly, and they can find that they have incurred very costly mistakes. Larger brands employ production managers who are responsible for the smooth operation of the management process to ensure mistakes don't happen (Burke, 2015).

The things that go wrong during the manufacturing stage are often due to the brand's lack of experience in working with manufacturers and suppliers, poor communication between the brand and the factory, or a lack of organization and planning to ensure everything is in place at the right time (Gehlhar, 2008). With many steps to monitor in the production process, it is easy to miss something vital or lose control due to timings slipping.

The production plan is a written document that incorporates all the steps in the process, integrating the design and manufacturing process to make sure the products are produced according to a set schedule and to the required quality (Burke, 2015). The production plan will include:

Figure 6.7 Critical path example

	Jan	Feb	March	April	May	June	July	Aug	Sept	Oct	Nov	Dec
Research	░	░										
Design			░									
Material sourcing				░								
Secure factory				░								
First patterns					░							
Sampling						░	░	░				
Editing colour									░			
Production										░	░	░

Critical path

The critical path is the timeline working backwards from when the products need to be delivered or ready for sale (Figure 6.7), allowing for sampling, production, material sourcing and delivery, shipping and potential delays along the process (Burke, 2015). It is necessary to include time for delays and errors in the plan, as there will always be unexpected delays or sampling may not run smoothly first time and the brand may need to sample the product again to get the perfect outcome.

The critical path needs to include all the steps of production from concept, design development, material selection, patterns, sampling, to production, with other elements added according to the brand's business model. The critical path should anticipate unexpected problems, as although production can be strictly managed, there are still things that happen out of the control of the brand, including factory shutdowns during holiday seasons in Italy and China or shipping delays due to bad weather (Burke, 2015).

Larger brands will have orders at various stages of completion as they work across several seasons or collections all at the same time. These brands are reliant on effective and efficient systems that keep track of every stage of the production process (Gehlhar, 2008), monitoring designs waiting to be made, designs that are in process, and others that are ready for delivery to the customer. While an Excel spreadsheet can capture this information, many brands today use production management software tools, with digital engagement integrated into the entire product development lifecycle to improve communication and efficiency across the supply chain (Black, Edwards and Miller, 2015).

NDA and manufacturing agreements

Brands must keep track of contracts and non-disclosure agreements (NDAs) that they have with their suppliers, partners and manufacturers. The NDA is crucial to ensure the brand's intellectual property is protected and the designs cannot be copied or shared. The brand should also insist on manufacturing agreements and contracts being signed, to make sure the production stays on track and that products are made to the quality standards set.

Quality control

Brands will often just presume that their manufacturer will provide the best-quality product or service, but this is often not the case. Quality assurance includes all the components including thread, zips, buttons and elastic, as cheap components can ruin a luxury garment and not meet customers' expectations. It also includes the sewing operations such as type and length of stiches, stitch tension, seam types, hems and buttonhole stitching (Burns, Bryant and Mullet, 2011). The brand has to insti-gate quality control processes and inform the factory and suppliers what they expect and have quality control checklists to ensure nothing is missed in the production process. The purpose of the production sample is to set the standard for production, as the brand can then compare all the production with the sample including seam allowances and stitching quality (Fashion Insiders, 2017). All fabrics, materials and trims should be checked as soon as they arrive; however, by this point the brand has usually already paid for it, therefore it is better to put quality control measures in place with the supplier before they are paid, and the goods shipped. A good supplier will send videos of the goods or fabric unrolled, or some will supply a sample cut of the fabric to check quality before the bulk of the order is shipped. If the goods are going direct to the manufacturer, then the brand should send a production manager to the site to inspect all the goods before production starts, as once the materials are cut, the responsibility lies with the brand not the supplier (Gehlhar, 2008). Many errors come from materials not being checked before production starts, and then it is often too late to negotiate with the supplier, rectify the mistake or have a backup plan to work around the faults.

An accurate Tech Pack will ensure unnecessary problems are avoided, giving the manufacturer clear instructions on how the product should be made and finished, setting the quality standard for each piece in the collection.

Tracking production materials

Most brands work globally, with production supplies such as fabric, buttons and zips being shipped from all over the world. Brands need a detailed plan and critical path to ensure all their supplies arrive at the right place at the right time, or the manufacturer will not be able to start the production run. The brand also needs to put quality control processes in place for the production materials to ensure the manufacturer has received the right product, as a CMT factory will cut, make and trim with whatever they receive.

Marker making/lay planning

Marking, which can also be called lay planning in some countries, is the process of arranging the pattern pieces on the fabric to make best use of the fabric and incur as little waste as possible. Marker making takes time and skill and not all designers are capable or want to create the marker. The fabric needs to be carefully cut depending on the grain lines, patterns and stripes. Poor cutting will result in a bad-quality prod-uct. Some brands will ask the factory to create the marker, but for brands that work on a zero-waste model it is recommended that they do this in-house, as not all facto-ries are able to produce this.

Garment labels

Along with the brand label, on every garment there needs to be clear labelling that adheres to the regulations and laws in the country where the product will be sold. The label will detail the fabric composition and country of origin, along with the care instructions for the customer. It is necessary for a brand to know the differences in legal requirements for products sold in each country in order to avoid paying penalties for failure to comply with their laws.

Cut and sew

A CMT factory cannot start a production run if elements are missing from the order such as a zip, thread or buttons. If deliveries are late, then the factory will delay the production run until everything has arrived and they may not have a slot in their diary for many more weeks.

Overproduction

Overproduction is a huge problem in the fashion industry, with many brands producing more products than they can sell, which has huge financial and environmental impacts. Brands end up with overproduction for many reasons, including sampling too large a collection and putting it into full production with the assumption that they will sell it all. It can also be due to manufacturers insisting on high minimum order quantities to get a better price. When developing and manufacturing a collection, brands need to only produce what they can realistically expect to sell, based on research and engagement with the potential customer.

Subcontracting

A growing concern in the manufacturing process is the hidden issue of subcontracting, where a brand's collection ends up being produced not in their chosen factory, but in a less favourable one that has unregulated working conditions. It is well known that some international manufacturers will agree a contract but then subcontract the order to another cheaper supplier without the knowledge of the brand. Subcontracting results in not only the products being made in awful working conditions, but also the products are likely to be poor quality or damaged. To avoid subcontracting, a brand should either work with local suppliers that they can regularly check on, or if working overseas they should consider hiring an independent production manager who can monitor where the collection is actually being produced.

Summary

This chapter has addressed the challenges occurring in the global fashion supply chain due to erratic economic and political conditions, as well as changing consumer demands for greater sustainability and transparency. It has detailed the areas that brands have to consider when finding and working with suppliers to ensure they can meet the brand's minimum order quantities and quality standards. It has also identified areas for improvement through the adoption of new digital technologies.

With the inherent risks in the fashion supply chain, brands have to develop effective and efficient business models to manage their suppliers and manufacturers around the world, with greater focus on not only cost efficiencies but also transparency, sustainability and corporate social responsibility. Brands need to develop efficient management processes that ensure reduced costs and better profits for the brand, effective inventory management, as well as improved quality and products that meet customer requirements.

Key terms

atelier	jobbers	production docket
bill of materials	marker	production management
blockchain	mills	sourcing
converters	minimum order quantity (MOQ)	specification sheet
critical path		subcontracting
cut, make, trim (CMT)	nearshoring	supply chain
ethics	non-disclosure agreement (NDA)	sustainability
full production package (FPP)	overproduction	tech pack
	production	transparency

Activity

Using the label within a piece of clothing, investigate the potential supply chain and issues for where the textiles and the final product were sourced and manufactured.

Online resources

The tech pack.

References

Alibaba (2020) Local vs global sourcing: the pros and cons, *Alibaba*, seller.alibaba.com/businessblogs/pxxf9hls-local-vs-global-sourcing-the-pros-and-cons (archived at https://perma.cc/6JBM-LC2Y)

Black, S, Edwards, M J and Miller, G (2015) What is digital about fashion design, *University of the Arts London*, ualresearchonline.arts.ac.uk/id/eprint/9790/1/WHAT%27S%20DIGITAL%20ABOUT%20FASHION%20DESIGN.pdf (archived at https://perma.cc/RGH2-7GNB)

Burke, S (2015) *Fashion Entrepreneur*, Burke Publishing, Ringwood

Burns, L, Bryant, N and Mullet, K (2011) *The Business of Fashion*, 4th edn, Fairchild Books, New York

Chen, C (2021) How fashion can tackle its supply chain crisis, *The Business of Fashion*, www.businessoffashion.com/articles/retail/how-fashion-can-tackle-its-supply-chain-crisis/ (archived at https://perma.cc/XG9D-GG3A)

Fashion Insiders (2017) The importance of quality control in fashion manufacturing, *Fashion Insiders*, www.fashioninsiders.co/toolkit/top-tips/quality-control-fashion-manufacturing/ (archived at https://perma.cc/YTC3-R3TN)

Fibre2Fashion (2019) 9 steps to formulate right sourcing strategy for the textile and apparel industry, *Fibre2fashion*, www.fibre2fashion.com/industry-article/8447/9-steps-to-formulate-right-sourcing-strategy-for-the-textile-and-apparel-industry#:~:text=%209%20Steps%20to%20Formulate%20Right%20Sourcing%20Strategy,information.%20Another%20essential%20is%20collecting%20supplier%E2%80%99s...%20More%20 (archived at https://perma.cc/8XDZ-FM4R)

Fish, I (2022) The search for fashion supply chain transparency, *Drapers*, www.drapersonline.com/topics/sustainable-fashion/the-search-for-fashion-supply-chain-transparency (archived at https://perma.cc/78T8-4YZB)

Forest Digital (2021) Impact of sustainable and organic fabrics within the fashion industry, *Forest Digital*, www.forestdigital.co.uk/2021/06/12/impact-of-sustainable-and-organic-fabrics-within-the-fashion-industry/ (archived at https://perma.cc/8HT5-XBXX)

Gehlhar, M (2008) *The Fashion Designer Survival Guide*, Kaplan Publishing, New York

Jain, S (2021) Blockchain technology in fashion industry, *Textile Learner*, www.textilelearner.net/blockchain-technology-in-fashion-industry/ (archived at https://perma.cc/T6FK-L4ET)

Londrigan, M and Jenkins, J (2018) *Fashion Supply Chain Management*, Fairchild Books, New York

McKinsey (2017) Supply Chain 4.0 in consumer goods, *McKinsey*, www.mckinsey.com/industries/consumer-packaged-goods/our-insights/supply-chain-4-0-in-consumer-goods (archived at https://perma.cc/6NWB-ZVXR)

McKinsey & Company (2020) Fashion on climate, *McKinsey*, www.mckinsey.com/~/media/mckinsey/industries/retail/our%20insights/fashion%20on%20climate/fashion-on-climate-full-report.pdf (archived at https://perma.cc/65FL-3U5Q)

Raghavan, M (2022) Council post: why fashion supply chain traceability is a tech challenge that begins with AI, *Forbes*, www.forbes.com/sites/forbestechcouncil/2022/03/18/why-fashion-supply-chain-traceability-is-a-tech-challenge-that-begins-with-ai/?sh=7cb3e8955f6d (archived at https://perma.cc/K3AZ-B9QY)

Serai (2021) Top supply chain issues in the fashion industry and how to address them, *Seraitrade*, www.seraitrade.com/blog/top-supply-chain-issues-in-the-fashion-industry-and-how-to-address-them (archived at https://perma.cc/E4Y3-BWEV)

Sewport (2022a) CMT vs FPP: which is best method for your business (& their benefits), *Sewport*, www.sewport.com/cut-and-sew-manufacturers (archived at https://perma.cc/7MH6-MBWD)

Sewport (2022b) Essentials of pattern making and why it's important to get it right!, *Sewport*, www.sewport.com/learn/pattern-making (archived at https://perma.cc/ZY5G-E9NF)

Sewport (n.d.) Fashion tech pack – avoid manufacturing errors (ultimate guide book), *Sewport*, www.sewport.com/tech-pack (archived at https://perma.cc/W3P6-AS3F)

The Sustainable Angle (n.d.) Future fabrics virtual expo: sustainability, *Future Fabrics Virtual Expo*, www.futurefabricsvirtualexpo.com/sustainability (archived at https://perma.cc/46XW-G6BA)

Tsolova, D (2020) Think globally but manufacture fashion locally, *Fashion Insiders*, www.fashioninsiders.co/features/opinion/global-local-manufacturing/ (archived at https://perma.cc/8C3N-P9ZY)

Case study
FREED

FREED is a Canadian brand that offers a range of vegan, cruelty-free, faux-fur outerwear and accessories for the whole family. FREED is the in-house brand from manufacturing specialists, Freed & Freed International Ltd, who have been the mainstay of the Canadian garment industry since their inception in 1921. Their sought-after expertise and technical capabilities led to the development and production of outerwear for heritage brands and major retailers around the world.

Female entrepreneur Marissa Freed is now the fourth generation leading the family business, inheriting not only the business but her father's business sense, tenacity and refusal to compromise quality, integrity or an ethical workforce. Today, under the leadership of Marissa, Freed & Freed is 85 per cent female-led with approximately 100 unionized employees, continuing a legacy of high-quality, locally made apparel.

Marissa took her passion for the business to have a positive impact on the world into the launch of new in-house label FREED, which launched in 2020. This label fulfils her desire to 'create the outerwear brand of dreams offering customers high-quality vegan faux fur outerwear in vibrant colours and easy-to-wear styles'. FREED's range is made by an ethical labour force and all products are entirely animal free, even down to the dyes, which are 100 per cent vegan. Sustainability and ethical production are important to Marissa, 'at FREED we want to make a contribution to positively impact the world our kids will grow up in, while offering luxurious yet fun and fashionable outwear that stands out'.

The brand sells internationally through luxury department stores and independent retailers, one of which is My Wardrobe HQ in the UK, which offers both sales and rental options, to make FREED pieces available to consumers who seek less consumption models.

Every year FREED takes on a new environmental initiative and the brand will always bring their fabric ends and past pieces back to the factory and repurpose them into accessories or new styles found in capsule collections. The brand's goal is to get as close to zero waste as humanly possible. The future of FREED is more than clothing, it is an initiative for positive change.

www.freedandfreed.com

Brand storytelling and management   7

LEARNING OBJECTIVES

After reading this chapter you should be able to:

- Explain what a brand is
- Describe the tools and processes used in developing a brand and a brand story
- Understand the five brand pillars used to build customer value
- Identify the components that are included in the development of a brand strategy

Introduction

If an organization wants to stand out from the competition in an oversaturated fashion market that is full of products from businesses around the world, it needs to create a brand not just products. The brand management role within a business is to create desire and build trust through various channels that will attract customers and build loyalty. Consumer behaviours have changed with the customer now seeking more than products – they want new experiences, look for transparency and authenticity from businesses they buy from, as well as a sense of community. They seek genuine brands that share their values, ethics and personality. This means a business has to add value through building brand stories and experiences that connect with their consumers on an emotional basis, so that they become and remain loyal customers.

This chapter will look at how a business can form itself into a compelling fashion brand that is relevant to the consumer, has strong brand stories and messaging, and a consistent style across all its touchpoints. It will look at the components that make the brand memorable to the consumer, as well as how the business connects its purpose and values to create a unique proposition that differentiates the brand from the competition. The chapter will look at the steps of brand development through brand pillars as well as building brand equity through the tangible aspects of the brand such as the logo and packaging, and the intangible factors including experience and emotional connections. It will also address the benefits of developing a brand strategy to communicate the brand messaging in a clear and cohesive way across all marketing activities.

What is branding

It is vital in the fashion industry to focus on branding when there are hundreds of businesses selling the same or very similar products. Businesses get confused about the meaning of branding and think their brand is the name on their label, which is not correct. A brand is more than the physical features of the logo, the name or the trademark, it is also how the customer perceives the brand, how they feel about it, and the emotional connection they develop towards the company and its products (Marion, 2022). There is not a clear definition for branding, though most describe it as a marketing process that creates a set of perceptions about your business, or, as Amazon CEO Jeff Bezos has been credited with saying, 'Your brand is what people say about you when you're not in the room' (Marketing and Creative Handbook, 2021).

The purpose of branding is to create such a strong identity that connects with a customer so that when they see the brand, the product or hear the business name, they intuitively know what the brand does, what it stands for and how they feel about it. While a product can easily be copied by other businesses, a brand is always unique. Branding can humanize a business by giving it a personality that a consumer can relate to, rather than just being another manufacturer who churns out products. By creating a unique personality and visual identity, as well as unique designs and signatures in the products, fashion businesses are more likely to attract a customer. Branding is not merely the design of the business or creating a logo, design and visuals, it is about defining the brand values and identity, voice and personality (Renderforest, 2021). If the business is consistent in their branding, ensuring that in every aspect of the organization they are loyal to their promises and values, then it builds trust with the customers, but also makes it more attractive to potential investors and stakeholders (Renderforest, 2021). No one will be interested in investing their time and resources in an unstable business that has no clear brand definition or rebrands itself frequently.

Foundations of creating a brand

The starting point of creating a brand involves the ideation and development of the design aesthetics, signature and range plan, but it also needs to include the development of the brand identity and brand stories to enable the business to connect and resonate with the consumer. A clothing brand is not just about being as good as your best design but also the business you need to create around it (The Brand Boy, 2022). A top priority for a business is to define its identity, determining what type of business they want to be, what their attributes will be and what values and opinions they will have. This will inform the decisions they make about the key brand messages, the language they will use, the tone of voice as well as all the visual elements of the business. All these processes need to connect with the consumer in order to create with a brand story that entices, engages and enthrals the customer (Figure 7.1).

Creating a brand involves numerous elements that need to be integrated to form a consistent message that will entice the consumer away from other brands, engage with them to build a sense of community and enthral them with exciting offers and experiences that keep them loyal to the business. Fashion brands tend to work on specific elements of brand development at various times, rather than thinking it as the creation of an interconnected system that forms a cohesive whole (Hodges, 2020). A well-defined brand ensures that everyone within the company, as well as external customers, partners and stakeholders, understand what the brand is and what it does that is different. Terms used in brand development include:

- *Brand essence*: The brand essence is the thread that pulls together all the various parts of a business. It refers to the substance of the business, the functions, leadership and decision-making processes that form the foundation of the brand.

- *The brand purpose*: Why the business exists beyond just generating income and making a profit.

- *Brand vision*: The future of the business, the direction it will develop in and how it will impact on the consumer, the community and the industry as a whole.

- *Brand mission*: A brand mission provides a clear statement of the commitment the business is making and the reputation it aims to develop.

- *Brand values*: The values, opinions and beliefs that the business will use as the guiding compass in the decisions and actions made (Houraghan, n.d.).

Figure 7.1   Brand storytelling

Each of these areas work towards creating a brand that is unique and stands out from the crowd. Developing a strong brand is transformative for the business, its people, its product and its success. There are many steps that go into creating a cohesive brand; it takes time and resources but is the biggest lever most companies have to improve profits and create a demand among customers. Larger well-resourced businesses may approach an agency to assist them with the brand development process, whereas smaller brands often have to struggle through and work it out themselves, but this often means they miss key elements that could affect their future success. Even if a business uses an agency to support the development of the brand, they still need significant involvement in the process and need to guide the agency, as the brand is the voice, the heart and soul and the story of the company, and for it to be authentic it has to come from the business founders.

The starting point of developing the brand is the process of identifying the target customers and competitors, which has been covered in-depth in earlier chapters of this book. The next steps look at image and tone of voice, integrating the purposes and values of the business in the brand messages and storytelling, and the development of the layers that add value to the business that form the brand strategy and brand management processes to ensure cohesion in all marketing approaches of the business. A business can use the brand pillars framework as the foundation for developing the brand and to inform the strategy.

Brand pillars

Brand pillars are the values and characteristics that form the DNA of a brand. They are the ingredients that make the brand unique, define the fundamental points that set the business apart from the competitors and determine how the company will communicate its message to the world (Giuliani, 2022). The brand pillars can be anything that the customers find important, such as innovation, engagement or express delivery, they are the things that differentiate the brand and should be valued and endorsed by the customers (Riserbato, n.d.). If a business creates the right brand pillars and communicates them effectively, then in the future when a customer describes the business they will mention elements from the brand pillars.

Figure 7.2 lists five categories – purpose, perception, personality, positioning and promotion – that are used by many fashion brands and are described in detail below. Brands can choose other pillars that are more relevant to their business or consumer, or call them different things such as identity, value and brand experience. Refining these elements to the brand will help convey an accurate and attractive brand image that will boost the business's reputation among existing and potential customers (Coastal Brand, 2022).

Figure 7.2   Brand pillars

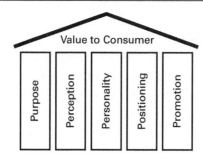

Brand pillar 1 – purpose

Purpose describes the very roots of the business; it is the reason the company was created and exists. The purpose is the foundation from which the brand mission, values and vision are formed. The purpose is outward facing, looking at the difference the business will make for people, community, the industry, the planet or even the world, whereas the brand mission, values and vision are inward facing as they determine how the company will act (Canva, n.d.). The purpose is the heart and soul of the business, it is what drives the business beyond making profit, it forms the culture among its people including customers and employees, and it builds brand legacy.

Brand pillar 2 – perception

Perception relates to feelings, experiences and thoughts about the business, both with customers and employees. When customers come across a brand, they will form instant perceptions about what that business or their products represent. This comes from the customers' feelings, not what the business says it does. While customers – not the company – hold the key to a brand's perception, they can be shaped, using the other brand pillars (Lischer, n.d.). To shape the perception, the business needs to conduct research into how customers or potential customers perceive the brand, to see if there are misperceptions and to discover ways that the brand can more effectively communicate to improve perception. The business needs to decide what they want the perception of their brand to be, including what words they would like their audience to use in relation to their business. These could be words or terms such as innovative, dynamic, experiential or enthusiastic, which would then be used to set the tone for all brand messaging, as if used effectively the consumer will then repeat them. The perception pillar is also about aligning internal and external communication, as a happy workforce creates a positive image of the company, which attracts a more positive brand perception.

Fashion brands have to consider how brand perceptions impact what customers buy and wear, as there can be associations related to image and social position of certain products or brands. These perceptions do not necessarily come from the quality or design of the product but more from how the consumer feels when they wear a particular brand or product, as they perceive it giving them greater status and self-worth.

Brand pillar 3 – personality

This brand pillar concerns the human characteristics and behaviours that define a brand, who they are, not what they do. A business, like a person, needs to have a personality, the elements that humanize it and make it easier to interact with its customers. The personality of a brand will influence all its visual elements, including designs and colours, as well as the brand's voice and messaging. Brand personality defines the brand's first impression and creates the connection and familiarity with the customer, even though the customers may not be consciously aware of it (Lischer, n.d.).

To develop the brand's personality, the business needs to review how it will describe itself, how it communicates across its channels, how it has a similar or different personality to its competitors, as well as ensuring that the personality is authentic to who the brand is. An example would be a young female fashion brand who would have a cheeky, girly personality, who would talk to their audience as if they were mates, sharing experiences and talking to them in colloquial language using words such as babe, basic or bae.

Brand pillar 4 – positioning

Brand positioning relates to the distinct place that a brand will hold in the mind of people who experience the business, including the employees, the industry, stakeholders and the customers. Marketing author Philip Kotler (2003) defined brand positioning as 'the act of designing the company's offering and image to occupy a distinctive place in the mind of the target market'.

Brand positioning is the strategy used to create associations in customers' minds that make them perceive the brand as different to others, more favourable and more credible than the competitors. Brand positioning is the reason customers will buy a product from a specific brand despite it being very similar to products from other companies. This is important in the fashion industry, with so many companies making the same or very similar products. There are different brand positioning strategies that companies can use including positioning based on quality, price, benefits, solution-based on solving a consumer's problems, or subjective, which implies no other company can offer a better solution or product.

A good brand-positioning strategy will ensure the brand's position is relevant to the customer, the messaging is clear and concise, the position is unique and desirable in the customer's mind and there is a distinct point of difference that can be recognized by the consumer. A good positioning strategy will be validated by consumers as it resonates with their needs and wants.

Brand pillar 5 – promotion

The brand promotion pillar includes all the diverse ways a brand will promote the business to introduce and entice the customer to engage with the company. Brand promotion aims to build a long-lasting relationship with the customer; it is different to product promotion, which just focuses on short-lived transactions (Lischer, n.d.). Many brands make the mistake of only focusing their promotional activity on product, but with customers now looking for experience over product, brand promotion has risen in importance. Businesses need to create a positive customer experience and association first that draws the customer in, before trying to sell the products. All brand promotions need to be consistent with the brand image, identity and tone of voice, so that wherever the consumer meets the brand they will feel that they are in the same space and having the same conversations (Coastal Brand, 2022).

Having identified and understood these brand pillars, a business can now start to build them in to their strategy and use them to create a brand identity that sets the organization apart from its competition. The brand pillars give the business a depth of character to build upon, a basis for brand storytelling and a promise to offer to the customer. Without these elements people will not feel compelled to engage with and purchase from the company.

Brand identity

Brand identity is the way a business will use different tools including visuals, messaging and experience to create a brand image that will engage with the consumer. The brand identity should emerge from the brand pillars to form elements including the logo, colours and fonts, the design signature, voice and tone, website and social media platform designs, content and messaging, advertising and packaging. All these elements of the brand identity need to be authentic and congruent, as overpromising or miscommunicating undermines trust, damages the reputation and leads to brand failure (Rukosuev, n.d.).

Visual brand elements

Visual imagery is highly important for a fashion brand as part of their communication and connection with the customer. Visual branding has five key elements – consistency, logo, typography, colour and imagery. For the first element consistency is key, as consumers need to see the same logo or imagery style over and over again before they recognize it and then trust it. While the world often calls for everything to be new and different, when it comes to branding it is the repetition that has the greatest effect. Fashion brands need a great logo, as this is used on products, labels, packaging and across all marketing and sales platforms. The logo needs to work in numerous ways without having to be altered or adjusted, which would damage the consistency and lose the impact. Brands should use consistent typography across all their marketing, opting for a primary and secondary font that they will always use. These fonts have to be easily read, particularly on the clothing labels, and a distinct font can make the brand's messaging instantly identifiable. Brand colours also need to be consistent and most brands limit their use to one primary colour and two or three secondary colours. There are a lot of theories behind the use of colour, as they can have significant emotional and psychological impact on the consumer. Using certain colours can cultivate stronger emotional connections between a brand and their customer, or due to cultural associations with certain colours the brand could either attract or repel consumer attention. For fashion brands their imagery style is vital in attracting the customer to their brand.

In an increasingly visual world, the need for powerful, impactful images has never been more important.

Too often brands only focus on the product, while the images are not given enough attention and budget. The images for a fashion brand need to tell a story, relate to and represent the customer and speak to them. Images bring the brand to life, giving it a personality and adding value.

A business can create a brand style guidelines document as part of its overall brand strategy, this would dictate how the business would use fonts, logos, colour palettes and styling to ensure all branding remains consistent. The more distinct, specific and cohesive these visual elements are, the more likely it is that the business creates a differentiated brand that is recognized and admired.

Brand voice

The brand voice is essentially how the brand's content sounds in people's heads. The voice defines and should embody the brand personality. It is the brand voice and tone that seeps into all of the business's communications, whether on the website, social media, podcasts, through customer service, as well as in advertising and PR. Brand personalities are just like the personality of human beings, they have certain emotional or personal qualities that attract us and make us like them. To develop the brand voice, a business would need to consider again who the customer is, how they talk, what personalities they connect with and how the brand will talk to them. A brand voice can be professional, friendly, authoritative, conversational, informative and hundreds of other adjectives that might be relevant to a brand. Businesses need to choose a voice that makes sense and resonates with their customers. A consistent voice makes the brand recognizable across all channels when the consumer engages with the brand's content.

Brand promise and values

The brand promise describes the quality of products, service and experience that the business will offer the customer. If a brand delivers on the promise – in other words they meet the standards in their product, service and experience that they have declared – then it will build a stronger brand value in the mind of the customer. The brand promise needs to speak to the target customer and tell them what they can expect, and the unique qualities and benefits they will get from purchasing from the business. The brand promise includes the tangible benefits, the things the customer can see and touch as well as the intangible benefits, which are the things the customer feels and experiences. Every brand needs to develop the range of benefits that they offer, such as quality, value and unique design. It could be that the product solves a problem, or that it makes the customer feel better than other brands. Businesses can determine the benefits that add brand value from the areas they identified in the brand pillars, such as being environmentally conscious or supporting ethical production.

Brand messaging

Brand messaging refers to the practice of delivering a unique story and value proposition for the business. Effective brand messaging conveys who the brand is, what they do and why the customer should care, and the value proposition is the value that the company promises to deliver to the customer. This needs to be a unique element or service that will inspire, persuade, motivate and make the customer want to buy the brand's product.

Brand messaging looks at the core motives that gives a company purpose and needs to describe the business and its products quickly and concisely in a language that the customer understands. To develop the brand message, businesses needs to consider how they can easily capture what they do and what benefits they offer within one or two sentences or within an image style. Many brands make the mistake of describing their brand in too much detail, writing long descriptive missives to describe their inspiration and design style, or use industry language that consumers do not relate to. Effective brand messaging has to be honed to speak to the specific customer and tell them what benefits they will get.

Brand messaging needs to be constantly evaluated, reviewed and refined to make sure that it resonates with the intended customers. If the audience is engaging positively with the brand's messaging and content then great, but if response and engagement is low then the brand will need to adapt its messaging to better meet the consumer need (Coastal Brand, 2022).

Brand storytelling

If the purpose of branding is to stand out in the marketplace and create a loyal customer base around shared values, then a business needs to determine what their brand is and what story they will tell.

> Storytelling is universal to human experience, an ancient and powerful tool used by all cultures to share history and experiences.

Stories help us find order in things that happen in the world, as well as help us see how others think and feel, which enables us to empathize with others. Studies suggest that the more compelling the story the more empathetic people become (National Geographic, n.d.), as telling stories make details more memorable than being given dry facts. Studies of human psychology have found that if we are told something through narrative, we are more likely to relate to the message, absorbing it further and remaining engaged from start to finish (Robertson, 2012). Storytelling gives a brand the opportunity to communicate on a human level and make a direct connection with consumers. The business needs to look beyond the product and service they deliver and develop their unique and authentic brand story that will appeal to consumers, draw them in and add value to their lives. Brand storytelling is a marketing method that uses a creative narrative to connect a brand to its customers. The narrative can draw on the company history, purpose, inspiration, goals, products and services to create a robust brand story. For the luxury market, businesses also draw on the stories of their head designers or creative directors, who add a more human element to their storytelling. Every brand needs a story to transfer its messages and values to the audience. Creating an emotional bond with the audience is one of, if not the most important, branding strategy a brand can use (Renderforest, 2021).

Brand storytelling is important because it offers companies the opportunity to personalize their brand and form a deeper connection and sense of community with their customers.

> The winning formula for consumer engagement is storytelling. A great brand story will entice, engage and enthral the customer.

Brand stories can embrace different elements including provenance, social action, purpose and consumer experience stories (The Story Mill, n.d.). Purpose-driven businesses and those with strong social action stories around diversity, sustainability and ethics build greater connections with their consumers, as their brand storytelling builds greater affinity and desire. Customer-experience storytelling shows how the brand fits into the customer world by solving their problems, satisfying their desires, or fulfilling their sense of self. Provenance storytelling builds on the heritage of the business or the people leading it, as consumers are inspired by passionate business leaders and disrupters.

Some brands make the mistake of listing facts about their business instead of crafting a story that will engage, inspire and move people. If a brand does not have a story to tell, then they are just selling product and that really limits their chance of success. While brand storytelling is a powerful marketing technique, it has to be authentic and the brand has to be able to deliver on the promises it makes. They cannot just add in buzzwords or key phrases and not deliver on them. There are currently many brands that use words such as sustainable or ethical in their brand storytelling without explicitly sharing how they deliver these. Today's modern consumer is very marketing savvy and knows when a brand is being false or misleading with its descriptions, using terms, phrases and even charity-giving in an inauthentic way.

Brand experience

A fashion brand that truly values its relationship with the customer will seek to offer a great brand experience at each and every touchpoint. No matter how the consumer discovers or interacts with the brand, whether through the website, social media, in a store or at an event, the brand will take every opportunity to give that customer an experience they will not forget. To achieve this a brand needs to make sure that all its branding, activities and marketing are consistent in relaying the brand identity and make its brand storytelling come to life. Manavi Pandey (2022) describes brand experience as 'awakening a holistic sensory experience to build an all-rounding relationship between customers and a brand. The business uses every customer touchpoint to develop a holistic brand experience'. Brand experience is important in this era of high competition, when a business needs to find ways of offering a better experience than its competitors. A business can stand out with brand activations that increase brand awareness, create delightfully memorable experiences and ultimately generate sustainable growth in sales (Tsatsawani, 2020).

Laurence Parkes (2019) identified five main facets to build an extraordinary brand experience: think, sense, feel, do and connect. These facets represent the way people become engaged with a brand. 'Think' is the process of engaging the consumer's intellect through experiences relating to the brand's purpose. 'Do' is the experience the customer gets from engaging or getting involved with solving problems. 'Connect' attracts the consumer looking to be part of a community. 'Feel' can come from emotionally engaging experiences that make the customer feel good. 'Sense' is about immersing customers in the brand through experiences that appeal to their five senses. Human memory is highly associative in nature – and multiple sensory stimuli such as music and scent will create neural connections that ensure consumers remember experiences.

With fashion being such a creative space, creating brand experiences should be a natural extension for future-facing brands. As consumers have moved online to purchase product, brands are having to think of new ways to interact with their customers by either changing the focus of their bricks-and-mortar stores to more experiential spaces or using brand activations to reach customers on a more intimate level where they live. Brand activation refers to the process of increasing awareness of and engagement with the brand through any number of experiences, either online through digital campaigns, through pop-up shops or taking the brand to cultural events or festivals (Shrum, 2019). According to colloquial wisdom, people never remember what you did, only how you made them feel. While memories degrade and the details of the event may fade away, the emotional connection to the brand remains strong and can be built on in further positive interactions (Tsatsawani, 2020).

The future of fashion will be experiential, as brands need to excite and engage their consumers in different ways from their competitors. Brand experience strategies can embrace both physical and digital elements, and brand activations can have a huge and lasting impact on brand growth and product sales, which is why it is important to do them often and do them right.

Brand equity

Brand equity refers to the value a company gains from its name recognition and is determined by the consumers' perception of the business. Brand equity can be positive with the consumer thinking highly of the brand, or it can be negative if the consumer perceives that the brand underdelivers on its promise or fails to live up to expectations. Brand equity is achieved by the business working through the processes of identifying brand pillars, brand identity and brand experience to shape positive perceptions of the business. Marketing theorist Kevin Lane Keller (2013) developed Keller's Brand Equity Model, which declares the four steps to creating a successful brand as brand identity; brand meaning, which is the performance and image of the brand; brand response, or the perceptions and judgements the consumer makes about the brand; and brand resonance, which relates to the connection between customer and brand.

Strategic brand management

A brand strategy is a vital business tool that ensures the company has a plan in place to actively influence how people perceive the business. A brand strategy will provide clarity on how the consumer perceives the brand currently, as well putting in place a plan to increase the company's credibility, reputation and customer experience. As a brand is a consumer's perception about a business, then the brand strategy is the best possible roadmap to create an emotional connection with the ideal customer through articulating the core values of the organization (Kusumadjaja, n.d.).

An effective brand strategy helps the business communicate its core values. Jon Persson (2021) advised that: 'People don't buy what you do, they buy why you do it. If you want to attract loyal customers, you need to figure out what your brand stands for and how to communicate that to consumers'. Customers can be overwhelmed by the noise and choice in a crowded fashion market, yet they are astute and not easily fooled by low-level marketing techniques. Therefore, a business has to be authentic and honest, creating a genuine brand proposition and experience that it will live by and a brand promise that it can deliver. Customers' expectations are high and over time as they engage more with the brand they want to increase the connection and understanding of the business to determine that it meets their expectations, needs and matches their value perceptions.

This concept is captured in the brand layer model shown in Figure 7.3, where initially the consumer comes across the brand in action, then over time as they get to know the brand better they peel back the layers to understand the brand personality and the brand values. The consumer reaches brand essence when they have a total understanding and emotional connection with the very core, or heart and soul of the business, and have a positive perception about the company, service or product.

The purpose of a brand strategy is to identify opportunities and weaknesses in the brand experience, embed accountability and consistency throughout the organization, focus the marketing on the brand's key messages and add value for the customer and also the business. There are many steps that go into creating a cohesive brand strategy – and the core components of purpose, emotion, engagement, intelligence

Figure 7.3 Brand layers

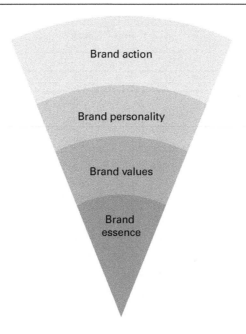

and consistency should be included. Developing a strategic plan to maintain brand equity or gain brand value requires first of all a comprehensive understanding of the brand, the customer and competitors, as well as the company's overall vision and purpose. The strategy goals will answer certain questions about how the customer perceives the brand, what qualities they will identify and what words they would use to describe the brand.

Figure 7.4 incorporates the types of elements that a business can include in its brand strategy, but as every brand is different there is not one framework to use for developing a brand strategy, but most will include these elements.

Visual identity

Visual brand identity evokes emotion and for fashion brands their visual identity is the first point of contact a consumer usually has with the business. Images are everything in fashion and without good images the business will struggle to connect with the consumer and sell its products. Brand visual identity is the set of characteristics that the brand will use across all its channels to invoke a feeling of the brand. The identity includes the logo, colours, typography, photography and film. Within the brand strategy, a business should include the development of a brand style guide, a simple document that details the guidelines of how the brand should look, sound

Figure 7.4 Brand strategy

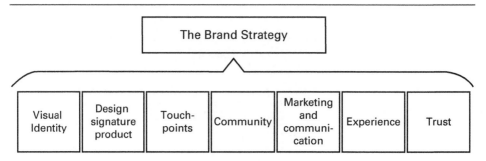

and feel. The purpose of the guide is to ensure the brand maintains its consistency in how it is presented to the world, as it can be hard to maintain consistency as a business grows and more people get involved in the management. Components in the brand style guide will be the brand messaging, brand purpose and values, the brand personality, logo design and use, tone of voice, typography, colour palette and guidelines for the creative direction of images, videos, films and graphics. All the brand's documents, images, social media platforms, website and marketing materials need to be consistent with the brand identity and messaging, therefore regular reviews are needed to ensure everything is cohesive and consistent with the brand guidelines.

Design signature product

In Chapter 5 (on design) we discussed the need for a fashion business to create a signature style, design feature or product. This signature would consistently create brand awareness, an emotional connection with the customer, and can form a community around the brand that builds trust. All of these points increase positive customer perception of the brand.

Touchpoints

Customers come across brands in many different ways and these are called touchpoints, places where the customer sees or experiences the brand such as through advertising, packaging, products, social media or through email marketing campaigns. A business needs to anticipate all the brand touchpoints where the consumer could discover the company and they need to convey a consistent tone and feel in every brand touchpoint. If all the touchpoints are on brand and messaging is consistent, then it creates a strong brand experience for the customer.

Community

A brand community brings together loyal customers of the business so that they can connect, engage and share brand experiences. Consumers become emotionally invested in brand communities, they share their experiences with friends and family and become brand ambassadors, which increases positive perceptions of the brand. The brand strategy needs to determine the ways the brand can connect with consumers and build the community, as well as build opportunities for the community to interact with each other.

Marketing and communication

Branding is what drives marketing within a business. The branding strategy helps the business align all its marketing efforts, to ensure that they stay 'on-brand'. The brand strategy will include all the elements of brand tone of voice, visual identity, messaging and brand promise and can function as a framework for the development of marketing ideas and campaigns. The clear and concise brand messaging and visual identity from the brand strategy will form the basis for all marketing activities to attract new customers and connect with the existing ones.

Experience

When there are so many options to choose from these days, customers will seek to buy from companies they like. This means a brand has to incorporate how it will create positive customer experiences within its brand strategy. The strategy will determine how the business will build brand experiences, based on its purpose and values, which will build relationships with customers, increase engagement and awareness, and improve brand perceptions.

Trust

Consumer behaviour has always been influenced by the trust they have in a brand. In 2021, Richard Edelman declared that research of 14,000 consumers indicated that trust is the new brand equity and consumers are ranking trust higher than brand love (Edelman, 2021). This change in behaviour is the result of global health, climate, economic and political issues that have led consumers to seek brands that they perceive will make life and society better. The aim of the brand strategy is to determine the actions that will position the brand as trustworthy. Trust can be gained through communicating the brand's purpose and values, delivering consistent brand experiences, authenticity and transparency, and engagement with the consumers.

Developing a brand strategy takes time and a meticulous understanding of what the brand aims to achieve, aligned with the business purpose and identity, as well as an in-depth understanding of the consumers' expectations and perceptions. The purpose of the brand strategy is to put in place effective brand management processes to increase brand awareness, measure and manage brand equity, and effectively position the brand in the market. Brand management is the process of ensuring that all messaging, visuals and communications from the brand are consistent to portray the right image, values and benefits to the customer (Walden University, n.d.). A precise and efficiently executed brand strategy will impact positively on all aspects of a fashion business, helping the brand meet consumer needs, create emotional attachments and outshine competitors.

Summary

Developing a great product or service will only take a business so far. It is the brand identity, equity, messaging, values and storytelling that takes a fashion business to the next level. The brand resides in the customer's mind as a result of the perceptions they make whenever they encounter the name, logo, product, social media and marketing messages of the business. This chapter has introduced the elements of brand building, including developing a clear brand position, communicating brand values and storytelling, and forming a differentiated brand identity. It identified that determining the brand pillars of purpose, perception, personality, positioning and promotion builds a brand identity that stands out from the rest of the market. The strongest brands are those that are built around purpose and values, as these businesses own a special place in the market and in the heart of the consumer. The formation of a brand is reliant on a unique value proposition and storytelling that connects with and inspires the consumer. Developing a strong brand is crucial if the business wants to grow to become a mega brand like Chanel or Gucci, or if they want to license their name for other income generation streams in the future. A strong brand is a consistent one. If the messages and branding are consistent, then the business will create greater awareness and build more trust and loyalty with the customer.

Finally, building a strong brand does not happen by accident, the business needs to put time and effort into it, but the results are worth it, as consumers pay more for their favourite brands and products, are more brand loyal and they will also tell others about brands that make them feel great.

Key terms

branding	brand messaging	purpose
brand essence	brand perception	storytelling
brand equity	brand pillars	tone of voice
brand experience	perception	touchpoints
brand identity	positioning	

Activity

Choose one luxury fashion brand and list five reasons why customers wear the products that feature their brand logos.

Online resources

Downloadable versions of the product star, brand strategy and brand pillars.

References

Canva (n.d.) What is brand purpose and why it is important, *www.canva.com*, www.canva.com/learn/brand-purpose-important/ (archived at https://perma.cc/BK2P-3HKZ)

Coastal Brand (2022) The ultimate guide to brand pillars, *Web Design Company & App Development agency Myrtle Beach*, coastalmediabrand.com/the-ultimate-guide-to-brand-pillars/ (archived at https://perma.cc/G5QA-KGHX)

Edelman, R (2021) Trust, the new brand equity, *Edelman*, www.edelman.com/trust/2021-brand-trust/brand-equity (archived at https://perma.cc/ZXL6-XR6W)

Giuliani, M (2022) Everything about brand pillars and why they matter, *Planable*, planable.io/blog/brand-pillars/ (archived at https://perma.cc/UP88-M8PM)

Hodges, N (2020) The importance of an integrated system for branding, *Studioother*, www.studioother.com/blog/the-importance-of-an-integrated-system-for-branding (archived at https://perma.cc/3QGW-H9LC)

Houraghan, S (n.d.) 26 branding elements for an effective brand strategy, *Brandmaster Academy*, brandmasteracademy.com/branding-elements/#:~:text=Brand%20Communication%20Elements%201%20Brand%20Name.%20The%20brand,always%20the%20one%20that%20should%20be%20told.%20 (archived at https://perma.cc/9BEQ-KCPW)

Keller, K L (2013) *Strategic Brand Management*, Pearson, Boston

Kotler, P (2003) *Marketing Management*, Pearson/Prentice Hall, Singapore

Kusumadjaja, L (n.d.) The main purpose of brand strategy, *Melinda Livsey*, melindalivsey. com/journal/the-main-purpose-of-brand-strategy (archived at https://perma.cc/SS97-JDQX)

Lischer, B (n.d.) The 5 brand pillars that every business needs to succeed, *Ignyte*, www. ignytebrands.com/brand-pillars/#:~:text=What%20are%20the%205%20Brand%20 Pillars%3F%201%20Purpose.,Personality.%20...%204%20Perception.%20...%20 5%20Promotion.%20 (archived at https://perma.cc/3Q77-PCQR)

Marion (2022) What is branding?, *The Branding Journal*, www.thebrandingjournal. com/2015/10/what-is-branding-definition/ (archived at https://perma.cc/Y946-TSNS)

Marketing and Creative Handbook (2021) Your brand is what other people say about you when you're not in the room, *Marketing and Creative Handbook*, mch.co.uk/your-brand-is-what-people-say-about-you-when-youre-not-in-the-room.shtml (archived at https:// perma.cc/EE4U-Y7ZW)

National Geographic (n.d.) Storytelling, *National Geographic*, education.nationalgeo graphic.org/resource/storytelling (archived at https://perma.cc/NDC2-G54X)

Pandey, M (2022) What is brand experience? *Feedough*, www.feedough.com/brand-experi ence-how-to-strategies-and-examples/ (archived at https://perma.cc/6EQN-TQ9B)

Parkes, L (2019) What is brand experience – and what brands are benefiting from it?, *My Customer*, www.mycustomer.com/marketing/strategy/what-is-brand-experience-and-what-brands-are-benefiting-from-it (archived at https://perma.cc/DXW6-BTLC)

Persson, J (2021) Why brand strategy is important, *Cult Method*, cultmethod.com/articles/ why-strategy-matters/#:~:text=%20Why%20is%20brand%20strategy%20 important%3F%20%201,a%20clear%20brand%20strategy%20helps%20keep...%20 More%20 (archived at https://perma.cc/Z5VE-D4AF)

Renderforest (2021) What is branding? Why is it important?, *Renderforest*, www.renderfor est.com/blog/what-is-branding-the-importance-of-branding (archived at https://perma.cc/ J5VT-9VJH)

Riserbato, R (n.d.) The beginner's guide to brand pillars, *Blog.hubspot.com*, blog.hubspot. com/marketing/brand-pillars (archived at https://perma.cc/ZHW8-RAC2)

Robertson, D (2012) The power of storytelling, the key to consumer engagement, *The Guardian*, www.theguardian.com/media-network/media-network-blog/2012/may/23/ storytelling-key-audience-consumer-engagement (archived at https://perma.cc/63LT-52E9)

Rukosuev, D (n.d.) What is brand identity?, *Professional Academy*, www.professionalacad emy.com/blogs/what-is-brand-identity/ (archived at https://perma.cc/7CJT-NS5X)

Shrum, H (2019) Why brand activation is the future of fashion, *LinkedIn*, www.linkedin. com/pulse/why-brand-activation-future-fashion-hogan-shrum (archived at https://perma. cc/QLL9-SH7J)

The Brand Boy (2022) A Guide to start a clothing brand from scratch, *The Brand Boy*, thebrandboy.com/starting-clothing-brand-guide/ (archived at https://perma.cc/NP2N-A6BF)

The Story Mill (n.d.) Business storytelling, *The Story Mill*, www.thestorymill.co.uk/brand-storytelling/ (archived at https://perma.cc/8L6T-ZAZH)

Tsatsawani (2020) The five pillars of successful brand activation, *Samplexafrica*, www.samplexafrica.co.za/post/the-five-pillars-of-successful-brand-activation (archived at https://perma.cc/7XL9-VSY8)

Walden University (n.d.) Five reasons brand management is so important, *Walden University*, www.waldenu.edu/online-bachelors-programs/bs-in-business-administration/resource/five-reasons-brand-management-is-so-important (archived at https://perma.cc/443T-AP6Z)

Case study
KIHT Collective

KIHT Collective creates mix-and-match gym wear with a purpose. Designed to make their customers feel amazing inside and out, the brand uses performance fabrics, trend-led styles and cute designs while being ethical and sustainable. The brand has been gaining considerable attention since its launch due to the design style and quality of their slow-fashion capsule collections, as well as the strong sense of community that forms the brand's DNA.

The label was founded by Danielle King, a passionate designer and entrepreneur, who created the purpose-driven brand with the aim of doing more good than harm to the planet and its people. Having spent 10 years in the fashion industry helping to build the 'fast' fashion model for some of the biggest online brands, and witnessed the impact of what it is like behind the scenes of the fashion industry, Danielle knew that the industry needed to change things for the better, which led her to develop KIHT Collective, launched during the Covid-19 pandemic in July 2020.

The brand seeks to be honest and transparent in the process of developing and making their conscious collections, sharing information on their approach to ethical practices, sourcing factories, low carbon footprint and recycled packaging. The brand carefully selected their manufacturing partner in Portugal and all their factories are audited and fully compliant with Portuguese and EU law. They buy the wastage (the pieces that have not passed their strict quality-control processes but are still wearable) from their factory and donate it to charity to ensure it is not incinerated or sent to landfill. The brand also plants a tree with every KIHT purchase, teaming up with the Tree Sisters charity who work to restore ecosystems and livelihoods while increasing protection against the extremes of climate change in multiple regions of the tropical forest belt.

KIHT's aim is to strive to be as sustainable and as ethical as possible and to build a brand and business as a force for good, not just profit.

www.kiht.co.uk

Innovation and technology   8

LEARNING OBJECTIVES

By the end of this chapter, you will be able to:

- Understand how innovation and technology is changing the management of fashion brands
- Discuss how technology is impacting the design, manufacturing, sales and marketing processes
- Explain the innovations fashion brands will integrate in future business models

Introduction

The future of fashion lies in the constant development and adoption of innovation and technology to survive and address the challenges in the industry and the volatile market. Fashion technology refers to any technological advancements that are used in the industry to improve fashion production or consumption. The use of technology in fashion has grown throughout the sector and is used across the board by designers, manufacturers, retailers and customers. Innovation is essential to keep the industry agile and improve the working processes of fashion production as well as continually improve the consumer experience. With fashion being the second most polluting industry in the world after oil (Bliss, 2019), the industry needs to embrace opportunities that technology and innovation can bring to improve the sector.

The advancement of innovation and technology in the fashion industry is accelerating at incredible speed, with the Covid-19 pandemic forcing brands to embed technology throughout their business functions. Changes are shaking the industry to its core and making brands rethink their business models to ensure they are making the most of innovations across every part of their business. The 2022 State of Fashion Technology report described how brands are using digital tools in customer-focused day-to-day operations, but declared they now need to expand the breadth and depth of technology application to address the challenges of the volatile market (Business of Fashion and McKinsey & Company, 2022). The magnitude of change is making it hard for brands to keep up, but those that are embracing change will stand to benefit greatly, making them more attractive to investors, while ultimately others will be left behind.

This chapter addresses many of the fields of technology and innovation that fashion brands are starting to adopt, as well as areas of future potential development. As the speed of change is happening at a pace, there will be new innovations launching on a constant basis over the next decade. It will therefore become even more challenging for fashion brands to stay ahead unless they invest in digital innovation and experiment with fresh approaches to creativity and commerce.

Innovation and technology in the fashion industry

There is big change coming in the fashion industry that will alter the current digital environment and brands will need to be innovative and agile to ensure they are not left behind their competitors. The day-to-day systems of running a fashion label are increasingly intertwined with the digital world. Brands are embracing the latest technologies to push the limits of manufacturing, production, marketing and wearability, using the latest in artificial intelligence, mobile commerce, 3D printing and blockchain (Kochar, 2022).

Since the birth of the internet, technology has evolved at a pace with millions of people and organizations around the world embracing the opportunities that it offers. Very quickly, technology has evolved from dial-up modems to the wide integration of email, through the dotcom boom and crash, to today's reliance on the internet for work, life and entertainment. Consumer adoption of mobile technology and social media platforms such as Instagram, Facebook and TikTok has played an important role in the progression of technology with user-generated content forming the backbone of increased connectivity and communication (Vyas, 2022). Consumers have become empowered through their use of digital technologies. They are much more informed, selective and in charge – using digital channels before, during and after making their purchases (Lay, 2018). The customer cares about how they look not only in real life but on digital channels too, seeking fashion that makes them feel good in real life and online.

Technology has already changed how fashion is designed, manufactured, marketed and consumed but the market is still evolving, with innovations on the horizon that will change the industry again. At the forefront of this change is Web3, which refers to the next generation of the worldwide web.

Web3

The advancement of Web2 resulted in a centralized system ruled by a small group of businesses such as Facebook and Google, who are able to control the data gathered, monetize aspects of the web, as well as decide what content can and cannot be shown (Vyas, 2022). The next iteration of the internet, Web3, will have a strong emphasis on decentralized applications that make extensive use of blockchain, machine learning and artificial intelligence technologies to challenge the dominance of the powerhouses and put the power back in the hands of the people: 'In the context of Web3, the concept of decentralization refers to the process of decentralizing power away from an authority, organization or location so that no individual or individual entity makes decisions on behalf of all parties' (Vyas, 2022). Web3 will work towards a fairer and more transparent internet and facilitate greater interaction and lifelike experiences. The fashion industry is already employing Web3 to offer innovative showcasing in the metaverse, create NFTs, accept cryptocurrencies, protect intellectual property and offer greater transparency on sustainable practices through the blockchain.

Along with Web3 there are numerous other emerging forms of technology and innovation that the fashion industry needs to invest in. The State of Fashion Technology 2022 report identified five imperatives to make fashion brands more resilient and sustainable (Business of Fashion and McKinsey & Company, 2022), these included:

- Metaverse reality check – brands need to separate the hype around the metaverse from realistic opportunities to generate sustainable revenue streams.
- Hyper-personalization – using emerging technologies a brand can provide more personalized experiences for its consumers.
- Connected stores – brands need to address the role of physical stores in a digital age and through technology provide a smooth omnichannel experience to their consumers.
- End-to-end upgrade – new digital tools can be used to analyse the value chain to develop more efficient operating systems.
- Traceability first – brands need to use Big Data to ensure greater sustainability across their supply chains.

The diagram in Figure 8.1 identifies all the elements of the business of fashion that are impacted by new digital technologies and innovations. These elements are discussed in more detail in the next section.

Figure 8.1 Technology and innovation elements

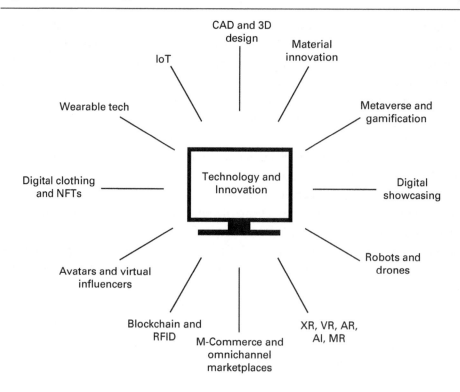

Innovation and technology in design and manufacturing

The increase and integration of technology in fashion is leading to innovation in the way that fashion is designed and made, enabling brands to develop smarter and more sustainable clothing. Fashion and supply chain technology is enabling brands to streamline their processes and increase efficiency through the use of data analytics, social media tools, artificial intelligence and augmented reality, which helps to guide their purchasing and business decisions (DHL InMotion, 2018).

Computer-aided and 3D design

Computer-aided design, or CAD, refers to design programs that are used in fashion designing to create sketches, flat drawings, pattern making and tech packs, among other things. Fashion design software allows users to create 2D and 3D designs, which more accurately communicate design ideas for sampling and production.

3D is at the heart of many of the technological advancements happening in fashion. It can be used to generate imagery and is needed for brands wanting to embrace virtual reality, augmented reality, animation and gaming (Hackl, 2021). 3D printers have opened up new possibilities with designers being able to consider on-demand production and development of supplementary design elements such as embellishments, buttons and accessories in their design processes. For luxury brands, designers can combine high-level design skills with cutting-edge technology to create new levels of conceptual art using 3D printing.

Leading the field in fashion is CLO3D, an intuitive designing process that many fashion schools, designers and brands have embraced. CLO3D integrates product lifecycle management and 3D design tools to facilitate a seamless and efficient digital workflow (Hackl, 2021).

Internet of Things (IoT)

The Internet of Things (IoT) refers to physical objects or 'things' that have technology embedded within them to allow the exchange of data or, in simpler terms, to talk to each other. The things can be everyday items such as a smartwatch talking to an app. Through connected devices and automated systems, it is possible to collect information, analyse it and create a solution to help someone with a particular task (Islam Kiron, 2021).

The fashion industry is heralding IoT as one of the most exciting emerging technologies. It can enable data sharing, which benefits fashion brands by helping them better understand their customers' needs, as well as improve experience, design, shape and fit, and optimize product assortment. IoT offers a natural solution for the design of fashion garments, as brands will be able to seamlessly integrate technology between fabrics, adding connectivity to clothes to provide anonymous data back to the brand. Using low-cost radio-frequency identification (RFID) and Bluetooth Low Energy (BLE) chips in garments, the lifecycle of clothing can be tracked beyond production to collect data about usage and longevity, which could improve future product developments (Brown, 2018).

In the future, IoT will become an integral part of the fashion industry and brands need to continue to push design innovations using IoT in the development of smart clothing, responsive wear and multi-functional designs.

Wearable technology

Brands are using IoT to innovate the design and development of wearable technology such as smart clothing and using new innovations and technological advancements to push the limits of what wearability means. Design developments have included clothing that monitors heart rate, body temperature, or a baby's sleeping patterns, as well as footwear that monitors step count and uses biometric data to improve gait and performance. There are a huge number of developments in sportswear in particular, such as the NADI X yoga pants that use built-in sensors that vibrate to correct the users' posture during yoga poses (Kochar, 2022).

Designers can now use low-cost RFID sensors to track the lifecycle of clothing and collect data covering everything from usage to customer satisfaction and comfort. Design developments being explored include space-age concepts such as flexible solar panels being incorporated into clothing so you can charge your smartphone on the move (Bhana, n.d.) to clothing that changes colour according to the wearer's mood.

Digital clothing design and NFTs

Digital clothing is taking the industry by storm with a wealth of fashion brands at luxury and fast-fashion levels all exploring the market and starting to offer digital collections alongside their physical fashion ranges. This tech-driven trend is set to completely overhaul the way customers see style, as they take steps to craft and style online identities to match the image they want to broadcast online (Ledger, 2021). Digital clothing was initially introduced in the gaming world, where players could buy virtual clothes for their characters, and it quickly became apparent that there was money to be made creating skins for games such as Fortnite or League of Legends. With fashion giants like Puma, Gucci and Louis Vuitton experimenting in the space, a rapid acceleration towards digital fashion's adoption is on the horizon (Ledger, 2021). The financial rewards are enticing for brands. Mass-market brands can aim for low-value, high-volume digital fashion selling thousands of skins in a game such as Fortnite for under $5, whereas luxury labels can sell digital fashion as NFTs at a premium price point of $200–$2,000, but in much lower volumes (Maguire, 2022).

Across the fashion and luxury industries brands are offering NFTs (non-fungible tokens) for every type of product from leisurewear to shoes to watches.

NFTs are unique digital assets that have been verified by blockchain technology, which records transactions to give the buyer proof of authenticity and ownership, and offer enhanced customer experiences.

The popularity of NFTs has emerged alongside the rise in metaverse-related initiatives, with fashion brands looking to offer digital designs alongside their physical products. Digital collectibles are offering a new level of exclusivity and the concept fulfils the consumer desire to virtually experience wearing luxury or designer clothing that they cannot afford in real life. It is difficult to predict where the development of digital clothing and NFTs will go in the future as the pace of technological advancement is only accelerating, but what is clear is that the brands that don't invest heavily in digital product creation today will be left behind (Hackl, 2021).

Manufacturing processes

Technology and innovation in fashion manufacturing have included new digital printing technologies such as 3D printing and the integration of robots and tracking systems within the processes. The making of fashion demands resources that have huge environmental impact. Across the industry there are research and development projects working to discover innovative ways to make the processes more sustainable. One of the major areas for innovation is to develop new manufacturing processes for reducing waste, such as new software systems that enable factories to work towards zero waste by monitoring, mapping and measuring leftover fabrics, which can then be reintroduced in the supply chain (Knox, 2022). The industry is also looking to use technological advances to improve communication, and cloud computing enables brands and factories to work more collaboratively from many parts of the world at the same time. This can optimize product development by giving everyone access to relevant data, which makes communication faster and more effective, but also eliminates waste and delivers better-quality products at the right time (Kochar, 2022).

Factories are implementing more innovative robotic technologies, using automation to connect CAD software from design to the making process and sewbots to speed up the construction or using new technology to meld elements together instead of using glues. There are already robots that can make custom seamless knit garments on demand using 3D modelling software (Knox, 2022). Robots can offer greater safety measures in factories, as they can be used for more dangerous tasks such as repetitive sewing, lifting, spraying, or be used in less amenable working spaces. Robots are more widely used in warehouses for selection and movement of materials and goods, which can make distribution more effective.

Innovation in the way clothes, fabrics and materials are manufactured has not kept pace with the acceleration of how they are designed and marketed. Fast fashion still represents a relatively low-tech production system, only slowly becoming more tech- and sustainability-focused (DHL InMotion, 2018), meaning greater focus on innovation in these areas is essential for the industry.

Material innovations

Brands looking to improve their impact on the environment have to consider material innovation as a primary area of development, as approximately 80 per cent of a brand's environmental footprint comes from the raw materials they use (Turk, 2021). The fashion industry is racing to develop new materials to offer sustainable alternatives to improve environmental impact. Natural fabrics from plants such as silk, linen and organic cotton, as well as Lyocell, which is made from sustainable wood pulp, are more sustainable than man-made fabrics that are petroleum based such as polyester and nylon, as these could take hundreds of years to biodegrade, if ever (Fashion United, 2022). With advances in science and technology, the future of fashion will include innovations in sustainable and ethical fibre alternatives, often called next-generation materials. The market is being flooded with new options made from a host of natural materials including pineapple and banana leaves, seaweed, orange fibres and leather replacements made from mushrooms, apples and cactus, to name a few. While many of the next-generation materials come from natural sources, others are being developed from new technological processes that can recycle materials including creating fibres from recycled plastic waste.

Blockchain

Through the process of design to manufacturing and then into the sales process, blockchain is the link that helps the fashion industry track and maintain transparent records of each garment from the raw materials to the finished product that arrives in store. Blockchain technology is a digital ledger that records a series of records and data known as blocks, recording all the linked transactions to the block, which are stored in a cryptic manner for security and safety purpose.

The revolutionary aspect of blockchain technology is that once a time-stamped block is added to the blockchain everyone can access and verify it, making it impossible for anyone to tamper with, destroy or steal information that is within the blockchain (Crypto Daily, 2021). A blockchain is managed communally in an autonomous manner and this decentralized infrastructure means that it cannot be controlled by any one person or group. A blockchain is a standardized and automated system ensuring all partners are obligated to record transactions, giving greater transparency and diminishing the potential of subcontracting or counterfeit products. For sustainable fashion brands looking to offer greater transparency, integrating blockchain into their management processes is the best option. It will determine the origin and supply of raw materials, through the manufacturing process to the shipment of the product to the consumer, providing immutable records as every transaction will be verified.

One of the biggest challenges in the luxury fashion market is counterfeiting and brands go to great lengths to preserve exclusivity and eradicate copying (DeAcetis, 2021).

With blockchain technology, manufacturers and brands will have greater intellectual property protection, as the sources of each product can be tracked and authenticity can be verified and tracked through the lifecycle of the product. Vincent Quan told Forbes that blockchain technology provides total transparency of product from inception to end use. This single technology can allow consumers and brands to track and trace the legitimacy of any product from luxury fashion to basic necessity, identifying sustainable sourcing and the source of all merchandise along the supply chain, which builds trust between brands and their stakeholders (DeAcetis, 2021). The benefits of blockchain are numerous, as identified in Figure 8.2.

Whether for the consumer or the brand, the transparency, security and accountability benefits from blockchain are what the industry needs to solve many of its challenges. The integration of blockchain therefore will continue to increase and transform the shape of the fashion industry in the years to come.

Innovation and technology in fashion retail

In the fashion retail environment innovation and technology have radically changed how fashion is now sold. Fashion brands have embraced every type of new digital technology from connected stores, digital price tags, smart mirrors, self-checkout to blockchain in order to improve their business models and offer a better consumer experience. Innovation is happening across all sales channels with brands using new technologies in physical stores as well as online in e-commerce, m-commerce and social media, integrating systems to offer the omnichannel experience the consumer demands. Brands are

Figure 8.2 Benefits of blockchain

| Digital passport or ledger that records all transactions | Transparency offering audit trail | Security encrypted transactions | Automation efficient streamlined processes | Autonomy decentralized system means no single owner |

benefiting from RFID technology and cloud computing to gather analytics in real time to manage their inventory more efficiently and effectively.

Hyper-personalization

While shoppers may be using a host of different channels to purchase fashion, one underlying theme is that they expect brands to provide them with product choices and experiences that are tailored to their individual preferences. Personalization is one of the buzzwords in the fashion industry, but today that means far more than using the customer's name in an email or wishing them happy birthday. Beyond this the industry has generally confined personalization to marketing recommendations for customer sub-segments, based on past purchases or online browsing history. There is scope to go further, as technology is now available to help businesses work with all types of data across channels in real time (Business of Fashion and McKinsey & Company, 2022).

Hyper-personalization takes considerable time and resources but developments in AI technology, which can analyse customer data and look for patterns, has the greatest potential to identify customer intentions. This will result in brands getting the right product in the right place at the right time.

Brands that develop advanced AI models, such as those that use size and fit algorithms, and incorporate behavioural data such as login time and add-to-cart behaviours, will be able to provide one-to-one experiences that build long-term loyalty (Business of Fashion and McKinsey & Company, 2022).

In-store

Technology has enhanced the in-store shopping experience through augmented reality, which allows a customer to learn more about the product, through to contactless payments and self-checkout through in-store kiosks, handheld computers, scanners and printers.

The use of smart mirrors is increasing across the retail environment to enhance customer service and experience. Smart mirrors are AR-based solutions that can be programmed to display product and styling options, or social media feeds, as well as giving customers the opportunity to try products on their virtual models that are displayed on the mirror. A smart mirror uses RFID tags along with augmented-reality technology, so that when the customer brings a piece of clothing in front of the mirror it scans and stores the image of it and then scans the user to create a virtual model of them wearing the scanned piece of clothing (Sharma, 2018).

E-commerce

The Covid-19 pandemic accelerated the growth of online shopping, and fashion brands at all levels of the industry noted that the functionality of the e-commerce sites needed greater investment to meet the engagement demands of fashion consumers, as well as increase their operational efficiencies.

Fashion e-commerce is a saturated market with more online fashion stores than ever before, which makes it difficult for a fashion brand to be discovered or to retain a customer's attention. The results from advertising spend have plummeted, forcing fashion brands to prioritize activities that build customer loyalty and greater customer lifetime value (Roach, 2020). Fashion brand websites can no longer be warehouse-style pages purely listing products. A brand's site needs to engage, inspire, educate and connect with its consumers. Brands need to be innovative in developing an e-commerce world that entertains and engages their consumers using all the digital tools available from video to avatars, XR experiences to brand activations, using AR and VR technologies to create immersive experiences. Alongside the entertainment value, brands also need to ensure they develop great customer service creating frictionless, easy checkout as well as using technologies such as chatbots to assist customers 24 hours a day.

While the front-of-house development of an e-commerce site is essential for customer engagement, the behind-the-scenes infrastructure of the site needs to work efficiently. E-commerce automation has huge potential with new software programs joining the market daily, which brands can use to make their sites more proficient.

M-commerce

Mobile commerce, or m-commerce, refers to the use of handheld devices, mobile phones or tablets to make purchases. Mobile technology is getting more advanced and easier to use every day, from social media shopping to smart wallets. As consumers now spend most of their time with their mobile devices in their hand, m-commerce benefits from being in the place where the fashion consumer is spending a lot of their time. The rapid growth of mobile commerce is attributed to the growth of wireless communication networks, mobile commerce apps and improved device infrastructure (CFI Team, 2020).

While it used to be difficult to shop on a smartphone, the development of digital wallets with fingerprint and facial recognition has meant the checkout process has become much easier, so consumers no longer need to input excessive information each time they want to purchase. Mobile technology is the main link between physical and digital, with brands now working on 'click and mortar' business models that enable the customer to use their mobile device to track the location of goods in-store, check out on device and complete online transactions and delivery options or connecting with immersive AR or VR experiences.

Social media

The development of sales channels on social media such as Instagram and TikTok mean that brands can be present in their customers' favourite places and sell product to them there, rather than having to entice them away to another platform to purchase. Social media stores give brands much greater visibility and provide them with more opportunities to make a sale. TikTok has successfully integrated stores into its platform giving brands not only the opportunity to market and promote their label and products, but also giving the consumer the chance to research, read reviews and purchase all in one convenient location.

Brand apps

As identified above, mobile is the future of retail and, with consumers constantly connected and within reach of a device, it gives brands the opportunity to open new communication channels with their customers. There are a host of discovery app platforms that fashion brands use such as Shop Style, who will then point the consumer to the brand's website, or fashion labels are developing their own bespoke app, which allows them to control the relationship right through to purchase.

Omnichannel

As today's consumers discover brands via a range of different channels including those identified above, brands have to take advantage of using technology to connect every touchpoint. Omnichannel commerce offers customers a connected buying experience across all channels. It is a necessity for consumers who are yearning for an optimized omnichannel experience that gives them the opportunity to purchase at any point during their journey, whether that is on digital marketplaces, social media, search or in-store, and they are rewarding businesses that provide it (Big Commerce, 2022).

Omnichannel relies on innovation and technology, using a world of screens and devices to connect online with physical stores. It also includes the integration of different digital channels and social networks like TikTok and Instagram, with many customers discovering brands on social platforms before any others. There is continuous evolution and change in the development of shopping features on social channels, which means brands need to be agile in order to adapt their omnichannel strategies to changing algorithms.

Omnichannel innovation will unlock more opportunities for brands to offer a frictionless shopping experience in the future, enabling the consumer to buy fashion in new formats and through novel places with the touch of a button. The future will not be e-commerce or m-commerce or any other iteration – it will just be commerce, as all the channels are integrated into an omnichannel approach.

RFID

RFID refers to radio-frequency identification and is a method of using tags that transmit a radio signal for businesses to be able to track their goods. RFID has been a gamechanger for fashion retail, as the process of being able to easily identify and track items has improved stock management processes. RFID has created a more seamless connection between online and offline, allowing brands access to a product at any point across the retail network, both in distribution centres and in-store (Dickinson, n.d.).

Brands are now able to have up-to-date, accurate stock counts across multiple stores and warehouses, as well as in the supply chain. For distribution and online shopping, RFID-enabled inventory tracking speeds up the picking, packing and delivery of product and ensures that the information shared with consumers about available merchandise is correct.

Fit technology

Returns and fit have been a huge challenge within the fashion industry, so brands have welcomed innovations in fit technology to provide a solution to the vast number of returns consumers make. Fashion brands have historically focused on detailing sizing for their products online, but the most important element is 'fit', not size. Customers often order multiple sizes or return clothing with the reason stated as wrong size, but they mostly mean it is the fit that is wrong. Brands create product that are sized according to the brand's fit models, and while this may work for some customers, there are also going to be a large number of people who won't fit into that garment (Douglass, 2022). Innovations in fit technology use a combination of AI, AR and 3D scanning software to enable consumers to create photo-realistic images so that they can visualize how clothing will fit, which will encourage more accurate purchase decisions.

Robots and drones

Areas of innovation that are on the cusp of development include in-store robots and drone delivery. While robotic technology is already being used in manufacturing, there is further potential for robots in-store either creating small-scale production or as sales or customer service assistants. Drones have already been tested and are being used in warehouse settings. Technology is now being developed for drones to be used for the delivery of e-commerce orders. These drones can either be air based, or more realistic options include ground-based robots for last-mile kerbside deliveries.

Brands will need to embrace all the innovative opportunities that are being developed for fashion retail in order to remain commercially viable in the future. Brands need to be prepared to experiment with new technologies, to enhance their operational efficiency as well as improve customer experience.

Innovation and technology in marketing and promotion

The most obvious developments in fashion have been apparent in marketing and promotion, with huge media attention given to brands expanding into the metaverse and innovations in the development of digital assets such as non-fungible tokens (NFTs) and gaming skins. According to The State of Fashion Technology report 2022, virtual fashion will continue to edge closer to the mainstream (Business of Fashion and McKinsey & Company, 2022) and brands will have to negotiate the hype around the metaverse to find their position in this new marketplace. Fashion brands cannot ignore the fact that, in 2021, global spending on virtual goods reached around $110 billion, so while many experiments in the metaverse are currently marketing exercises, innovative fashion brands have the potential to earn significant revenue from activities in the metaverse (Business of Fashion and McKinsey & Company, 2022).

Metaverse

The term metaverse refers to a virtual-reality, collective shared space in which users connect with each other through physical, virtual and augmented reality (Figure 8.3).

Figure 8.3   Metaverse

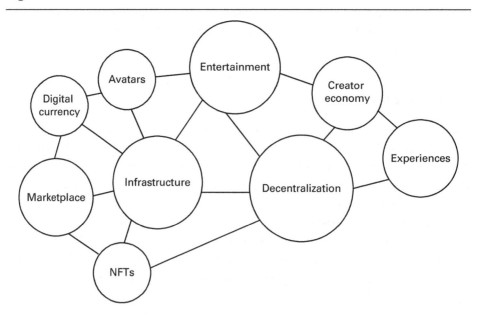

The purpose is to create a virtual world that simulates human experience and emotions. Vaibhav Sharma (2021) describes it eloquently on Quytech: 'The metaverse encompasses the entire social and economic structure that exists in both the actual and virtual worlds. Avatars, content and goods may all travel around freely. It's a living, breathing experience that never pauses or finishes like a game.'

Fashion brands have been quick to jump in to the metaverse, experimenting with the ways they can connect, engage and create new revenue streams. Businesses have the potential to augment their digital transformation strategy by exploring product development, brand placement, customer engagement and financial gains in this virtual world (Furlonger, Uzureau and Kandaswamy, 2022).

Some brands may have jumped in too early without a proper understanding of how the metaverse works or the implications behind it, while other brands are embracing the challenge and finding a whole world of possibilities opening up. The experiments that some brands have made with metaverse principles, such as virtual fashion, extended reality, gaming and non-fungible tokens (NFTs), demonstrate the impact that virtual activities can have as marketing and community-building tools for fashion (Business of Fashion and McKinsey & Company, 2022). However, the metaverse is still in the early development stages and its full potential and its challenges are still to be discovered, but there is no doubt that there will be substantial growth that will lead it to become the norm in the future.

Gamification

Gamification is a marketing process of turning something into a game in order to boost engagement and sales. As brands seek new ways of gaining consumer attention, combining the creativity of games and fashion enables them to showcase their collections in different formats to new audiences.

Market research firm EMarketer estimates that the number of gamers worldwide in 2022 will surpass 3 billion people, over one-third of the world's population (Lebow, 2021), and *Vogue* reported that, in 2019, 63 per cent of mobile-game consumers were women (Pithers, 2019), which offers huge commercial opportunities for fashion brands. The fashion industry is aggressively moving into the gaming arena, with both fast fashion and luxury labels creating skins to dress avatars on platforms like Fortnite or Roblox, as well as developing their own branded games.

Gamification makes luxury fashion more democratic, enabling brands to connect with a whole new market of customers who may not be able to afford the collection in real life. Using in-game currency, consumers are able to buy the designer collections of their dreams. For all fashion brands, gamification gives players a chance to be immersed in the world of the brand, building engagement and connection in a fun way while increasing purchaser intent.

Artificial intelligence (AI)

Artificial intelligence (AI) is technology that enables a computer to think or act in a human way. AI is used in programmes to analyse and contextualize data in order to provide information or automatically trigger actions, for example internet search engines, face recognition software, Alexa or Netflix offering recommendations on what else we may like, chatbots on websites, as well as email spam filters (BBC, 2019).

Fashion brands are integrating AI in their processes to analyse data, boost sales, forecast trends and enhance their customers' shopping experiences. This includes adding chatbots and in-store touchscreens, or using AI algorithms to track customers' journeys so that the brand can match them with the right products. Alongside customer service technology tools there is also potential for trend forecasting and supply chain management, which could be the most profitable avenues for AI. Brands can use real-time inventory tracking to save time, improve warehouse management and operations, as well as using data to create the right product at the right time (Kochar, 2022).

AI opportunities are increasing across all areas of the industry from design, all the way through to delivering the product into the consumer's hands. As AI processes advance and improve it can only give brands a greater chance of commercial success.

Augmented reality (AR)

Augmented reality (AR) adds an enhanced version to the real world, enhancing it through computer-generated visual, audio or sensory digital elements. AR utilizes the existing reality through a device of some sort, such as using the camera facilities on a smartphone or tablet and then putting an overlay of digital content into the environment, for example Pokémon Go or Snapchat's AR bitmojis (North of 41, 2018). Consumers are used to interacting with AR on a regular basis now through the use of social media filters, as well as through QR codes, which became a necessity during the Covid-19 pandemic.

AR can offer fashion consumers rich immersive brand experiences, giving them access to additional content about the product or the brand through QR codes or trigger images. This has been particularly beneficial to luxury brands, who can increase the perceived value of their products through brand storytelling, which customers can access through AR touchpoints.

One of the greatest advantages of AR for fashion brands is the development of AR fitting-room technology, which places an item over live imaging of the customer, so they can check the size, style and fit of a product they are thinking of buying (Dopson, 2021). With concerns about the high level of returns due to poor fit, AR fit solutions could radically improve this industry challenge.

Virtual reality (VR)

Virtual reality (VR) is used to describe a computer-generated, 3D environment that offers immersive experiences for people to explore and interact with. VR is dependent on using reality headsets, which can generate the sounds, images and sensations to replicate a real environment or create an imaginary world. VR is a totally immersive experience that can engage all five senses (North of 41, 2018). Fashion brands can use VR to connect their consumers with products or provide experiences where they can immerse themselves in the brand's world, such as catwalk shows or through in-store or digital activations.

Mixed reality (MR)

Mixed reality (MR) is a hybrid reality version, or a blend of physical and digital worlds to produce new environments and visualizations where physical and digital objects co-exist and interact in real time. The key characteristic of MR is that the synthetic content and the real-world content are able to react to each other in real time (North of 41, 2018). Unlike VR, which takes the customer to another virtual dimension, MR superimposes images on the natural surroundings (Arthur, 2016), such as through the use of holograms.

Extended reality (XR)

Extended reality (XR) is an umbrella term used for VR, AR and MR (as shown in Figure 8.4) and refers to all real-and-virtual combined environments and human-machine interactions generated by computer technology and wearables. The future is XR, as the different reality elements will all integrate in the future for people to interact with the real and virtual worlds in seamless ways, without needing to mention extended reality's distinct categories and their underpinning technology (Scribani, 2019). The term XR will be easier to understand by consumers and recognizes the intersection of all the VR, AR and MR technologies and how they will work together in the future to change our everyday lives.

Figure 8.4   XR is the future

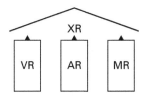

Avatars and virtual influencers

An avatar is a digital image, created as 2D or 3D animations or computer-generated imagery (CGI), that represents a real person who is used in digital realms. The rise of the metaverse and gamification, and the blurred lines between reality and virtual experience, have resulted in a raft of fashion brands introducing avatars and virtual influencers in order to offer greater consumer engagement and drive new revenue streams. Kate Nightingale (2022) explained the psychology behind some businesses using brand avatars, as research has shown that a significant inhibitor of online shopping is the absence of pleasurable experiences, social interaction and personal consultation by a company representative. Brands using avatars have resolved these issues, as the avatar leads the customer to perceive the information on the website as more credible, increases their satisfaction and makes their attitude towards the product more favourable (Nightingale, 2022).

Consumers are becoming more drawn to having an online representation of themselves and using their virtual identities as a form of digital self-expression. As the technology advances, enabling the development of more realistic avatars, consumers can create a collection of identities that are closely linked to their real-world selves, with avatars representing their work or personal lives that they can use to interact across their platforms, communities and games (Correia, 2022).

During the Covid-19 pandemic, fashion saw a rise in virtual influencers as brands turned to CGI influencers to leverage their connected social media followings to promote the label. Luxury brands rushed to engage CGI influencers such as Noonoouri and Lil Miquela to be the faces of their campaigns, finding that while they are not real, their influence is (Dodgson, 2019). The next stage of this comes from TikTok introducing avatars as a means to allow users to re-create themselves as virtual beings in the metaverse. It shows a growing movement towards new forms of user-generated content and the potential of digital nano-influencer campaigns further blurring the physical and online worlds. Fashion brands have a fantastic opportunity to help users personalize their avatars through branded clothing, and in the future hyper-realistic and emotive avatars will enable customers to make better purchasing decisions by being able to see their avatars trying on products (Pearse, n.d.).

Digital showcasing

The global pandemic forced the fashion industry to pivot from real-life events to digital showcasing. Brands developed a host of new creative ways to show their latest collections through virtual catwalks, fashion film, podcasts, interactive websites, virtual showrooms, VR experiences and gamification. Post-pandemic, many brands have continued to use digital showcasing or combined it with a return to physical events to amplify their brand narrative and widen their market (Kessler, 2022).

Brands have rushed into creating virtual events with varying success. The first metaverse fashion week was watched with interest but did not hit the mark, with many in the industry feeling the technology was glitchy and often detracted from the collections. Vogue reported on the events stating that 'much may have been left to be desired, but there's hope for the future' (Kessler, 2022).

Digital showrooms have addressed the challenge of how fashion brands can show their new collections to wholesale buyers who are unable to travel internationally or want to cut travel costs (Browzwear, n.d.). Various platforms, such as Joor and ByondXR, have joined the market offering interactive, highly visual virtual showrooms where brands can conduct sales meeting and take orders. These worked well for established brands that already had relationships with a store, as the buyer knew the brand's quality and fit, but newer labels experienced extremely poor results.

Summary

The only constant in fashion is change, and the rapid expansion of innovation and technology in the industry has impacted the way brands do business from design and manufacturing to sales and promotion. Digital transformation is essential for brands that want to thrive and grow in a volatile, saturated market and that transformation has to be embedded in every aspect of the organization's culture. As Web3 matures, gaming surges and NFTs become the norm, virtual fashion will be in high demand. Consumers will continue to demand more and brands will have to constantly innovate to meet their demands for great sustainability, transparency and engagement. This chapter has discussed the need for the industry to develop innovative practices to reduce environmental impact, developing more sustainable practices as technology advances. Digital is here to stay and brands need to build a robust infrastructure to take advantage of the new opportunities. Fashion brands will need to be brave and step outside their comfort zones to embrace innovation, but time is of the essence as consumers are actively seeking brands that are taking an integrated approach to digital transformation.

Key terms

3D design	e-commerce	mixed reality
artificial intelligence	extended reality	NFTs
augmented reality	gamification	omnichannel
avatars	hyper-personalization	RFID
blockchain	Internet of Things	smart mirrors
CAD	m-commerce	virtual reality
connected store	metaverse	Web3

Activity

Investigate how luxury brands like Louis Vuitton, Tommy Hilfiger, Gucci and Balenciaga are using new technologies to offer enhanced and immersive customer experiences.

References

Arthur, R (2016) Hololens' mixed reality to transform London Fashion Week Show, *Forbes*, www.forbes.com/sites/rachelarthur/2016/09/16/hololens-london-fashion-week/?sh=3c6a856c2ec1 (archived at https://perma.cc/P6W6-VWYE)

BBC (2019) What is AI? What does artificial intelligence do?, *BBC*, www.bbc.co.uk/newsround/49274918 (archived at https://perma.cc/9UKA-R3BE)

Bhana, Y (n.d.) The challenges wearable tech poses to the fashion industry, *Toppan Digital Language*, toppandigital.com/translation-blog/the-challenges-wearable-tech-poses-to-the-fashion-industry/#:~:text=Wearable%20tech%20is%20a%20trend%20that%E2%80%99s%20engaging%20the,the%20mix%2C%20fashion%20is%20moving%20into%20new%20areas (archived at https://perma.cc/RNV6-9X78)

Big Commerce (2022) The guide to omnichannel commerce, *Grow Big Commerce*, grow.bigcommerce.com/rs/695-JJT-333/images/guide_0622_omni_guide_gb_gb.pdf?mkt_tok=Njk1LUpKVC0zMzMAAAGFUyRMhVcxSGhXRtK3k11vSOhh__7-LCbkJ0DNfMWVMs9yBAWuCuHWIiA2T5C2qfQGwuxJZmnI_7BpiLKZgAL7mZEF_2Ec3WhHGbQT446amSb0dOU (archived at https://perma.cc/CN5U-8A9M)

Bliss, D (2019) The huge toll of 'fast fashion' on the planet – and why the answer could be circular, *National Geographic*, www.nationalgeographic.co.uk/environment/2019/06/the-huge-toll-fast-fashion-the-planet-and-why-the-answer-could-be-circular (archived at https://perma.cc/A3TA-AYSQ)

Brown, M (2018) How Microsoft is shaking up fashion with mixed reality, AI, and IoT, *Windows Central*, www.windowscentral.com/microsoft-fashion-mixed-reality-ai-iot (archived at https://perma.cc/XVL8-R828)

Browzwear (n.d.) Reshaping the value chain through digital showcasing as the fashion industry adapts to the new norm, *Browzwear*, browzwear.com/blog-reshaping-the-value-chain-through-digital-showcasing-as-the-fashion-industry-adapts-to-the-new-norm/ (archived at https://perma.cc/P6KS-QDYV)

Business of Fashion and McKinsey & Company (2022) The State of Fashion Technology, *McKinsey*, www.businessoffashion.com/reports/news-analysis/the-state-of-fashion-technology-industry-report-bof-mckinsey/ (archived at https://perma.cc/E4XB-6J9J)

CFI Team (2020) Mobile commerce, *Corporate Finance Institute*, corporatefinanceinstitute.com/resources/knowledge/ecommerce-saas/mobile-commerce/ (archived at https://perma.cc/ZXJ7-H2S3)

Correia, S (2022) Your digital identity in the metaverse: design your avatar, *Digital Nexa*, blog.digitalnexa.com/your-digital-identity-in-the-metaverse-design-your-avatar (archived at https://perma.cc/XNJ7-95U5)

Crypto Daily (2021) The future of fashion with blockchain at its core, *Cryptodaily*, cryptodaily.co.uk/2021/12/the-future-of-fashion-with-blockchain-at-its-core (archived at https://perma.cc/R37H-XTYE)

DeAcetis, J (2021) Innovative blockchain technology creates new opportunities for the high-end fashion industry, *Forbes*, www.forbes.com/sites/josephdeacetis/2021/03/27/innovative-blockchain-technology-creates-new-opportunities-for-the-high-end-fashion-industry/?sh=236effc0c68e (archived at https://perma.cc/NZW9-E5L9)

DHL InMotion (2018) Fashion technology and innovation shape the future of fashion, *DHL InMotion*, inmotion.dhl/en/fashion/article/fashion-technology-and-innovation-shape-the-future-of-fashion (archived at https://perma.cc/4BNP-LJ43)

Dickinson, S (n.d.) How to enable an efficient omnichannel strategy in fashion, *Checkpoint Systems UK*, checkpointsystems.com/uk/blog/how-to-enable-an-efficient-omnichannel-strategy-in-fashion/ (archived at https://perma.cc/FX74-EB66)

Dodgson, L (2019) Fake, computer-generated Instagram influencers are modelling designer clothes, wearing Spanx, and attending red carpet premieres, *Insider*, www.insider.com/cgi-influencers-what-are-they-where-did-they-come-from-2019-8 (archived at https://perma.cc/7Q6Z-7CVJ)

Dopson, E (2021) What are virtual fitting rooms and why should retailers use them?, *Shopify*, www.shopify.co.uk/retail/virtual-fitting-rooms (archived at https://perma.cc/7GF7-DZSJ)

Douglass, R (2022) Shopping is about fit, not size, *Fashion United*, fashionunited.com/news/business/shopping-is-about-fit-not-size-bods-founder-christine-marzano-talks-virtual-avatars-and-sexy-tech/2022070648490 (archived at https://perma.cc/S5M3-JLWA)

Fashion United (2022) The rise of 'green' materials heralds a new era in fashion, *Fashion United*, fashionunited.com/news/fashion/the-rise-of-green-materials-heralds-a-new-era-in-fashion/2022071248607 (archived at https://perma.cc/FMS6-7N4S)

Furlonger, D, Uzureau, C and Kandaswamy, R (2022) Wondering how to capture opportunity in the metaverse?, *Gartner*, www.gartner.com/en/articles/how-to-capture-opportunity-in-the-metaverse (archived at https://perma.cc/U38K-NFPQ)

Hackl, C (2021) Fashion in 3D: an opportunity for greater innovation, *Forbes*, www.forbes.com/sites/cathyhackl/2021/10/17/fashion-in-3d-an-opportunity-for-greater-innovation/?sh=35141dc7a5a2 (archived at https://perma.cc/R23W-T599)

Islam Kiron, M (2021) Application of Internet of Things (IoT) in textile and fashion industry, *Textile Learner*, textilelearner.net/internet-of-things-iot-in-fashion-industry/ (archived at https://perma.cc/XL9D-P8BA)

Kessler, A (2022) Is metaverse fashion week the future of the industry?, *British Vogue*, www.vogue.co.uk/fashion/article/metavese-fashion-week-decentraland?utm_social-type=owned (archived at https://perma.cc/723K-E2JT)

Knox, B (2022) 22 UNIQUE fashion innovations changing the industry in 2022, *The Vou*, thevou.com/fashion/fashion-innovation/ (archived at https://perma.cc/Y8FE-WCQS)

Kochar, S (2022) Top 9 technology trends reshaping the fashion industry in 2022, *Techpacker Blog*, techpacker.com/blog/design/top-9-fashion-technology-trends/#:~:text=As%20customers%27%20real%20lives%20become%20increasingly%20intertwined%20with,the%20limits%20of%20manufacturing%2C%20production%2C%20marketing%2C%20and%20wearability (archived at https://perma.cc/CD64-Z9MF)

Lay, R (2018) Digital transformation in the fashion industry, *Deloitte Switzerland*, www2. deloitte.com/ch/en/pages/consumer-industrial-products/articles/ultimate-challenge-fashion-industry-digital-age.html (archived at https://perma.cc/24H5-BNSK)

Lebow, S (2021) Gaming's growing population, *Insider Intelligence*, www.insiderintelligence. com/content/gamers-make-up-more-than-one-third-of-world-population (archived at https://perma.cc/TKF5-RBAK)

Ledger (2021) Digital fashion and NFTs: what is it all about?, *Ledger*, www.ledger.com/ academy/digital-fashion-nfts-what-is-it-all-about (archived at https://perma.cc/VQ86-PZ7P)

Maguire, L (2022) The digital designers making millions from in-game fashion, *Vogue Business*, www.voguebusiness.com/technology/the-digital-designers-making-millions-from-in-game-fashion?uID=c3f9f40646d5511ecf991a0757a713a5f2179c9953c544ca6c f2da3ef904a7bb&utm_campaign=newsletter_weekly&utm_source=newsletter&utm_ brand=vb&utm_mailing=VB_FUTURE_EDIT_250522&utm_medium=email&utm_ term=VB_VogueBusiness (archived at https://perma.cc/R9E9-8384)

Nightingale, K (2022) Metaverse psychology – brand avatars, *LinkedIn*, www.linkedin.com/ pulse/metaverse-psychology-brand-avatars-kasia-slowikowska-?trk=eml-email_series_ follow_newsletter_01-hero-1-title_link&midToken=AQGHLbDVWrJzFw&fromEmail= fromEmail&ut=08-oROyoLLSWk1 (archived at https://perma.cc/M5EL-96TM)

North of 41 (2018) What really is the difference between AR / MR / VR / XR?, *Medium*, medium.com/@northof41/what-really-is-the-difference-between-ar-mr-vr-xr-35bed1da1a4e (archived at https://perma.cc/8ETV-H95U)

Pearse, J (n.d.) Why retail brands need to maximize their use of avatars, *New Digital Age*, New Digital Age, newdigitalage.co/social-media/why-retail-brands-need-to-maximise-their-use-of-avatars/ (archived at https://perma.cc/HVA4-Z6EB)

Pithers, E (2019) How fashion got the gaming bug, *British Vogue*, www.vogue.co.uk/ arts-and-lifestyle/article/fashion-and-gaming (archived at https://perma.cc/L98L-3GQJ)

Roach, A (2020) The future of e-commerce: how e-commerce will change in 2021 and beyond, *Oberlo*, www.oberlo.com/blog/future-of-ecommerce (archived at https://perma. cc/FTR5-2VH2)

Scribani, J (2019) What is extended reality (XR)?, *Visual Capitalist*, www.visualcapitalist. com/extended-reality-xr/ (archived at https://perma.cc/XT37-2LB8)

Sharma, V (2018) Virtual mirror technology – it will change the way you shop, *Quytech Blog*, www.quytech.com/blog/how-virtual-mirror-technology-will-change-the-way-you-shop/ (archived at https://perma.cc/J75G-5YJ2)

Sharma, V (2021) What is the metaverse? beginner's guide, *Quytech Blog*, www.quytech. com/blog/what-is-metaverse/ (archived at https://perma.cc/G3FF-PFPY)

Turk, R (2021) How material innovation can change the fashion industry, *Fashion United*, fashionunited.com/en/news/fashion/how-material-innovation-can-change-the-fashion-industry/2021030138518 (archived at https://perma.cc/XP2Q-PJTF)

Vyas, A (2022) Introduction to Web3 and the metaverse, *Nexa*, www.yourglobalvillage-bookstore.com/post/design-a-stunning-blog (archived at https://perma.cc/LS87-2RQC)

Case study
My Wardrobe HQ

Photo credit: Emily Batters

MY WARDROBE HQ (MYWHQ) is the UK's first fashion rental marketplace and has become the leading destination for renting or buying contemporary and luxury womenswear fashion. Founded by Sacha Newall and Tina Lake in 2019, and chaired by retail expert Jane Shepherdson, this powerhouse of women has created the groundbreaking new platform with sustainability at its core: renting out current and past season collections from big-name designers, as well as selling pre-loved pieces from covetable wardrobes, extending the lifecycle of a garment by up to 15 times. MYWHQ also offers an additional way for brands and retailers to sell through pieces that either didn't make it into production or didn't sell through at the end of the season, saving more products from going to landfill as well enabling brands to recoup some costs.

Sustainability drives every decision MYWHQ makes, and in their drive to becoming fully sustainable they have partnered with dry cleaners who only use non-toxic biodegradable detergents and eco-couriers who deliver all parcels on a fleet of eco-conscious modern vehicles. MYWHQ use their social shopping platform for education, encouraging their consumers to buy better and buy less, and helping them discover that better-quality items are often made with more stringent processes that don't – or have less of – an impact on the environment. Where possible, on some products there is a calculator that shows exactly the savings made to the planet by buying, resale or renting.

The brand believes fashion rental is the solution to consuming fashion in a sustainable way, but their unique model means that if the consumer totally loves the piece then they can buy it, and when the time comes to pass it on they can list it back on the platform. MYWHQ believes that the only way to change behaviour is through income growth on both sides of the equation, so they enable both luxury fashion brands and their consumers to generate funds.

www.mywardrobehq.com

Driving sales 9

LEARNING OBJECTIVES

By the end of this chapter, you will be able to:

- Identify the different sales channels that fashion brands use
- Explain the process of using a sales funnel to increase sales
- Describe the wholesale, e-commerce, direct retail and social selling strategies for fashion brands

Introduction

Selling fashion is not easy. The fashion brands that develop effective sales strategies are the ones that will stay in business. In a highly saturated market with thousands of brands selling similar items, it can be really difficult to stand out, attract the buyer's interest and persuade them to make a purchase. The reality of running a fashion brand is that without sales there is no business, just a very expensive hobby and a load of products that could end up in landfill.

Other chapters in this book have addressed the challenges of changing consumer behaviour, with the customer now looking for brands that they can have an emotional connection with, changing from seeking high-quality products for cheaper prices, to seeking emotional rewards from their experiences as a consumer (Kim and Johnson, 2013). Brands must develop strategies that offer memorable, immersive experiences to make the consumer feel good. If the brand is selling direct to the consumer, then it is imperative that they determine experiential strategies that will attract their customers to make a purchase. If they are selling through a third party or wholesale, then they need a strategy to offer their stores additional benefits that will make their brand more appealing to the buyer, but also offer them added values to pass on to their customers.

This chapter will look at the different channels fashion brands can use to sell their products and the challenges they can face with each method, including wholesale, direct to customer and through third-party marketplaces. The chapter will discuss why social selling is taking over from traditional selling methods, and how an omnichannel approach is essential to deliver consistent brand experience across all the brand sales channels.

Sales channels

There are four main sales channels (Figure 9.1) for a fashion brand to sell their collection through:

- *Wholesale* is a business-to-business model. Brands sell a bulk order of pieces of the collection at a lower, wholesale price to store buyers, who will then place the brand's pieces in their retail shops.
- *Dropship marketplaces* is a business model that involves a fashion brand agreeing with an online platform, or another fashion business store, that they will sell the brand's collection, but the marketplace does not buy the product or hold the stock. The brand will simply list their product on the site for a set fee and commission, and when orders are placed they ship the goods to the customer.
- *Online* is an e-commerce or m-commerce model when the brand sells their collections direct to their customers, at a higher retail price, through their online channels including websites, online stores, social media or apps.
- *Retail* is a consumer-facing model involving the brand directly selling their collection to the customer at a higher retail price through their own physical stores, events or pop-up shops.

These sales models and their challenges are explained in more detail below. As the industry pivots post-pandemic and responds to changing economic conditions, brands have to consider different sales channels in order to establish their businesses, increase market share, generate higher returns, and have more control over their management and production processes.

Figure 9.1 Sales channels

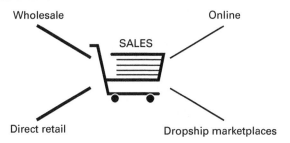

Sales funnel

For the different sales channels a brand has to consider the sales funnels they need to develop for each method. A sales funnel is a process that tracks the customer journey from when a potential consumer meets the brand to when they make a purchase. Companies in all sectors use funnels to track potential customers as they move through the sales process, as this helps the business identify their strategy, know what works and what they need to adjust. Understanding the sales funnel is key to tracking prospect engagement and closing deals, and changing customer expectations means sales funnel strategies must evolve (Gustavson, 2021).

The AIDA model represents the traditional stages of a sales funnel (Figure 9.2). The AIDA principal was coined by US advertising and sales pioneer Elias St Elmo Lewis in the late 1800s (Dragon 360, 2011) and is still used in business every day for marketing, advertising, sales and content creation. The sales funnel aims to take the customer from the top to the bottom through the steps of awareness, interest, desire and action:

- *Awareness*: In this first stage, the potential consumer discovers the brand. To achieve this the brand has to work to raise awareness of the label through numerous means including online, in person, through social media or encouraging word-of-mouth recommendations.

- *Interest*: Once the consumer has awareness of the brand, this next stage is when they start to show a genuine interest in the brand and its products and services (Gustavson, 2021). At this point the brand has to work hard to make a connection with the potential consumer to start to establish a relationship with them. This is a crucial stage when the potential customer may keep looking for other options or be drawn away due to awareness of another brand or product.

- *Desire*: In the third stage, the consumer shows a desire to purchase as they feel the product or service meets their needs. This can also be called the decision stage. It is at this stage that the brand really needs to work on delivering emotional

Figure 9.2   Sales funnel buying stages

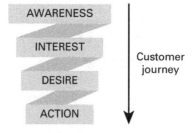

branding strategies that focus on sensory branding, storytelling, cause branding and empowerment to build the desire in the consumer. Brands can use emotional branding as a way to engage their customers, appealing to their needs, aspirations, dreams and ego (Kim and Sullivan, 2019). At this stage, the consumer can still change their mind if the experience does not fulfil or add to their desire to own the piece.

- *Action*: In this final stage the consumer makes the decision and purchases the product. The brand needs to ensure the potential consumer can easily take action to purchase – whether that is checking out online or in-store, the final stage needs to make the purchase process as smooth as possible for the consumer. They must ensure that there are no barriers to purchase, such as slow checkout, too much unnecessary information required or unfavourable payment terms.

All fashion brands need to develop a sales funnel as part of both their marketing and business strategies in order to remain customer focused. In a volatile market where customers are not always brand loyal, a fashion label needs to remain vigilant and always be looking to identify and attract new customers, as well as maintaining the relationship with current ones. The key to building a successful sales funnel for a clothing brand is understanding how the customers' brains work and what they need in order to purchase from the brand (Steven, 2021).

Wholesale

Fashion brands that want to sell their products business-to-business (B2B) through department stores or independent retailers need to develop a specific wholesale strategy. This strategy must position the brand in a way that will make it appealing to the stores, as well as being economically viable for the business.

Historically, wholesale B2B sales models were the preferred choice for luxury and start-up fashion brands, as they wanted the prestige of selling through high-end fashion retailers and large department stores around the world (Burke, 2015). Selling through wholesale gave labels credibility by being associated with well-known store names, enabled them to have brand alignment next to their potential competitors, increased their brand awareness and gave them potential to be in stores around the globe. In the past the other advantages of wholesale were that it was less risky for the brand, as they just had to create a sample of each piece to show to the wholesale store buyer and did not have to invest in putting the collection into full production until they had guaranteed orders. As stores used to pay a deposit when placing orders, there was minimal risk for brands as the deposit would cover most of the production costs. Using the wholesale model meant the brand did not have the responsibility of finding consumers, selling the product to them, or managing the retail environment and worrying about the overheads.

However, the reality of the wholesale business model is now very different, which has resulted in many brands either choosing other sales models that offer them better returns, or they have been forced to find alternative models in order to survive. Stores no longer pay deposits and expect the brand to take responsibility for driving customers to the store through PR activity. The majority of department stores around the world no longer buy the collections of emerging fashion brands, instead asking for pieces on a sale-or-return basis. On top of all of this, the wholesale payment terms offered by many stores are debilitating to smaller brands, with late payments and terms of up to net 270 days. This means wholesale is not actually financially viable for most smaller brands, as it does not offer them the profit margin to scale the business, and the onerous payment terms cripple their cashflow. This new model of wholesale means that the level of risk has now moved from the store to the brand, resulting in more emerging fashion designers adopting a direct-to-consumer model, wooed by the promise of higher margins and a closer relationship with the customer (Sherman, 2016).

If brands do wish to still proceed with a wholesale business model, or have already established wholesale accounts, then they need to build their wholesale strategy based on facts gathered from primary and secondary research. The brand also needs to prepare all the necessary documents and set the terms and conditions that they will need to execute a successful wholesale strategy.

What do wholesale store buyers want?

Wholesale store buyers look for brands that have a buzz about them, with lots of press features, an established customer base and a really engaged following on social media with people engaging with the brand, proving that there is interest in the label and its products. The wholesale store buyer would expect the brand to drive this customer base towards their store to buy the product. A buyer does not want to take a risk on a brand, as they need to hit their targets and profit margins, so they look for brands that they think will sell through well. The buyer also has to consider merchandizing, bearing in mind the visual and creative side as well as ensuring the analytical and assortment planning of the brand's product will fit in-store (Giordano, 2017). Buyers look for brands that have a consistent design aesthetic, which leads them to often watch a brand for at least three seasons to ensure the brand has a solid design signature and quality before they buy.

Primary and secondary research

Brands have to be realistic about the stores that they wish their product to be featured in. They need to conduct both primary and secondary research to make sure their brand is right for the store before they waste the buyer's and their own time. The research has to determine the store's customer, price points, aesthetic and product range to confirm they match those of the brand. Too often brands make assumptions without ever actually researching or visiting the store. Brands all over the world will reel off the same list of stores that they want to be in, such as Harvey Nichols, Harrods, Lane Crawford, Saks, Liberty, Joyce, amongst others. Yet all of these stores have very different fashion customers, focus on different types of products and brands, and have varying price points. Store buyers get very frustrated with brands that approach them with no knowledge or understanding of their store and customers. With larger department stores, the fashion department might include numerous sub-departments such as international brands or contemporary, and the brand needs to research which section they would fit best within. From the research, the brand can create a database of potential stores, but the next challenge is finding the name of the right buyer who is responsible for buying product for the department the brand wants to be in (Burke, 2015). For smaller independent stores the owner is often the buyer, but for larger stores the brand would need to search on channels such as LinkedIn to find the names for buyers of particular product categories.

Contacting buyers

Buyers are bombarded daily with emails and phone calls from fashion labels, agents and sales reps from around the world, therefore brands have to make sure they have all the important information ready to share with them and develop an effective approach to contacting them in order to stand out (Giordano, 2017).

The majority of brands only contact store buyers during the main buying seasons, which are predominantly based around the traditional fashion calendar of Spring/Summer in August to October and Autumn/Winter in December to February. During these times the buyer's inbox is absolutely jammed with requests from brands. In the buying season, the buyers organize and attend sales appointments, but they have often already decided which brands they will have in-store and apportioned their budgets months in advance. A better strategy is for a brand to build a relationship with a buyer outside of the buying season and maintain it all year, using the drip method to keep the brand name at the top of their minds. The drip method is simply reminding the buyer in subtle ways about the brand (Giordano, 2017), its products, any latest news or press, sending through different information on a regular basis so that they learn more about the business over time.

Pitching to buyers is really difficult with a brand having to make hundreds of cold calls and send numerous emails yet often they get no response. The success comes from brands that consistently follow up with a prospect. On average 43 per cent of people give up after their first 'no' from a buyer, but contacting a potential buyer is not just about making a sale, it is about building and maintaining a relationship in the hope that the sale will happen organically (Giordano, 2017).

Look books

The look book is one of the main documents that a fashion brand creates to entice the store buyers and wholesale accounts. In the highly visual world of fashion, the brand needs to communicate their design ideas, brand storytelling and quality of their products in a highly effective way, conveying their brand essence effectively to catch the buyer's attention (Omotoso, 2018). The look book can be either a physical printed version or digital, and features images of a new collection or key products in a visually appealing way that will encourage sales. It can include a combination of stylized editorial photography as well as e-commerce-style product images. The main criteria for a look book is to present that product in detail so that the buyer can clearly see what they are buying. Brands need to invest time and money into creating a great look book, using a professional team of photographers, models and stylists to showcase the brand and its products in the best way possible.

Line sheet

The line sheet is the second main document and it is sent along with the look book to provide the details of the collection. The look book showcases the collection through beautiful images and the line sheet gives the facts, figures and details. The line sheet is the selling tool to help the buyer from a retail store understand and place orders for the collection (Omotoso, 2018). Details in line sheet need to include the season date, collection name, size and colour options, fabric composition, design details, as well as the wholesale price and recommended retail price (Table 9.1). It can also include details of the packaging bags, boxes and hangers offered with the product as well as any exclusive designs or colourways that the brand can offer to a store. The line sheet is a flexible document that can be tweaked according to the store or country the brand is approaching, as the buyer will want to see pricing in their own currency.

The line sheet should also include the brand's terms and conditions such as delivery times, minimum order quantities, shipping and payment terms. The terms and conditions make it very clear for both sides about what is expected when placing an order and covers the brand in case of late payments as well as protecting them from any misunderstandings or queries later on. The brand should also detail copyright and design rights, as well as information about product inconsistencies if handmade, or any other areas relevant to the brand. For the buyer to place an order, they need to know the minimum order quantity (MOQ), the delivery date, along with pricing and payment terms.

Table 9.1   Line sheet

Name	Image of product	Colour	Fabric	Sizes	Wholesale price	RRP
Name or number of the piece	Include an image, sketch or outline drawing of the piece	List all the colours and prints the piece is available in	Detail the fabric composition	List the size range for the product	Include prices in £, €, $ or the currency of the country you are selling to	
1.						
2.						

When setting the terms and conditions, brands have to decide on their payment terms, with many asking for a 30 per cent deposit on order with the remaining 70 per cent balance paid on delivery. For a more established relationship or repeat order from the store, then the brand may set net payment terms such as net30, which would require payment 30 days after delivery. However, in reality, brands set net payment terms for net60, net90 or even net120. These unfavourable terms result in brands waiting months to receive payments, which is not an efficient or feasible model for most businesses, so they need effective negotiation skills to persuade store buyers to accept better terms. The prices for each product quoted on the line sheet are normally 'ex-works', which means it is just the price of the piece and does not include shipping, import duties and insurance.

The final section to include in a line sheet would be the returns and exchange policy to cover the brand if a store returns goods that they perceive to be poor quality, faulty pieces or an incorrect order is delivered. A fashion brand needs to set clear terms on which they will accept returns, or their exchange policy, in order to avoid any misunderstandings.

Trade fairs

Alongside calling and emailing buyers, brands can participate in trade fairs that store buyers attend. A trade fair brings a whole range of brands together under one roof and there are trade fairs, shows and exhibitions all around the world. Brands need to research the trade fairs to ensure they choose one that is attended by buyers who place orders for their kind of product and at their price points, as the fairs can vary in who attends. Taking part in a trade fair is very expensive so they need to make sure they don't waste money by participating in the wrong one.

Social media

Before the rise of Instagram store buyers mainly used trade fairs to discover brands, but today, social media plays a large part in how fashion buyers discover and reach out to emerging brands (Yu, 2019). Brands need to take a strategic approach to their social media content to ensure it appeals to store buyers as well as direct customers.

Sales agents, showrooms and distributors

Many brands struggle to sell their collections due to lack of contacts or understanding of the sales process. In these cases, they often turn to employing a sales agent or rep to take over the sales negotiations, set the terms and conditions, and introduce the brand to new export markets (Burke, 2015). Sales showrooms are spaces where numerous brands come together to showcase their collections to buyers. These are managed by sales agencies who bring buyers to the event and support the sales negotiations. Contracts with sales agents and showrooms are set for a period of time such as a season, or annually, and state the commission fees on sales as well as any additional fees for the brand to be included in showrooms and events.

Another sales option is working with a distributor who will buy goods directly from the brand at a significant discount and then they will sell on your collection to stores in their agreed territories. A distributor has the sole rights to sell the brand products in a particular country, meaning the brand or any of its partners are unable to also sell in that territory.

Finding a good sales agent, showroom or distributor can be challenging, and due to the added costs of paying the commission and fees the brand may have to increase its prices significantly to cover the extra costs, or risk selling at a loss. When working with agents, distributors and showrooms the brand may have no direct relationship with the store buyer, which means if at some point in the future they decide to change agents then they may lose some accounts.

> To wholesale a collection successfully a brand needs to develop a specific strategy for this sales method and be prepared to spend time on research and preparation for it to achieve results.

For most brands, it can take several seasons before they get a buyer from their target stores to even look at the collection. Then the likelihood is that the buyer doesn't place an order, instead advising the brand that they will continue to 'watch them' or will see them again next season. As wholesale strategies become more challenging due to the changing economy and industry, and with the crippling payment terms stores now offer, the majority of fashion brands no longer see wholesale as their main sales strategy.

Dropship marketplaces

An alternative method of selling that is similar to wholesale is dropshipping. This model involves a store selling a fashion brand's product, but they don't own the inventory and they don't carry the stock. With this model, the store will include product in their online shop and, when an order comes in, the store will send the brand the details and tell them to ship the product direct to the customer within an agreed timescale. The benefits of dropship for a brand are that they still hold their stock while having access to a wider global market through the platform. The difficulties come from having to finance and produce the product and keep it to one side just in case an order comes through from the site. This may not be the most cost-effective way of managing stock for many brands.

The marketplace model has been growing significantly over the past five years, with businesses including Amazon, Zalando, Not Just a Label, Wolf and Badger, to name a few offering a new way for brands to sell. A marketplace is a platform that brands pay to be featured on, then the marketplace takes responsibility of sales and marketing to drive customers to the platform. This can be hugely beneficial for brands to access a wide customer base in areas where they don't have any traction, helping them gain feedback on their products in new territories. With many of these marketplaces having a global reach, this is perfect for a designer whose attempts at wholesaling in the territory have been thwarted (Tsolova, 2017). This model is also proving popular for brands who are opening their own e-commerce sites to other brands to increase the product offer to their customers, in order to keep them returning to the site. With the decline of department stores around the world, the marketplace model is filling the space they have left (Parisi, 2020).

Online

When the wholesale market started to become more challenging for brands, many of them turned to e-commerce as their future sales strategy. However, the success rate for most brands was really slow, as e-commerce democratized fashion industry competition and even with contemporary strategies many fashion brands suffer from stagnant sales (Kim and Sullivan, 2019). Fashion brands often mistake e-commerce as an easy strategy, working on the assumption that by having a site the consumer will automatically find them. In a highly saturated international fashion market, brands have to work really hard and deliver substantial marketing activities to drive consumers to their sites. Poor customer service can lead to failure on e-commerce, as customer expectations are quickly outpacing most brands' ability to make shopping feel unique (SAILTHRU, 2022). Fashion brands must develop an e-commerce strategy that focuses on flexibility and convenience for customers and constantly adjusts and adapts the shopping experience to meet a wide range of customer needs and expectations (Modern Retail, 2022).

The global pandemic changed the face of fashion sales with online business models becoming the standout success story (Business of Fashion, 2022) and the growth of online has not slowed down, reflecting a longer-term trend. Fashion brands will need to keep investing in their digital applications in order to stay ahead of the competition and keep their connection with consumers who can be easily swayed to look elsewhere online. Clare Lawson told *The Drum* that the drivers of loyalty have changed, with consumers demanding value-added experiences rather than points and prizes, and 70 per cent of Generation Z saying that experiences are what drive their loyalty (Bradley, 2022).

One of the biggest challenges that has arisen from the increase in online sales is the return process, with the National Retail Federation and Appriss Retail reporting that more than $761 billion in merchandise sold in 2021 would be returned by consumers, a return rate of 16.6 per cent (Modern Retail, 2022). Customers expect brands to offer easy and free returns and exchanges, but this process presents complex financial and logistical challenges to brands as well as environmental impacts. The cost of returns has become too expensive for some brands, resulting in them starting to charge customers for online returns.

Direct retail

The fashion industry continues to adjust and adapt to the changes brought about by new technology and social media platforms, and while online offers huge advantages for brands across the fashion industry, there is still a place for direct retail. Consumers are still demanding opportunities for face-to-face contact with brands, and businesses no longer have to rely on third parties to have a physical retail store. Direct retail relates to opportunities for the brand to interact directly with their customers through flagship stores, pop-up shops, trunk shows or events.

Larger fashion brands are scaling their physical presence with expensive and inspirational flagship stores to showcase their brand essence and what they have to offer (Di Somma, n.d.), whereas smaller labels are making the most of the opportunities from pop-up shops. Physical stores, as well as trunk shows and events, give a tangible meeting point for a brand's community to meet with the brand and each other, which fulfils their demand for greater engagement and connection.

Many in the fashion industry have embraced a hybrid business model of online and pop-up shops to offer a convenient and immersive experience to their consumers. With the current high level of empty store fronts, brands are able to easily find spaces if they want their own store. Brands can also join the growing number of collaborative organizations like Lone Design Club, who facilitate space for a group of different designers to come together to create a unique retail space. Trunk shows and sales events in stores, hotels or galleries can also offer a unique, engaging experience to build relationships between the brand and its customers.

While the wholesale business of the past is bankrupt, shifting to a direct-to-consumer model is scary for brands and requires them not only to develop a new business model, but also invest in technology, marketing and a reconfigured supply chain (Human B, n.d.). Brands entering the direct-to-consumer business model are often enticed by the higher profit margins they can get from retail pricing, but they need to have sufficient funding to pay for the production of inventory to fill a store, as well as a substantial marketing budget.

Social selling

The definition of social selling is a strategy that involves using personal contacts and social networks to find potential customers, build trusted relationships and increase sales. This sales technique helps brands develop more effective sales lead generation and builds more authentic and meaningful relationships with potential customers. Building and maintaining relationships is easier within a network that the brand and the customer trust (LinkedIn, n.d.), and brands adopting this method of selling their collections have been finding greater success than through traditional wholesale models.

> Social selling is not a separate approach to sales, it is the foundational method to use across all the brand's sales channels including wholesale, retail, online or marketplaces, as taking a relationship-building approach will improve a brand's chance of success in any of the channels.

While social selling uses what may appear to be an informal business model, it is a proven strategic approach that works, with a report in salesforce declaring that 78 per cent of social sellers outsell brands who don't use this approach (Crawford, 2019). Brands need to develop a strategic plan and understanding of how social selling works, they cannot just use social channels as another way to bombard potential customers with advertising. Social selling relies on insight and empathy (Crawford, 2019) and brands need to focus on the 'social' part of researching, connecting and interacting with people to build a relationship with them rather than selling product. If a brand is being social with their customers and building a genuine relationship with them, then the customer learns more about the brand, feels part of it and trusts it, so then the sale becomes a natural part of the process rather than a forced, hard sell to a stranger.

The benefits of social selling are vast and while it does help a brand build better relationships with professional partners including store buyers, magazine editors and industry partners, the greatest benefit is the ability to build direct consumer relationships without needing to rely on third parties. Brands are also able to get direct feedback from their customers on what they want and like, helping the business create products that have a greater chance of selling. The four steps of a social selling strategy include:

- Developing a professional brand with well-designed digital channels including e-commerce and social media selling pages.

- Creating a refined list of potential customers or customer types to target.

- Delivering activities that engage with the consumer such as brand activations and events, newsletters, social content and live shopping.

- Building a trusted relationship with the customer through interesting and relevant information and content that meets their needs, not what the brand wants to sell.

A social selling strategy involves both digital and physical tactics including social media, physical events and parties, newsletters, brand activations, live shopping, trunk shows and pop-up shops (Figure 9.3).

Live shopping

Live shopping refers to a real-time, live-streamed event hosted by a member of the brand's team, or an influencer, who talks through and sells the product on social

Figure 9.3   Social selling

platforms. Live shopping is possible now on many platforms including a brand's own website or through Instagram, TikTok, YouTube or Alibaba, to name a few. Live shopping events are interactive, fun and offer consumers the personal assistance of an in-store shopping experience from the comfort of their homes. The interactive element provides the connection and engagement consumers require, allowing them to ask questions, interact with each other and share their experiences. Elisa (2022) states that live shopping will increase conversion rates, views, comments and contact time as well as increasing sales.

Social media and e-commerce stores

E-commerce relates to selling products online through all digital channels. This is a broad term that means the brand's own website or online shop as well as through apps and social media on any other online platform.

The primary e-commerce platform is the brand's own webstore, which is an essential part of the strategy for any fashion brand, but as technology advances brands have other digital options that they can also embrace. The online shop needs to be aesthetically pleasing, have great content, provide an easy user journey to get the customer through the buying process quickly, offer a secure checkout process and gather the data needed for the brand to increase repeat sales. Product descriptions are a primary tool in offering brand transparency through detailed product descriptions as well as helping with search engine optimization (SEO).

Alongside the webstore, brands are now able to create stores on Instagram, TikTok, Facebook, Pinterest and many other social media sites. These are all critical elements of a social selling strategy as this takes the brand into the place where the customer is already hanging out, exploring and communicating with brands. Social media enables a brand to authentically talk to potential customers, share the brand storytelling and their values, and bring the customer into the brand's lifestyle. A Forbes article reported some research from GlobalWebIndex who found that social media is one of the main places that consumers use when looking for more information about a product brand or service, and the option to use a 'buy' button would make them more likely to purchase (McCue, 2018). Brands need to remember that followers are not customers, so they need to create a strategy that turns their followers into leads by providing great content and building genuine engagement and relationships through their pages.

Events, trunk shows, parties and pop-up shops

The social selling strategy involves developing various routes that a brand can use to get in front of potential customers. Pop-up shops can be solo shops or brands can participate in shared stores. For a pop-up to be successful, a brand needs to deliver numerous marketing approaches to get the consumer in the store, as they may not organically just 'pop in', whereas trunk shows, where the brand takes their product to the customer, can be hosted in any place that the brand's consumer already visits such as private member clubs, corporate companies, hotels, gyms, or school and church groups. Trunk shows can also be within another store, boutique or gallery that does not sell the same kind of merchandise as the brand.

Events and parties offer brands an opportunity to offer their consumers immersive brand experiences to increase brand awareness as well as sell product. The purpose of all brand activations is to keep them exciting, engaging and creative in order to build a buzz about the brand, increase customer relationships and make more sales, both at the event and in the future.

Email newsletters

The main purpose of the social selling strategy is to build and maintain relationships with customers that will drive consistent sales through an online store. The prompt or stimulus for online sales is often a newsletter/email campaign that prompts the customer to visit the site. Fashion brands that are using intelligent email marketing campaigns not only prompt sales but build relationships with customers. The key to success is the content. Brands must provide their audience with content that adds value, that is entertaining, informing or solves their problems. Most brands make the mistake of using email newsletters to heavily promote the brand or advertise products – this approach does not engage the consumer and can result in them unsubscribing.

Omnichannel

Customers now shop through multiple channels and the market is totally saturated with thousands of sites and social media platforms selling fashion product, which makes the business of selling fashion much more complex. Brands now have to develop well-planned strategies if they want their products to be available in all the places where their customer is present, using a combination of physical stores, digital channels and marketing channels. Omnichannel is a term used to describe a strategy that provides a seamless shopping experience across all channels where the consumer will engage with the brand. Many brands offer multi-channels where their product is available, but these may not be directly aligned, whereas omnichannel ensures that whichever channel the consumer chooses the experience is consistent and integrated with the others (Muras, n.d.).

Omnichannel is necessary as consumers no longer distinguish between different channels and can quickly switch from online store to physical store to social media in seconds, and they expect the brand experience to be the same wherever they discover the brand. Executing a successful omnichannel strategy requires a brand to research and map the customer journey to ensure they deliver a personalized experience at each stage to empower the consumer to buy from them wherever they are (Shopify, 2020).

Figure 9.4 includes many of the channels that fashion brands can now use as part of their omnichannel strategy. According to Shopify, in an omnichannel environment, 'the world is truly your storefront — a world of screens, devices and touchpoints your target market is using' (Shopify, 2020). The omnichannel strategy links marketing and sales to ensure that every brand touchpoint is a potential point of sale. Many brands are using some of the sales methods noted but are missing out on a wider range of digital channels including gaming, mobile apps, podcasts, chatbots and live broadcasts, as well as considering the renaissance of printed catalogues or the potential of AR-enabled shoppable magazines.

The omnichannel experience is more than giving consumers more places to buy – the true power of omnichannel is realized when the channels work together in harmony to immerse consumers in a highly personalized experience that also respects the stage of the buying cycle the consumer is in (Shopify, 2020).

Figure 9.4 Omnichannel

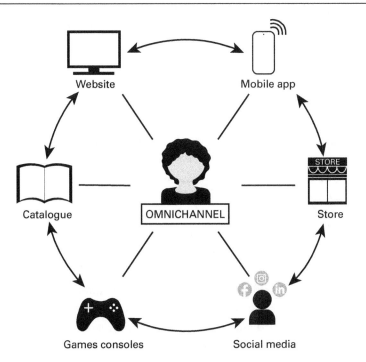

Returns

Whichever sales channel brands are using, one of the greatest concerns is the ever-rising rate of returns. With the rise of e-commerce has come an increase in returns, as consumers have found that returning purchases can be easily managed with often no cost to themselves. In an article on Fashion United, CNBC are quoted as saying that retailers expect about 16.6 per cent of the total merchandise customers purchase to be returned (Fraser, 2022). Fashion brands have to anticipate a certain number of returns, but high return rates severely affect the company's bottom line.

Brands need to develop a returns strategy that is simple, frictionless, cost-effective and sustainable as it plays a significant role in building customer relationships and loyalty, and improves the customer experience (Modern Retail, 2022). However, many brands are now only offering free returns for goods returned to their stores and are charging consumers for online returns. They hope this approach will fix the logistical and environmental challenges as well as the financial costs of processing online returns. As the BBC reported, a return in a shop can be processed and put back on the rail for resale quickly, but items returned via a courier have to be sent to a warehouse, unpacked and cleaned before being available for resale (Smith, 2022).

To minimize returns, businesses have to look at the reasons for return, which for fashion brands are often due to poor quality, sizing or fit of products. Many brands are looking at investing in new fit technology to reduce return rates, using AI sizing and visualization technology to eliminate multi-size ordering for shoppers (Fraser, 2022). There are numerous apps now in development that offer virtual fitting rooms that brands will be able to integrate into their sales channels.

Summary

This chapter has shown that it can be very difficult for brands to successfully drive sales, as the market is saturated with thousands of brands selling similar items. With consumer behaviour also changing, brands must offer the experiences and emotional connection that the customer demands, as well as great products at good prices. Brands can no longer rely on one sales method, they have to develop new omnichannel sales strategies, using every channel that they can, in order to place their brand and products in front of the customer.

While wholesale is not dead, the power dynamic between brands and retailers has shifted (Vogue Business, 2020). Brands that once relied almost entirely on wholesale accounts to succeed can now operate more diverse business models that include direct-to-consumer digital, digital activations, physical stores and social selling. A brand can connect directly with their consumer, making it no longer necessary to rely on third parties or intermediaries to grow their business or sell products. Through direct connection with the customer, brands can find out what their customers want and need, enabling them to create product to meet their needs and sell it at better profit margins.

Key terms

AIDA	live shopping	sales funnel
direct retail	look book	social selling
dropship	marketplace	trunk shows
e-commerce	m-commerce	wholesale
line sheet	omnichannel	

Activity

Select a fashion brand and research the different sales channels it uses to connect with its customers, including wholesale, direct retail, marketplaces and online.

Online resources

Wholesale line sheet and terms and conditions example, and social selling strategy elements.

References

Bradley, S (2022) How do you solve a problem like... eroding customer loyalty? *The Drum*, www.thedrum.com/news/2022/01/25/how-do-you-solve-problem-eroding-customer-loyalty (archived at https://perma.cc/A346-PDY2)

Burke, S (2015) *Fashion Entrepreneur*, Burke Publishing (n.p.)

Business of Fashion (2022) The state of fashion 2022: global gains mask recovery pains, *The Business of Fashion*, www.businessoffashion.com/reports/news-analysis/the-state-of-fashion-2022-industry-report-bof-mckinsey/ (archived at https://perma.cc/MFR9-L8L9)

Crawford, R (2019) What is social selling and how does it work?, *Salesforce*, www.salesforce.com/blog/guide-to-social-selling/ (archived at https://perma.cc/TP6W-95GW)

Di Somma, M (n.d.) Retail brand strategy: role of the flagship store, *Branding Strategy Insider*, www.brandingstrategyinsider.com/retail-brand-strategy-role-of-the-flagship-store/#:~:text=Flagship%20stores%20are%20an%20excellent%20way%20for%20a,Green%E2%80%99s%20call%20to%20%E2%80%9C%20romance%20your%20customers%20%E2%80%9D (archived at https://perma.cc/95KS-V4DC)

Dragon 360 (2011) Who created AIDA? *Dragon 360*

Elisa (2022) Live shopping in fashion retail, *Elisa*, elisa.io/e-book-on-live-shopping-in-fashion-retail/ (archived at https://perma.cc/F7QV-GZ5X)

Fraser, K (2022) Return reduction is the hot topic at 2022 The Lead Summit, *Fashion United*, fashionunited.uk/news/fashion/return-reduction-is-the-hot-topic-at-2022-the-lead-summit/2022071864178 (archived at https://perma.cc/L32R-KF3M)

Giordano, N (2017) How to expand your fashion wholesale business and grow your brand, *StartUp Fashion*, startupfashion.com/how-to-expand-your-fashion-wholesale-business-and-grow-your-brand/ (archived at https://perma.cc/P3A5-CMUW)

Gustavson, J (2021) What is a sales funnel? (and how is it changing?), *Salesforce*, www.salesforce.com/blog/what-is-a-sales-funnel/ (archived at https://perma.cc/44DB-6S9Z)

Human B (n.d.) Growth strategy for fashion brands – fashion business solutions, *Human B*, www.humanb.com/growth-strategy-for-fashion-brands (archived at https://perma.cc/A8VK-JGGT)

Kim, J and Johnson, K (2013) The impact of moral emotions on cause-related marketing campaigns: a cross-cultural examination, *Journal of Business Ethics*, 112(1), pp 79–90

Kim, Y and Sullivan, P (2019) Emotional branding speaks to consumers' heart: the case of fashion brands, *Fashion and Textiles*, https://fashionandtextiles.springeropen.com/articles/10.1186/s40691-018-0164-y (archived at https://perma.cc/MXS9-BBKP)

LinkedIn (n.d.) What is social selling?, *LinkedIn*, business.linkedin.com/sales-solutions/social-selling/what-is-social-selling (archived at https://perma.cc/6SVH-2VTJ)

McCue, T (2018) Social media is increasing brand engagement and sales, *Forbes*, www.forbes.com/sites/tjmccue/2018/06/26/social-media-is-increasing-brand-engagement-and-sales/?sh=3c558cf57cb3 (archived at https://perma.cc/8DU5-ZJKT)

Modern Retail (2022) The retailer's guide to returns and reverse logistics, *Modern Retail*, www.modernretail.co/wp-content/uploads/sites/5/2022/06/HAPPYRETURNS_Guide-to-Returns_060222.pdf (archived at https://perma.cc/9253-JAEZ)

Muras, A (n.d.) What is omnichannel? The advantages, disadvantages and pitfalls, Business.trustedshops.com, business.trustedshops.com/blog/what-is-omni-channel (archived at https://perma.cc/T7RY-VLZH)

Omotoso, M (2018) What is a fashion look book and how to create one?, *Fashion Insiders*, fashioninsiders.co/toolkit/how-to/what-is-fashion-lookbook/ (archived at https://perma.cc/9MTP-YDLK)

Parisi, D (2020) Across fashion sites, the marketplace model is catching on, *Glossy*, www.glossy.co/fashion/why-the-shift-to-the-marketplace-model-is-accelerating/ (archived at https://perma.cc/3YMG-YXCY)

Sailthru (2022) Six ecommerce conversion hacks your brand needs in 2022, *Sailthru*, www.sailthru.com/marketing-blog/six-ecommerce-conversion-hacks/ (archived at https://perma.cc/NK8L-G5BA)

Sherman, L (2016) Does luxury fashion still need wholesale showrooms?, *Vogue Business*, www.voguebusiness.com/consumers/does-luxury-fashion-still-need-wholesale-showrooms-nicholas-k-maggie-marilyn-misha-nonoo (archived at https://perma.cc/2DRY-E7LV)

Shopify (2020) Omnichannel commerce guide, *Enterprise Plus Shopify*, enterprise.plus. shopify.com/rs/932-KRM-548/images/Omnichannel_Commerce_Guide.pdf (archived at https://perma.cc/WSP3-8VP9)

Smith, C (2022) Zara starts charging shoppers for online returns, *BBC News*, www.bbc. co.uk/news/business-61423753 (archived at https://perma.cc/W2FT-NSDW)

Steven, K (2021) How to build a sales funnel for clothing and fashion brand, *Khris Steven*, khrissteven.com/sales-funnel-for-clothing-brand/ (archived at https://perma.cc/N3F8-GUPF)

Tsolova, D (2017) The questionable future of fashion wholesale? *Fashion Insiders*, fashioninsiders.co/features/opinion/the-questionable-future-of-fashion-wholesale/ (archived at https://perma.cc/Y2QA-U2EP)

Vogue Business (2020) How to fund a fashion business without venture capital, *Vogue Business*, www.voguebusiness.com/companies/how-to-fund-fashion-business-without-venture-capital-hsbc (archived at https://perma.cc/K3XE-SVRV)

Yu, A (2019) What does a fashion buyer do?, *Fashion United*, fashionunited.com/education/news/fashion-careers-what-does-a-fashion-buyer-do/2019011825674 (archived at https://perma.cc/X84P-7XEL)

Case study
Pala Eyewear

Founder John Pritchard developed the concept for Pala following travels to Africa in his earlier life, where he learnt about the lack of access to eyecare and discovered the empowerment that comes with a new pair of spectacles or corrective surgery. Pala is a brand on a mission, founded on the ambition to produce high-quality, long-lasting sustainable sunglasses while seeking to deliver lasting change, empowerment and opportunity through funding eyecare projects across Africa.

The brand's social impact business model determines that for every pair of sunglasses sold, Pala gives back to eyecare programmes across Africa, providing grants directly to vision centres, dispensaries, screening and training programmes through their charity partner Vision Aid Overseas. Pala is making a difference, with more than 11,000 sight-impaired people having had their lives positively changed thanks to receiving a pair of prescription glasses or corrective surgery, and the brand is now working with Vision Aid Overseas to build and equip a new vision centre in Sierra Leone.

Pritchard's ambition for Pala is to be the most sustainable eyewear brand on the planet. This is a huge challenge but one that the team wholeheartedly embraces, and the brand promises transparency in communicating its progress towards this goal. As a manufacturer Pala understands the responsibility to drive, measure and benchmark its performance. The brand focuses on innovation to ensure they choose materials for every component of their product – from the lenses to the packaging – that are better for the environment. The transparency in the supply chain has enabled the brand to achieve accreditation with B-Corp. This evidences that as a company Pala is committed, for the benefit of their employees and business operations, to have a materially positive impact on society and the environment as a whole.

Pala is taking an active part in leading the conversation about how to make the eyewear industry more circular and address the challenges of how to make recycling into a more scalable and commercially viable option.

www.palaeyewear.com

Marketing and promotion 10

LEARNING OBJECTIVES

By the end of the chapter, you will be able to:

- Explain the process of marketing for a fashion brand
- Describe the 10Ps of marketing
- Understand different marketing approaches including digital marketing
- Explain the communication channels a fashion brand can use to connect and engage with their consumers

Introduction

A fashion brand cannot jump straight into marketing, they need to develop their brand pillars and storytelling first to ensure that they have a concise story and clear messages to use in their marketing activities. Marketing without a brand strategy can result in mixed messages that could damage the reputation of a label. Branding and marketing work together but it is imperative that they are approached in order, as branding begins within the company and marketing begins with the consumer. If marketing is successful, the brand will live inside the hearts and minds of the consumers and seeing or hearing the brand name will prompt positive perceptions and emotions, leading to an engaged, loyal customer base. The work that was done in the previous chapter on branding will have determined the brand pillars, storytelling and promise to the customer, so the brand would now be ready to move on to marketing and promotion. Marketing is what the brand will do to attract customers to the business through the product, messaging and delivering those branding promises. The chapters on the customer and competitors also feed into the marketing process and should be reviewed again in relation to marketing.

This chapter explains the elements of marketing that are relevant to fashion brands in today's market. It addresses the approaches that brands need to take to respond to changing consumer demand for new experiences, authenticity in their relationships with brands, and transparency in the design and making process.

Today's customer is marketing savvy, not easily fooled, and they tune out many elements of promotion and advertising. This chapter looks at how brands can develop authentic marketing and promotion strategies that create valuable experiences that connect with consumers, draw them into the brand and make them loyal, regular customers.

What is marketing?

It is easy to confuse marketing with advertising and promotion, and while these are two rudiments of marketing, there are many more elements to it. Marketing is a process that is embedded deep within a company and its business plan. Through market research, analysis and understanding of the ideal customer's interests, needs and wants, the marketing process touches on all aspects of a brand, including product development, pricing, merchandizing, distribution methods, sales and promotion. The marketing process is fundamental to the business performance because it addresses the most important aspects of the environment in which the business operates. It ensures that a business reaches the right consumers with the right product at the right price, place and time.

Marketing is a fundamental cornerstone of every fashion business and it is not about promoting and selling products, it is about engaging with the consumer to bring them into the brand's lifestyle and tapping into their aspirations and dreams. Marketing used to focus on one-way broadcast or just pushing out messages, but the world and the industry has moved on, as consumers no longer want to be talked *to*, they want to be talked *with* (Council, 2017). Today marketing focuses on brands creating conversations and engagement with consumers, using multiple channels including public relations, influencer marketing, experiential marketing, digital marketing and content marketing (Business of Fashion, n.d.a).

Marketing is a process, a string of interlinked actions that all need to be addressed to achieve the ultimate goal of customer satisfaction. It has to be a continual process, which is relentlessly worked on in order to main market position and keep the customer.

Figure 10.1 shows the marketing process, a wheel that needs to keep turning with various actions that keep it in motion. A fashion brand may need to keep several wheels in motion, as each one will focus on a specific target group. Starting at the top of the wheel the brand will identify a specific consumer and then circle around to analyse how big is the market for that specific customer, then analyse the competition and see what other brands are targeting the same consumer group. If the market is big enough and there is not too much competition, the brand will analyse the distribution channels for that consumer, which means the ways that they can reach them, before moving on to the marketing mix for that consumer. This link in the

Figure 10.1   The marketing process

process means brands need to ensure they have the right product at the right price, etc, for that customer – the 10Ps marketing mix is covered in more detail below. Having developed the marketing mix the brand will then review their finances to ensure that it is a financially viable decision to market to that specific consumer, as the brand may need to lower prices, or invest in new products or communication channels. If the financial analysis is favourable, then the brand will go ahead and start a marketing campaign to attract that customer, but this is not the end of the process. If a brand does not review and revise, they will struggle to maintain their market position, as the consumers and competitive environment constantly change. A flaw with most marketing plans is that they are written to cover a 12-month pe-riod, but in today's volatile environment circumstances can change quickly, which can render the brand's carefully crafted plan obsolete (Bly, 2018).

Market research

Every business needs accurate and detailed information in order to be successful. Market research is an integral part of business planning and provides a wealth of information about prospective customers, the competition and the industry in general. Good market research will provide the brand with relevant data to identify the target group, product differentiation and competitive advantages needed for the marketing strategy. The primary and secondary research identified in earlier chapters, including identifying the customer and competitors as well as the environmental scanning business tools, all feed into the marketing strategy. In the development of the strategy, a brand needs to revisit their PESTLE and SWOT analyses, to ensure that they have an external and internal view of the environment in which their company operates in order to identify a competitive advantage. Without the research that these business tools provide, the brand may miss out changes in the industry, consumer behaviours and new technologies, which could be disastrous. Another major business model that needs to be used in developing the marketing strategy and any future campaigns is the PACE model (Figure 10.2), which was introduced in Chapter 1 on Putting the customer first. This model concerns the changing behaviours of consumers who seek brands that offer greater protection, acceptance, connection and engagement.

The PACE model is important for brands to include in their marketing strategy, as it will drive how the brand will adapt its activities, storytelling and behaviours to meet the needs of future consumers.

The marketing mix – the 10Ps

The marketing mix is the combination of factors that a brand can use to create an effective strategy to promote its business, products and services. While the basic marketing mix is often referred to as the 4Ps of marketing – product, place, price and promotion – for fashion brands it is essential that they augment this with additional factors that make up the 10Ps of marketing. The 10 elements are product, price, place, promotion, people, process, physical, packaging, personality and proof (Figure 10.3). This formula of 10 elements has to work together as if they were musical instruments in an orchestra – no instrument is more important than the other, each has a part to play and it is when they all come together in a symphony that beautiful music is made (Denney-Stone, 2015).

- *Product:* A fashion brand needs to create a unique product or range of products that stand out in a saturated market, with clearly defined tangible and intangible benefits that will make it appealing to the consumer.

- *Place:* A fashion brand can sell their products in numerous places both online and in physical stores. A brand needs to sell their products in places where their customer can discover and/or easily access it. The places need to offer the buying experience that the consumer expects or desires.

- *Price:* The price of the product needs to make sense to the consumer, as well as be profitable to the brand. The pricing of the product can affect the consumer's perception of value, and the pricing architecture for the product range needs to be consistent and appropriate to the market and customer.

Figure 10.2   PACE model

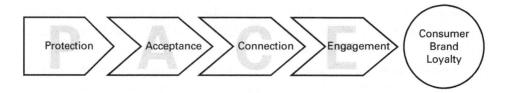

Figure 10.3   The 10Ps of fashion marketing

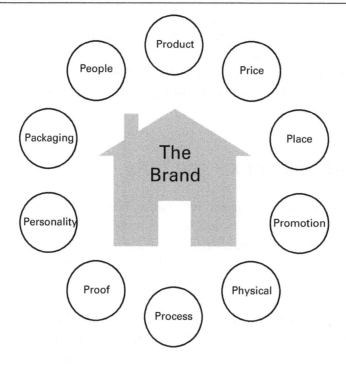

- *Promotion:* Promotion covers the many different ways a brand can promote their brand and products, including advertising, sales funnels, PR, sales promotions, content marketing and social media. The brand needs to use the right channels that connect with the target audience in a way that will appeal to their emotions and provide a return on investment.

- *People:* The people factor relates to both the people in the organization as well as the current and potential consumer. The brand needs to ensure that they have the right people on the team who can represent the company, grow the business and connect with the consumers. They also need to identify the right target consumer to ensure that the marketing efforts hit the target, as a scattergun approach could fall on stony ground.

- *Processes:* The processes are the services that a brand offers their customers to ensure an easy and enjoyable shopping experience, both online and in person. The processes can include easy checkout, apps, automated systems and programs, payment terms, delivery and return processes, as well as the omnichannel systems that make it easy for the customer to see, find and purchase products on any channel.

- *Physical evidence:* The physical evidence of the 10Ps relates to the tangible elements that the consumer can evidence in their connections with the brand. These elements can include an impressive building, great website, the brand's brochures and advertising, the brand imagery and content, staff uniforms and store windows. Well branded physical evidence can be highly reassuring and persuasive to potential customers as it builds trust and creates emotional connections.

- *Packaging:* With an increase in online shopping, packaging has become a priority for most brands as it adds to the customer experience, and if done badly consumers are more likely to return goods. The purpose of packaging is to protect what is inside from damage, but it is also the first thing the customer will see from any online purchase. Cheap or ugly packaging can affect the perception your customer has of the value of the product.

- *Personality:* A vital factor of marketing is the personality of the brand, the brand owners and staff teams in an era when consumers look for authentic, transparent engagement with a brand. The brand's personality helps it to connect and engage with a customer and helps form a community around the brand of like-minded people.

- *Proof:* This refers to the reviews, testimonials or customer content that help other customers make a decision. In today's online world, we are used to looking for proof before we decide to make a purchase, and if there are no reviews or they are less than positive we move on to a similar product or brand. Social proof or happy customer reviews are one of the biggest drivers for new customers to make a purchase, with influencers playing a large part in the social proof process.

When a brand defines their 10Ps, they will have a marketing mix that will position the brand with a unique selling proposition (USP) to their customers. A brand should not be unique in only one element, such as just product or just price, because this leaves it open to being copied. The unique combination of elements from the 10Ps marketing mix is what will enable the brand to stay ahead of the competition.

Neuromarketing

Neuromarketing is a form of market research that studies customer behaviour and how it affects their buying patterns. Understanding neuromarketing is essential for fashion brands, as emotions greatly influence the consumer's choices and decisions when purchasing fashion (Murray, 2013). Neuromarketing uses emotional triggers to promote a brand based on the psychological traits of the target customer. Brands use neuromarketing to increase sales and create emotional triggers in their customers, using a host of different tools including storytelling, inspiring fear, altruism or social proof.

Tell stories

Stories trigger emotions and a good story will create positive thoughts. Customers love stories, as they appeal to their decision-making processes in a way that facts and figures don't. Brand storytelling can include the purpose, as well as the elements that make the brand and the product unique.

Inspire fear

An unusual approach but this is the fear of missing out rather than abject terror. Brands use this technique by creating limited edition pieces, or through time limited offers, which can incentivize the customer to see now and buy now.

Altruism

Altruism, or giving back, can be a powerful tool for building customer recognition and loyalty. As today's consumer is looking for authenticity and transparency, a brand should only use altruism if it is authentic. There needs to be a genuine reason, a clear purpose and an authentic connection between the charity and the brand or product. Genuine altruism can work and will provide a connection and sense of belonging for social-conscious customers.

Social proof

Social proof is evidence of how other customers have experienced the product and loved it, which encourages other customers to buy as well. One happy customer always makes another one.

Digital marketing

Digital marketing is the use of digital technologies to find, engage and connect with consumers and market the brand and its products to them. With so much competition for users' time and attention, it is important that a brand invests in developing unique approaches for each of the main channels of digital marketing, including website, email, social media, SEO, m-commerce, display ads and click per view (Figure 10.4). While digital advancements bring lots of positive results, there are also challenges around consumer data privacy, accurate segmentation of audiences, validating campaign performance and measuring return on investment, which have all become more complicated. Brands are also having to adapt to digital marketing approaches, which are more informal, with more interactive engagement needed to attract consumers (Behl, 2021).

E-commerce and m-commerce

Having an e-commerce website is an absolute imperative for every fashion brand post-pandemic. A fashion brand's website needs to deliver a brand experience through inspirational storytelling, as well as being a platform to sell product, with branded messaging, style and aesthetic that is cohesive across all platforms. The website is the brand's shop window, so it needs to be user friendly, aspirational, up-to-date and entice the consumer to stay.

A website needs to work as effectively on a mobile phone as it does on a laptop. Shopping through mobile phones has continued to grow from strength to strength for the fashion sector and m-commerce growth is predicted to continue for fashion sales (Behl, 2021). Mobile marketing is an essential tool in a brand's strategy as consumers spend their lives now on phones – making payments, getting directions, playing games and shopping – and they are ready to get closer with brands through text. Mobile devices are becoming their most important shopping tool and 58 per cent of shoppers say that texting is the ideal way for brands to communicate with them. Of the marketers who have already employed a mobile strategy, 41 per cent report that they have seen increasing text opt-in rates (Bluecore, 2022).

Figure 10.4 Digital marketing channels

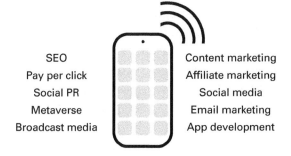

SEO
Pay per click
Social PR
Metaverse
Broadcast media

Content marketing
Affiliate marketing
Social media
Email marketing
App development

Brands can now create a bridge between online and in-store shopping through mobile integration to provide a truly omnichannel experience. From maps to apps to QR codes, the brand can connect the physical with the digital experience through their consumer's device and texting them can be a great place to start (Bluecore, 2022). Shoppers want personalized messages that sound like any other text message they get, and the brand has to take this deeper than just using a customer's first name or congratulating them on a birthday (Bluecore, 2022).

Search engine optimization

SEO (search engine optimization) needs to be part of a brand's long-term marketing strategy to make sure their site is highly visible to search engines such as Google. Having a good presence on search-engine results pages (SERPs) increases traffic to the website and increases the chance of customers discovering them. SEO involves using keywords in all content that match the phrases a customer may be searching for in order to improve product searches. SEO also includes keyword optimization, meta descriptions, link building, site speed and crawl rate optimization.

Pay per click

Pay per click (PPC) is a paid form of digital marketing advertising that brands use to push their name to the very top of the search-engine results pages. This is crucial, as many users instinctively click on the paid links at the top of Google and no longer scroll down very far. With PPC the brand can set their own budget and monitor the results they are getting, as well as tracking the amount it costs to get a user to click on an advert.

Social media

Social media is saturated with brands and content; therefore, it takes a significant amount of time and effort for a brand to stand out and connect with potential customers. With careful, effective targeting, a brand can build brand awareness, increase engagement, make sales, or drive traffic to its website. As social media channels constantly change their algorithms, brands need to regularly adjust their activity to achieve results. If brands are going to run social media adverts and sponsored posts on their platforms, they need to be clear on their objectives to ensure they get a return on investment such as an increase in engagement or sales.

Content marketing

Content marketing is an essential part of the digital marketing process. Mediums include blog posts, videos, ezines and social media stories and posts, as well as a variety of other digital content that provides information and connects with the brand's audience. Brands have to craft content that tells the brand's story as well as bring the consumer into the brand with user-generated content.

> A marketer is someone who makes decisions, develops and executes the marketing strategies for an organization, whereas a marketeer is someone who connects and engages with consumers, building relationships. In today's digital world, brands need to think like a marketeer and act like a creator!

Email marketing

Email marketing is one of the biggest drivers to online sales and helps keep a brand top of mind with consumers; the downside is that consumer inboxes are flooded every day with automated emails. Brands need to manage their email marketing campaigns effectively or it can be a waste of time. A good email newsletter can keep an audience engaged, build strong customer relationships and expand reach (Samson, 2022).

Email newsletters are a powerful way of connecting with a customer on a regular basis. By using platforms such as Mailchimp or Active Campaign, brands can create impactful campaigns that offer more personalized engagement with their communities. The content of the email is the important factor, using it as an opportunity to engage, educate or inform the customer about subjects they are interested in, the purpose of the brand, how products are made, or bringing the customer into a community rather than just promoting products. According to Mailchimp, one in every five emails will be opened if it is well crafted; brands can connect with customers where they live, on their phones and on email. Email campaigns give brands a good return on investment reach (Samson, 2022).

Affiliate marketing

Affiliate marketing uses a third party such as an influencer to promote products using a unique tracking code and the brand pays them a commission on the sales they generate. Brands use this type of marketing as a way to reach new audiences and gain credibility through the affiliate's relationships with their following. There are different types of affiliate marketing but the recommended approach for fashion brands is 'involved affiliate marketing', which is working with affiliates who only recommend products and services they use and truly believe in (Hayes, 2022). This more genuine approach builds trust and shows brand authenticity.

App development

Since the growth in m-commerce, an app is a huge sales and marketing opportunity for a fashion brand. According to Launchmetrics, a successful fashion app can deepen connections with consumers, foster brand loyalty and drive sales (Launchmetrics Team, 2019). For an app to work effectively, a brand can offer exclusive offers, and add value through personalization, unique content and a greater sense of community. An app adds an additional feature to the brand's omnichannel retail model.

Broadcast media

Broadcast media refers to video and audio content, which was traditionally broadcast through TV and radio, but today includes distribution through the internet and apps. Fashion brands are initiating new forms of broadcast media into their marketing plans including podcasts, fashion film, video content and live streaming either as an invited guest on other platforms or through their own channels. Live shopping is a very commercially focused form of broadcast, which drives engagement and conversions and is predicted to be one of the biggest e-commerce trends of the future (Wynne Lockhart, 2022). Brands can also consider audio as well as visual platforms, with new platforms developed such as Clubhouse, Discord and Twitter Spaces where brands can engage with potential consumers through open conversations and discussions.

Metaverse

As new metaverse opportunities start to emerge, fashion brands are rushing to stake their claim in this new online network of 3D virtual worlds focused on social connection. The metaverse offers opportunities for brands to translate their values and brand storytelling in different formats, helping them connect with new audiences through immersive experiences. Every type of fashion brand needs to plan their participation in the metaverse, as this is where consumers will be spending time online, whether to work, play, socialize or shop (McKinsey and Company, 2022). Brands looking to enter the metaverse will need to improve their understanding of the roles that NFTs, gaming, avatars and virtual fashion will play in the future of their interactions with their customers and how they will sell products. They will also need to consider how they can express their creativity while remaining true to their brand ethos and purpose.

An introduction into the metaverse for many fashion brands has been gamification, with many of the luxury labels experimenting in this field by partnering with platforms like Roblox to test new forms of promotion (Spaziani, 2022). There has been a growth of brands creating their own virtual worlds, where consumers can represent themselves through personalized avatars, which can enjoy a host of experiences from attending virtual catwalk shows to visiting luxury hotels, villas or stores.

All these forms of digital marketing offer brand engagement that can be used to replace or augment traditional marketing approaches. The purpose of all activity is ensuring two-way communication with customers that helps build connections, truly engage consumers and build a relationship with them. Brands need to use digital marketing to provide a seamless experience for the consumer, regardless of which channel they encounter the brand on.

The marketing strategy

The marketing strategy is a working plan that acts as a driver for all the marketing and promotional activities of the brand. A major component of success for any fashion brand is having an effective marketing strategy, one that gives the business direction and clarity, while making sure it stays ahead of the competition. In the volatile fashion industry, a good marketing strategy that embraces all the new opportunities offered through digital marketing will keep the brand not only afloat but growing, while other brands flounder in confusion (Appnova, n.d.). The strategy identifies ways for the brand to be proactive and agile, keeping their consumer at the forefront of everything they do to ensure they are creating products and services that meet their customer needs. The strategy is based on the brand's research into customer profiles, competitor research, PESTLE, SWOT and the 10Ps marketing mix. It will include a situational analysis of the external environment and the current market as well as identifying potential changes, challenges and opportunities in the future.

The marketing strategy fits within the overall business plan, but it is also a working document that stands on its own to help the brand achieve its vision. To achieve this, the strategy needs to include SMART objectives, which means steps that are specific, measurable, achievable, realistic and timely. By setting these objectives, a brand can ensure it stays on track to success.

A marketing plan can be as unique as the brand – the example in Table 10.1 gives some of the generic headings that are used in most marketing strategies.

Table 10.1　Marketing plan template

Executive summary
The executive summary always comes first but is written last. It summarizes each of the sections below to give an overview of the plan.
Background
The history of the brand, why it was formed and the competitive advantage.
Situation analysis
Include research and information on the market, competitors, trends, demographics, PEST and SWOT analysis.
Competitive analysis
Competitor analysis and differentiation.
Customer analysis
Detailed consumer analysis and customer profiles.
The brand
The brand's purpose, unique selling proposition (USP), value proposition and explain the brand tone, voice, personality.
The marketing mix – 10Ps
The brand's 10Ps of product, price, place, promotion, people, process, packaging, personality, proof and physical evidence.
Objectives and goals
What the brand wants to achieve using smart objectives.

(*Continued*)

Table 10.1 (Continued)

The implementation plan
The activities needed to implement the marketing plan to meet the goals, including resources such as time, people and budget.

The marketing budget
Full breakdown of the costs to deliver the marketing activity.

Additional information

Fashion promotion

Fashion promotion is the thread that holds together all the different processes of a fashion brand. Fashion promotion links the brand and its products with the wider world, raising awareness and interest in a manner that will generate sales. The different aspects of fashion promotion include fashion journalism, advertising, visual merchandizing and PR. It is only the larger fashion brands that can afford to advertise their businesses, as paid announcements and media cost a considerable amount of money. However, all brands can develop a strong PR communications strategy.

Public relations (PR) aims to achieve understanding, influence opinion and behaviour, and improve the credibility and reputation of the brand. A good reputation is not earned overnight, it takes time, planning and sustained effort to establish and maintain goodwill and build relationships between a brand and its public. A fashion brand's public includes their current and potential customers, suppliers, partners, sponsors, or in fact everyone the brand comes into contact with. All PR activities have to be carefully managed and undertaken with integrity and honesty, as a brand's reputation is very fragile and can be quickly lost. While in the past, most public relations focused on third parties, or the intermediaries between the brand and the actual customer such as magazines, newspapers and department stores, more often than not now brands use PR to build relationships direct with the customer through their own channels such as social media.

There are many promotional approaches and techniques that fashion brands can use, from traditional routes such as selling stories into magazines and newspapers, to more cutting-edge elements such as gamification, podcasts or user-generated content. Business of Fashion advises brands that a strong PR strategy can result in organic media exposure, as well as influencer endorsements through celebrity placement, gifting, or wardrobe loans for events (Business of Fashion, n.d.b).

Larger, established fashion brands are more likely to recruit a PR agency to act on their behalf to build and maintain relationships with publications and stylists, write and send out press releases and generate press coverage, product placement and social media mentions. Smaller, independent brands often have to work on public relations themselves, communicating directly with their consumers while also trying to build relationships with journalists, editors and stylists.

PR has always played a primary role in fashion, but conventional approaches have been affected by digital advancements and changed due to consumers reading less and purchasing fewer magazines. Instead, customers look for more authentic content and brand storytelling that they can consume in bitesize pieces that capture their imagination and engage them. Consumers look for this type of content on social media or online sites, therefore brands need to focus their activity on the places where their customers are. Brands need to regularly review their PR tactics to ensure they are targeting their activity to someone who is listening and not just adding to all the 'noise' that everyone else is busy making.

Digital press pack

In order to participate in PR activities, firstly a brand needs to create a digital press pack to have everything ready to send to a journalist as soon as they have spoken to them. It is advised to create a press pack folder online on a site such as Dropbox or Google Drive. The digital press pack could include a profile of the brand, the latest press release, both high-res and low-res images of the collection, the latest look book, details of stockists and celebrity dressing, an image of the designer/brand founder and a price list.

Traditional public relations

The traditional approach to PR in fashion involved the brand raising awareness through press coverage and product placement in print magazines, journals or newspapers as well as on TV and film. These approaches rely on the brand employing a PR professional, either in-house or an agency, to build the relationships with the publications, contact editors and writers to feature the brand; creating and placing exclusive stories and features in magazines; product placement in shopping pages, as well as building relationships with stylists, so that they select the brand for their editorial shoots or celebrity clients. Traditional PR would also involve the organization and management of fashion events such as catwalk shows, presentations, installations and press days.

New approaches to PR

The advancement of new digital technologies has resulted in changes in the public relations process, making traditional approaches no longer relevant for fashion brands. Many of the fashion print magazines and newspaper titles that fashion brands would want to be featured in have closed due to diminishing reader numbers. Brands also recognized that traditional content in print press no longer connected with consumers who sought engagement, as well as it being difficult to measure any return on investment.

The advancement of social PR, sometimes called consumer PR, offers a more efficient and effective PR approach using the digital communication channels consumers are already using to participate in online communities. It offers the opportunity for two-way communication direct with current and potential customers, and enables brands to collect data through feedback and engagement. Social media is fast moving, providing stories straight from the source in real time, which has made it a much more effective communication channel for brands, allowing them to communicate and engage directly with their audience (Cicero and Bernay, n.d.). The growth of social media has had a huge impact on the fashion industry, influencing how brands now sell and promote their collections. Fashion houses used to build their businesses around the fashion week seasons, in order to introduce their brands to both store buyers and the press, but this business model is no longer necessary when the brand can talk directly to the customer. Rather than waiting months for a product to appear in a magazine or a store, the customer can now watch the latest catwalk shows from their couch, shop some collections direct from the catwalk, or buy the dress direct from a post on Instagram.

Social PR should now be integrated into the strategic organizational plan to ensure the brand is constantly talking directly to their current and potential customer. Brands need to be dedicating time to directly engage with followers, answer questions, share information and include them in the conversation. Social PR takes a more informal approach to meet the consumer's demand for more conversational messaging and conversation with real people representing the brand (Carufel, 2021). As consumers turn to social spaces to communicate, this does not just involve digital channels, they also want to meet brands in real life too. Fashion brands should integrate both physical and digital elements into their communication mix to interact with the current and future consumers across a range of channels.

Brand activations – the communication mix

Brand activations is a marketing and promotional discipline aimed at driving action through shared experiences, events and interactions. It is a communications mix that integrates all the brand's communication assets to a focused channel to make the brand known to potential customers and increase awareness and engagement through a brand experience (Figure 10.5). Brand activations have become an essential tool for brands that need to stand out from the thousands of others that are also trying to catch the consumer's attention (Send Pulse, n.d.).

An activation offers a more interactive, effective and experiential method to attract the consumer and make the brand recognizable. There are many different forms that can be integrated into the brand's activations and communications mix, as detailed below. All the elements of the marketing mix can be used to create brand activation campaigns that are interactive, creative and engaging in order to bring the consumer into the brand's world and lifestyle.

Interactive marketing

Interactive marketing is activity that focuses on consumer involvement and collaborative activities. Hubspot describe interactive marketing as a tactic that uses engaging imagery and videos to capture the consumer's attention and delight them, with call to actions to prompt the consumer to participate, comment or give feedback (Chi, n.d.). Interactive marketing also includes competitions, quizzes, polls, gifs or clickable content.

Figure 10.5   Brand activations – the communication mix

Sales promotions

Sales promotions do not have to mean price discounts. Brands should look at promotions that build loyalty to increase the lifetime value of customers, boost engagement and drive repeat purchases. This can be through early access to new products or sales, free shipping, member only discounts and charitable giving. Bolt reported that while engagement with loyalty programmes had gone down, consumers are returning as they actively look for reward points, cash back and discounts due to the economic crisis. The Bolt consumer report evidenced that, in 2021, 44 per cent of shoppers earned and redeemed points compared to 37 per cent in 2020 (Bolt, 2022). Brands need to constantly review changing consumer concerns and demands to tailor their loyalty programme to offer solutions that customers want.

Events and experiences

The fashion industry has always driven promotional activity through events, including catwalk shows, presentations, press days, launch events and parties. Every day in every fashion city around the world there are a lot of events to attend, which means competition is tough to get people to attend. It is challenging to create events that are memorable as well as achieving a good return on investment. Fashion events are notoriously expensive to produce, with Forbes reporting that on average in 2019, a 10- or 15-minute fashion show can cost anywhere from $200,000 to over $1 million (London, 2019). Sometimes in the excitement and glamour of fashion events, it is forgotten that brands need a return of investment to equal the expenditure. Events need to generate sale not just a few Instagram posts or column inches.

With many brands now turning away from fashion weeks to focus on consumer events, brand activation events create fun, memorable experiences that help customers remember the brand through direct engagement, understand the brand story and feel part of a unique community. A successful brand activation drives in-store or event traffic and greater social engagement that can travel beyond the event itself.

Advertising

Advertising is defined as paid for, non-personal communication through mass media channels used to promote a product, service or contact in a creative way. Consumers are bombarded with advertising every minute of every day online, in magazines, billboards and through TV and radio. It is therefore very difficult to get their attention. Advertising relies on repetition for success, so brands using a drip-feed method are more likely to gain attention and make the viewer notice their message (UK Essays, 2018).

PR

Brand activations provide public relations opportunities for brands to build relationships with customers as well as a chance to generate press coverage, social media and attention.

Influencers and ambassadors

Influencer marketing has been a popular strategy for many fashion brands who have been working with content creators and brand ambassadors to reach new audiences, raise brand awareness and generate sales leads. While working with an online content creator means a brand can benefit from their creativity and authenticity, influencer marketing can be tricky. It isn't about finding someone with a lot of followers, it's about finding the right person who has 'influence' over their community that will result in sales (Hall, 2022). Many brands have failed in their influencer marketing strategies due to lack of research, choosing the wrong person, or being distracted by the numbers of followers rather than looking at the influence. Spending money to gift products or pay influencers to promote the brand on an account with a large number of fake followers is money wasted. Research now shows that micro-influencers, those with less than 100,000 followers, tend to have more influence, trust and engagement within their social circle than big celebrities (Sahraee, 2022). Building a relationship with a brand ambassador can be more beneficial than working with an influencer, as they are perceived by consumers as more authentic followers of the brand.

Social media

Social media is now an indispensable part of the marketing strategy for a fashion brand, enabling them to have better engagement with their customers. For social media to be successful as part of the communications mix, brands have to adopt a 'content is king' strategy, which was identified by Bill Gates in an essay where he stated that content is where the real money is made on the internet (Davis, n.d.). Brands can use social media channels to tell stories direct to their consumers in the way the customer wants to see and hear it, offering authenticity and transparency in the stories they tell about their brand and products.

Brands are not limited in the channels they use, they just need to identify the ones that their potential consumers are already using, which can include Instagram, TikTok, LinkedIn, Facebook, Snapchat, Pinterest or Twitter, or audio platforms like Clubhouse and Anyone. As each platform has different benefits, content styles and followers, a brand needs to consider which ones to focus on and the type of content that will work on each channel.

Content and communications plan

The content and communications plan links into the brand and marketing strategies to ensure an integrated approach to how and through which channels the brand messaging is shared. It is essential that brands develop the right messages and content, as well as using the right media at the right time to attract and maintain their target audience.

The communications plan details the targeted audience, the distribution channels and the type of content to be shared, with an evaluation plan to measure engagement and success. The content plan pulls together all the marketing and branding assets, SEO and engagement tracking research, as well as the budget to achieve the goals. It is aligned with the sales funnel for the brand, as the content should achieve the outcomes of raising awareness, interest and desire. Along with realistic and achievable objectives, the content plan will detail the style and aesthetic that will be most engaging to the target audience including social media, blog posts, email marketing, campaign shoots or video content. In an increasingly visual world, the need for powerful, impactful images has never been more important. The images bring the brand to life, helping it stand out while giving it a personality and adding perceived value. Fashion brands need a library of images to use across all their platforms, including both still and moving imagery. Vogue reported that with endless e-commerce options, the way fashion products are shot and displayed is an essential purchase driver for brands and marketplaces (Schiffer, 2019). Brands need to consider every small detail from framing and lighting to the styling, as it can make or break the customer's decision to add to cart.

The success of a content plan is reliant on cohesive and engaging content as well as consistent engagement. Therefore, to execute the plan effectively, a brand needs to have a detailed schedule with dates and times for all content posting (Indeed, 2022).

User-generated content

As consumers no longer trust advertising as much as they have in the past, user-generated content has stepped forward as a proven way to help grow a brand and increase conversions. User-generated content refers to unpaid content that is created by the audience, when they share posts raving about a brand's products or services (Mazouri, 2021). This organic form of content can be far more effective and impactful than carefully constructed brand content, as it offers the greater authenticity and transparency that consumers are looking for.

Evaluation

Brands have to put evaluation into their communication plans to ensure they are achieving results from all their activity. They need to plan ongoing monitoring to evaluate each platform and be prepared to adapt their approach when consumers, the market or the platforms change. If their account lacks engagement or is not gaining new followers, then they may need to make a change such as new style posts or images, new hashtags, confirm their customers are still on the platform or try something completely different in order to be more successful.

Summary

This chapter has reviewed the elements of marketing that are relevant to fashion brands in today's market. It has looked at how brands need to develop authentic marketing and promotion strategies that create valuable experiences that connect with consumers, draw them into the brand and make them loyal and regular customers. For a brand to survive and succeed, they will always need to be a step ahead of the competition. Marketing helps a business adapt to a changing world and shifting consumer behaviours. The tools they use to connect with and sell to a customer today will change over time and there are constantly new challenges in trying to get a brand heard in a crowded marketplace. Marketeers need to be entrepreneurial in their approach, using every marketing and communication tool they can to reach out to and connect with their customers. This includes traditional print media as well as social media and new digital channels. Marketing activity will continue to move towards more experiential rewards that offer greater value to the consumer than discounts. Businesses need to build a community around their brand, rewarding loyal customers with one-of-a-kind experiences that they cannot get anywhere else. This chapter has detailed the benefits of a strong marketing strategy and the need to have a working marketing plan that acts like a daily driver of marketing activity for the business.

Key terms

activations	interactive	proof
affiliates	marketing	SEO
altruism	m-commerce	social PR
content	metaverse	user-generated content
experience	neuro-marketing	
influencer marketing	PR	

Activity

Choose a fashion brand and analyse their marketing and promotion activity to determine what they do well and what can be improved.

Online resources

PowerPoint presentation with marketing plan and 10Ps marketing mix.

References

Appnova (n.d.) 10 most effective marketing strategies for fashion brand, *Appnova*, www.appnova.com/marketing-strategies-for-fashion-brand/#:~:text=Every%20fashion%20brand%20needs%20a%20good%20marketing%20strategy,but%20also%20grow%20as%20others%20flounder%20in%20confusion (archived at https://perma.cc/JN3A-42EJ)

Behl, S (2021) Digital marketing for fashion industry: the ultimate guide, *Digital Vidya*, www.digitalvidya.com/blog/digital-marketing-for-fashion-industry-a-complete-guide/ (archived at https://perma.cc/E4QV-Z5W6)

Bluecore (2022) Retail SMS | retail text message marketing, *Blue Core*, simpletexting.com/guide/sms-marketing-for-retail/ (archived at https://perma.cc/2SJJ-9JVB)

Bly, R (2018) Why and when to review your marketing plan, *Entrepreneur*, www.entrepreneur.com/article/253483 (archived at https://perma.cc/U2U5-TNEY)

Bolt (2022) Industry report on loyalty programmes, *Bolt*, Bolt.com (archived at https://perma.cc/FQY2-65GG)

Business of Fashion (n.d.a) Fashion marketing and communications, *The Business of Fashion*, www.businessoffashion.com/education/collection/fashion-marketing-communications (archived at https://perma.cc/V6EJ-KMMK)

Business of Fashion (n.d.b) The basics | part 8 – marketing, *The Business of Fashion*, www.businessoffashion.com/articles/news-analysis/the-basics-part-8-marketing/ (archived at https://perma.cc/B9HZ-QK6A)

Carufel, R (2021) Consumers crave more personal, conversational brand messaging with local businesses, *Agility PR Solutions*, www.agilitypr.com/pr-news/public-relations/consumers-crave-more-personal-conversational-brand-messaging-with-local-businesses/ (archived at https://perma.cc/FEQ7-C6QP)

Chi, C (n.d.) What is interactive marketing [+ 15 inventive examples], *Blog.hubspot.com*, blog.hubspot.com/marketing/interactive-marketing (archived at https://perma.cc/A577-3C86)

Cicero and Bernay (n.d.) What is the difference between PR and social media?, *Cicero and Bernay*, www.cbpr.me/difference-pr-social-media/ (archived at https://perma.cc/5DZT-CMLH)

Council, F (2017) Council post: marketing is no longer a one-way street, *Forbes*, www.forbes.com/sites/forbesagencycouncil/2017/03/28/marketing-is-no-longer-a-one-way-street/amp/ (archived at https://perma.cc/B23V-RXNV)

Davis, D (n.d.) Content is king – why you still need great content in 2022, *Social Planner*, socialplanner.io/blog/content-is-king/ (archived at https://perma.cc/4F77-NXLT)

Denney-Stone, H (2015) The 10Ps of marketing, *LinkedIn*, www.linkedin.com/pulse/10-ps-marketing-helen-denney-stone (archived at https://perma.cc/AWQ9-UMET)

Hall, L (2022) Influencer marketing, *Digital Marketing Institute*, digitalmarketinginstitute.com/blog/influencer-marketing-guide?utm_source=Email&utm_medium=Email&utm_campaign=free-members-weekly-tips&mkt_tok=NjI1LUdYSi0xODcAAAGFTjX2v6U3sBaCqylmbO8EH8U824A1wgoECxxk4q0Vgufu1K5mPNVfe3TPUltdZnh8GSpBAjwSfsMmLKOTwcwU4G6MpFWh42-qiX7TnCxi4gjYsw (archived at https://perma.cc/Q3UK-GU33)

Hayes, M (2022) What is affiliate marketing and how to get started, *Shopify*, www.shopify.co.uk/blog/affiliate-marketing (archived at https://perma.cc/P6UE-9XF4)

Indeed (2022) How to create an effective communication plan, *Indeed Career Guide*, www.indeed.com/career-advice/career-development/communication-planning

Launchmetrics Team (2019) How these fashion apps are winning over consumers, *Launchmetrics*, www.launchmetrics.com/resources/blog/fashion-app (archived at https://perma.cc/2QUF-4H9S)

London, L (2019) How much does fashion week cost (and what is the ROI)?, *Forbes*, www.forbes.com/sites/lelalondon/2019/02/14/how-much-fashion-week-cost-what-is-roi/?sh=2afa4f805eec (archived at https://perma.cc/FB6S-U2QC)

Mazouri, H (2021) User-generated content, *Sprout Social*, sproutsocial.com/insights/user-generated-content-guide/ (archived at https://perma.cc/5YHV-NSJ8)

McKinsey and Company (2022) How the fashion industry can get into a metaverse mindset, *McKinsey*, www.mckinsey.com/industries/retail/our-insights/how-the-fashion-industry-can-get-into-a-metaverse-mindset (archived at https://perma.cc/ED7F-QZTY)

Murray, P (2013) How emotions influence what we buy, *Psychology Today*, www.psychologytoday.com/us/blog/inside-the-consumer-mind/201302/how-emotions-influence-what-we-buy (archived at https://perma.cc/DV3B-VJ2F)

Sahraee, Z (2022) Everything about micro influencers in 2022, *Blog.ainfluencer*, blog.ainfluencer.com/everything-about-micro-influencers/#:~:text=Micro%20influencers%20in%20comparison%20to%20other%20influencers%E2%80%99%20types,results%20and%20be%20more%20affordable%20for%20marketing%20campaigns (archived at https://perma.cc/4D5H-PFUB)

Samson, E (2022) Email marketing in 2022 (utilizing campaigns to drive sales), *The Big Commerce Blog*, www.bigcommerce.com/blog/email-marketing/ (archived at https://perma.cc/2RES-3RWG)

Schiffer, J (2019) How fashion brands use product imagery to sell their story, *Vogue Business*, www.voguebusiness.com/fashion/fashion-brands-use-product-imagery-to-sell-their-story (archived at https://perma.cc/Z7NS-4QQU)

Send Pulse (n.d.) What is brand activation: ideas and examples - definition, *Send Pulse*, sendpulse.com/support/glossary/brand-activation (archived at https://perma.cc/A2XW-BJ9B)

Spaziani, M (2022) How the fashion world is moving into the metaverse, *Inglobe Technologies*, www.inglobetechnologies.com/fashion-worl-and-metaverse/ (archived at https://perma.cc/X9WF-TVGX)

UK Essays (2018) Advertising and communication mix marketing essay, *UK Essays*, www.ukessays.com/essays/marketing/advertising-and-communication-mix-marketing-essay.php?vref=1 (archived at https://perma.cc/PR4X-7AAV)

Wynne Lockhart, J (2022) Live shopping: how to launch a live event (2022), *Shopify Plus*, www.shopify.com/enterprise/live-shopping (archived at https://perma.cc/48Y5-84NZ)

Case study Unhidden

Unhidden is a multi-award winning, socially responsible, adaptive fashion brand that creates stylish, inclusive and ethically made designs for people with and without disabilities. Unhidden was the first adaptive brand to become a member of the British Fashion Council and show on the official London Fashion Week schedule.

The brand has adopted a socially responsible approach that commits to more than just sustainable fabric goals, it also cares about the people throughout its supply chain. Unhidden also believes in radical transparency, providing customers with price breakdowns on their product pages on the website, as well as sharing information on its suppliers, makers and materials used in both the product and packaging.

Unhidden was founded by Victoria Jenkins, a garment technologist with 14 years' experience in the fashion industry, who became disabled in her twenties. Victoria had already realized that most of her old clothes did not adjust to her own new needs, but the main initiator of the line came from a hospital stay in 2016 when Victoria met a fellow patient who had survived cancer but was left with multiple other conditions. This patient was frustrated and struggling with constantly having to remove all her clothing in front of doctors and nurses to access her stomach, chest port, or cannulas for treatments or doctor appointments. She was unable to find clothing that was stylish and adaptable to meet her needs, so was having to rely on pyjama tops and loungewear. This encounter sparked the development of Unhidden and its aim to develop fashionable yet practical, universal and adaptive designs.

Unhidden is on a growth trajectory, continuing to develop ethically made, inclusive fashion as well as creating equity for the disabled and chronically sick community through representation and self-expression in fashion. Alongside the label, Victoria also writes, speaks and advocates on disability awareness, accessibility and inclusive design, including delivering a TEDx talk in summer 2022.

www.unhiddenclothing.com

Finance

LEARNING OBJECTIVES

By the end of this chapter, you will be able to:

- Identify different ways fashion brands raise finance
- Understand the basics of cash accounting
- Explain how fashion brands determine their prices

Introduction

Fashion brands, even those that are purpose driven or created for social impact, need to make a profit. Understanding and maintaining financial systems and managing financial performance is important to meet profit aims and ensure the business can survive. In any sector a business always needs time and money to grow, but in fashion it is common to take far more money and time than the founder initially thought, and it is always advised to extend the budget and time frame accordingly (Lovelace, 2017). It is not just at the start-up stage that fashion brands need money, they are renowned for needing constant and significant capital injections in order to enter new global markets, expand their products or open concessions or their own stores (Chitrakorn, 2014).

This chapter will look at the financial challenges that fashion brands face, as well as the basic accounting processes that fashion brands use. Just the mention of financial management and accounts can send chills through creatives, and brands set up by creative design talent can mean there is a lack of knowledge and understanding of accounting processes, which can lead to challenges or business failure. Even if they have the most amazing designs in the world, the business owner has to understand and manage their accounts to succeed and grow. Managing the money side of the business is as important as great design.

This book cannot deal with all the issues of financial management of a brand or give a guide on how to create a financially viable business in one chapter, therefore the advice for any brand would be to find a great accountant or financial adviser to ensure the business builds a strong financial foundation for future success.

Financial challenges for fashion brands

Start-up and smaller emerging labels often face failure really quickly, as they run out of money before they have even had a chance to enter the market or grow a customer base. This happens due to their lack of understanding of the market and due to their failure to build a robust financial plan. Too many start-up labels think that they will be able to instantly attract an investor or raise finance through a bank loan, but when this doesn't happen, they have no cashflow to build their business. The reality is that investors for start-up fashion businesses are the exception not the rule, and banks rarely offer loans to start-up fashion brands as they are seen to be too risky due to the high failure rate of fashion start-ups.

It is challenging to raise money to start the label, but the challenges will not stop, as fashion businesses continually face cashflow problems. Many labels have to self-fund in the beginning, which means they will stay quite small and only be able to grow their brand slowly. With a lack of financial backing, it can be impossible to take on a large wholesale order. While getting a big order from a major retailer might sound like a good thing, with a lack of financial backing the brand may not have the cashflow to produce the inventory in the short time needed or hire the necessary employees without any money upfront (Fashionista, 2018).

If a brand chooses to develop a direct-to-consumer business model then they can also have financial challenges, as they need to find the financial resources to produce the inventory they need to sell, as well as the costs of developing sales channels and e-commerce sites, marketing, distribution, events and promotion to drive consumers to their online to generate sales (Fashionista, 2018).

Every global fashion brand emerging from the Covid-19 pandemic is facing significant financial challenges due to supply chain disruption, changing consumer demand and persistent pressure on the bottom line (Business of Fashion and McKinsey & Company, 2022). With a growing cost of living, consumers are wary of making unnecessary purchases and the fashion brands are struggling to pay their own bills, turn a profit and focus on growth. The State of Fashion 2022 reported some of the challenges shaping the fashion economy, including the need for brands to ramp up their efforts towards sustainability, to reflect customer values in their assortments, supply chains and ways of working including technology advances (Business of Fashion and McKinsey & Company, 2022). To respond to these challenges, fashion brands need to find the money to invest in hyper-interactive digital environments and investment in e-commerce, NFT developments, gaming skins and virtual fashion as well as greater brand activation for improved consumer engagement.

For the near future, fashion brands will continue to face challenges that could have a great impact on their bottom line due to an ongoing volatile market and changing consumer demand.

Financing a fashion brand

It is cheap to come up with concepts and ideas to launch a fashion label, but incredibly expensive to make the dream a reality, start producing and selling collections. Hundreds of brands fail every year as they struggle to be financially viable. As discussed through this book, fashion brands are vulnerable to external forces such as the state of the economic environment, the power of suppliers charging higher fees and competitive brands that have more resources, which affect their finances. Many start-up labels fail to even get off the ground, as they have created a brand concept that is totally reliant on bringing in investment to launch the business but is not appealing to external investors. These emerging fashion businesses struggle to attract potential backers as they do not have the strong brand identities, product signatures and sustainable revenues that attract potential backers (Chitrakorn, 2014).

Sourcing finance for a fashion brand can come under four different categories (Figure 11.1). Equity funding means a brand gives a percentage of its business in return for money, whereas debt funding is money that the business has to pay back with interest. The brand can also generate money through sales of its product or through endowments such as grants or competitions, which is money that does not need to be paid back.

The most common ways that fashion brands bring money into their businesses include the following.

Personal savings

A designer who creates their own fashion label may decide to 'bootstrap' their business or fund it from their own pocket and savings. This is possible, if the brand is starting in a small way, with a small product run rather than creating a full collection. They fund their brand through savings they have built while working somewhere

Figure 11.1   Sources of finance

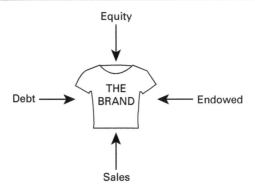

else, often at another label so that they learn about the business side of the industry as well as saving towards their own brand.

Friends and family

Many designers and entrepreneurs launch labels with financial support from friends and family, often by what is referred to as the 'bank of mum and dad'. Sometimes the support from a friend or family is gifted, other times it may be a loan. Personal support from friends and family needs to be carefully managed to ensure that everyone understands the terms it is lent on, in order to avoid conflict later, which can put a strain on relationships.

Bank loans and overdrafts

Banks and building societies can authorize loans if they are presented with solid business proposals, which need to evidence that the business is in a position to make the payments. Fashion is perceived as a high-risk industry due to being a highly competitive and volatile market, with a high dependence on e-commerce, which has the added risk of high returns (Miller, 2022). This makes most banks very wary of lending money, unless the business has substantial assets, or the business owner is prepared to take a personal loan secured against their home. Overdraft facilities, which are used to support the day-to-day cashflow of the business, are also difficult to secure due to the same risk factors.

Factoring

Factoring is a method of financing that gives brands access to working capital. It is a short-term plan that allows brands to receive a cash advance based on the value of their current invoices, so that they do not have to wait several weeks or months to receive their payments (Factor Funding Co, 2012). Factoring helps larger brands that have big wholesale orders, which they have to produce and ship before receiving payment from the retailer. The factoring company will consider the brand's written wholesale orders, credit check the company who has ordered and, if acceptable, then release around 80 per cent of the invoice order value to the brand. The factor will then take on the responsibility of collecting the invoice payment from the store. If the store fails the credit check, however, the factoring company would refuse to take on the invoice. Factoring only becomes a relevant finance option for brands with big enough business-to-business orders and is not suitable for brands that have a direct-to-consumer business model.

Grants

Fashion brands may be able to apply for grants for projects or specific purposes if they meet the funding body's criteria. Grants can be sought from government agencies or private funding bodies and, unlike loans, grants do not have to be paid back (British Business Bank, n.d.). There are often grants available for businesses that are looking to expand into certain markets or increase their exports.

Licensing

The dream for many brands is to get a licensing deal with another brand such as a beauty or accessories company to bring in another revenue stream. Licensing is a lucrative brand extension and a great way for a brand to expand and move into new product categories or markets. If a brand wants to develop licensing deals, then they have to have a brand name that is recognized and already successful, but this also brings risks as they need to ensure the licensing deal does not damage their brand name or reputation (Gaille, 2018).

Crowdfunding

Crowdfunding is becoming a popular method of raising finance for fashion brands, offering a way of testing the market by pre-selling a collection. Crowdfunding is a way of raising lots of small amounts of money from a large crowd of people and there are numerous platforms for crowdfunding including Kickstarter, GoFundMe and Indegogo. There are different types of crowdfunding campaigns but the most used ones in fashion are either equity based, or reward based.

Crowdfunding is not always the easiest option as it takes a lot of planning in order to make it successful but offers brands a way to gauge interest in their products (Tsolova, 2016). A brand will have to work on the campaign every day for the length of their campaign, sharing updates on social media, persuading people to support or share the campaign and using all their networks to push out the message.

Government loans

In some countries there are loans from the government to support start-up businesses, export or business growth. In the UK we have Start-Up Loans and access to funding for overseas trade fairs through the UK Fashion and Textile Association (UKFT). Brands from international countries are sometimes also able to access showcasing funds to take part in trade shows in key markets. Most of these government initiatives are loan based, which means the money has to be paid back, but they offer more favourable terms than banks.

Competitions

There are a number of competitions aimed at fashion businesses that offer cash prizes, such as the CFDA/Vogue Fashion Fund and the LVMH Prize. There are also many competitions such as incubator programmes or the British Fashion Council's NEWGEN initiative, where a brand can win support, mentoring and business advice with the aim of putting them on the right path to attract investors. All these competitions can be intense and very time-consuming, needing detailed business plans and sales projections.

Sponsorship

Sponsorships are a great way to raise money for specific projects that can offer mutual benefits to both parties, including increasing access to new markets and customers, attracting press coverage and increasing social media reach. In fashion, sponsorship is often secured from several partners for the brand to host events, fashion shows, fashion films and installations. In order to attract sponsors, brands need to be entrepreneurial, offer a host of benefits to their sponsors and develop inspirational marketing decks or proposal documents in order to stand out and open the conversation.

Business angels/venture capital

Investors can come in the form of 'business angels', who are wealthy private individuals looking to take an equity stake in small, high-risk businesses, or from venture capital firms who offer much larger-scale investments. Both types of investors take equity, a percentage of the business, in return for their investment. They may also provide business expertise and management as well as the cash, to ensure that their investment is wisely spent and that the business grows. Fashion brands are not particularly appealing to venture capital firms as they rarely offer quick or high returns, as fashion brands often have much slower growth patterns. Many investors look to get into the business in the early stages, when they can take a higher percentage of equity in return for their investment and then push the business for rapid growth. They can seek a high percentage of equity, as the business is worth very little in the early stages, so the brand has to give a much higher percentage of the company for the money. Brands need to make careful decisions in choosing investment partners, as they can change the dynamics of the company and there can be conflicts between investors focusing on the financial bottom line, looking for good margins and volume of sales, and the designer seeking to create slow fashion, luxury or sustainable collections that take longer to make a return on investment.

Pitching for finance

Getting money or investment into a business is not easy and brands have to work really hard to attract investment or secure money. Whether approaching a bank, an investment company, a sponsor, or setting up a crowdfunding campaign, the brand will need significant time to develop their pitch.

If looking for investors, it can be difficult for the brand to get in front of the right people and find the right investors that match with their business purpose and growth strategy. The brand has to remember that in exchange for the funds, the investor is usually given equity in the company. For some brands, this is a deterrent as it typically means the investor has some control over the company and is involved in business decisions. When creating the pitch to investors, the brand needs to set out what they want and what they will give (Fashionista, 2018). In some cases, it can be beneficial for them to take advantage of investors who have experience in growing similar businesses, as it can help them reach their potential quickly, accelerate growth and help them scale.

While finding investment for brands solely making fashion product is virtually impossible, investors are pouring record sums into fashion-tech and retail-tech start-ups (McDowell, 2021). Investors prefer digitally native brands with classic – rather than seasonal trend – products, and with a strong omnichannel strategy over a single online channel.

Before the brand starts to seek funding they need to prepare their business plans and pitch documents in order to stand out to potential partners. The pitch deck will need to include a compelling brand story around the unique point of difference; aims, objectives and key performance indicators; full financial breakdowns and projections; as well as the resource requirements including finance and staff, equipment, products and suppliers. The pitch needs to be full of rich data that evidences qualitative and quantitative data on past performance as well as future forecasts.

The pitch deck has to show that the brand is a good investment with great potential, or already holds a position of strength in the market. The business owner is an essential part of the process, there are few creative people who are analytical and process-oriented, but the business owner who has both these strengths is a force to be reckoned with and investors will snap up the opportunity to get involved (McDowell, 2021). A brand will need to have an official, independent valuation of the business in order to determine how much equity they will need to offer in return for investment. Brands have to get the facts and figures right and ask for the right amount of money to deliver the growth and success they promise. There is only one chance to get the money – the brand cannot go back and ask for a bit more money later because they didn't get it right first time. Pitching for finance is a skill that a brand or its founders need to develop in order to charm the investors, while also being able to talk through detailed business plans and financial projections.

Allocating money

If the brand has been successful in attracting finance, then they need to manage the process carefully and allocate the money in the ways declared in their pitching. A mistake many brands make is to start adding in additional costs for extra things they want because they are now cash rich, but they have to spend any investments carefully in order to meet the contracted terms.

Financial management

Once the brand has raised the finance, launched, or started to incur expenses and generate income, then it needs to put in place solid accounting systems to record business transactions, price its products correctly, calculate costs, manage the cashflow, monitor and evaluate systems to improve efficiencies and make effective plans for the future. Accounting plays a vital role in running a fashion brand, because as well as tracking income and expenditures, it ensures statutory compliance and provides investors, management and government with quantitative financial information that can be used in making business decisions (Woods, 2019).

This next section of the chapter looks at the elements of product pricing, cost management and business accounting.

Pricing strategy

Developing a correct pricing strategy is obligatory, as getting the pricing wrong and selling product at a loss or with minimal profit will damage the long-term success and viability of a fashion business. At the most basic level, fashion product is priced according to the fashion level that the brand sits at such as designer, bridge or diffusion, or budget. However, brands cannot just pick numbers out of the air to price their products at a certain level. They need to have a strategy that will allow a healthy profit margin and work across their different sales channels, without limiting their options. Prices also need to make sense to their consumers. As part of the pricing strategy the brand needs to consider how they will set the price of their products, what discounting they will offer and whether they will have mark-down sales and when. Brands also need to consider if they will offer deferred payment terms online, partnering with companies such as Klarna, Clearpay or Afterpay. Deferred billing gives the customers the option to buy things now and spread the payments, usually free of finance charges. Fashion brands are using payment instalment services as a marketing tool to attract younger price-sensitive customers, who are new to the concept of layaway (McDowell, 2020), and offers an alternative to debit- and credit-card payments.

In the fashion industry there is a divide between the majority of brands that are constantly lowering their prices with others who have developed new strategies to increase their pricing. Many high-street brands have been obsessed with discounting over the past few years, and the fast-fashion sectors 'race to the bottom' to always offer cheaper products has damaged consumer perceptions of what our clothes should cost now (Ewens, 2020). The frequent and extreme markdowns that feature all over the high street are damaging the industry, resulting in disappearing margins and driving fashion brands to the brink. Discounting can work in the short term but eventually brands have to raise their prices in order to preserve profit margins and get back to regular pricing. The problem is the consumer is now used to constant discounting and low-price fashion; they have become bargain hunters who are prepared to wait for sales rather than always buy 'new in' products. Though most consumers know that in order to produce really cheap product the brands must be cutting corners in exploiting workers and the environment, they still want to purchase cheap (Biondi, 2020). Therefore, brands are having to consider new strategies to incentivize consumers to buy at full price, or some brands are increasing their margins and prices at the start in anticipation of losses due to the inevitable discounting they will have to implement to make sales (Farra, 2021).

At the same time as the race to the bottom, luxury is getting more expensive, with the top of the market electing to raise their prices. In the height of global uncertainty both pre- and post-pandemic, Chanel has continued to increase its bag prices, not only due to an increase in production costs but because of strong demand. Business of Fashion reported that 'Chanel may feel its size and reputation grant some immunity from the ups and downs of the global business cycle' (Baskin, 2018).

Start-up fashion brands often make mistakes in their pricing at the start of the business, which can limit their future growth and wholesale opportunities. These newer brands may not consider future wholesale opportunities when setting their prices, but then later on realize that their retail price is far too low to offer a significant enough discount to potential retailers (Domenech, 2021).

The starting point of pricing is understanding the difference between wholesale and retail pricing. Wholesale pricing is what the brand charges a retailer who buys its products in large volumes. Retail prices are what the retailers charge the customers for the product after they have added on their mark-up, or what the brand charges its direct customers. This is called the RRP, or recommended retail price or list price, which standardizes the prices that all retailers will charge across different locations.

Wholesale pricing

Wholesale is the process of a brand selling their goods to a store at a wholesale price. The wholesale price is lower than the retail price, so the retailer will then add their costs and a margin for a healthy profit, which results in the higher price that they will sell the product at, but this cannot exceed what the customer will pay for it (Damen, 2022). Retailers are only interested in brands that can offer them a reasonable margin.

There is a standard industry formula that fashion brands use for calculating the wholesale price. Brands have to start with calculating the cost of making the garments, including materials, manufacturing and labour, as well as overheads such as rent and electricity (Baukh, 2020) and then the brand adds their profit margin, which in fashion is often calculated at ×2.5. This is the price the brand will charge the retail store for the product.

Retail pricing

Direct-to-consumer strategies mean a brand will need to work out the price for selling the product direct to the customer. If the brand has a wholesale strategy too, or may want to wholesale in the future, then they also need to consider the wholesale price and what the store will mark it up by to their customers. The retail price is the final price of a garment that is sold to the end consumers (Baukh, 2020).

Brands can easily get confused and will often sell their product to their direct consumer at the wholesale price. This a dangerous precedent that can damage the business in the future and prevent them from ever having the option of selling wholesale to stores. It will also mean they will have limited profit margin, which will make it difficult to scale the business. Similar to the wholesale pricing model, the brand will need to calculate its costs in order to calculate the retail price. Even if not wholesaling, the brand calculates the retail price from setting the wholesale price as detailed above. The retail price formula is set by taking the wholesale price and then adding a markup, which averages now around ×3 but can be anywhere between ×2 and ×5. By using this formula, brands will ensure they are priced competitively to the market while keeping the door open to wholesale as a future option.

Keystone markup

The model mentioned above is a form of keystone markup, a pricing methodology that retailers use that multiplies the cost basis by a factor of two (sometimes this can be up to 5× in the case of jewellery) to dictate the price for the next rung in the value chain. For a business that is not sure how to price a product, keystone pricing provides an easy starting point that is likely to ensure some profit. It is the simplest way to universally markup goods, as it is logistically impossible to uniquely price hundreds of different products to reflect market conditions and retail demographics – the theory being that retailer profitability was more of a function of units sold versus maximizing each product's price (Carroll, 2012).

Cost price strategy

Both wholesale and retail pricing rely on the brand working out their costs and this cost price strategy is recommended for fashion brands and used throughout the industry.

If a brand was to use the formula shown in Figure 11.2, a dress that cost a designer £100 to produce could then be sold to a retailer at a wholesale price of £250 once they have added their ×2.5 margin on top of the costs. That retailer could then markup the dress again by ×3 to make their own profit, bringing the final price up to £750, which would be the price on the ticket (Farra, 2021).

Product cost sheets

The easiest and best way to work out the cost of goods is to use a cost sheet template that gathers information together in one place of all the costs incurred in making each product. By using a simple, concise template, the brand can be sure to include all the elements that it has cost to produce the piece and make sure they haven't missed anything that could mean their pricing is incorrect and they are selling at a loss. Product cost sheets, as in the example shown in Table 11.1, can cover everything from design time, fabric, dying or printing, trims, embroidery, labels, manufacturing and labour costs to packaging, shipping and any other costs that go into making a final product ready to sell (Baukh, 2020).

Figure 11.2   Cost price strategy

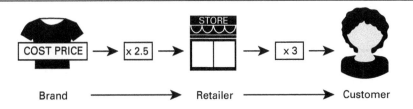

Table 11.1 Product cost sheet

PRODUCT COST SHEET			
DATE/SEASON	STYLE NUMBER/NAME		
PRODUCT DESCRIPTION			
COSTING:			
MATERIAL COSTS			
FABRIC	AMOUNT NEEDED	COST PER METRE	TOTAL
		TOTAL MATERIAL	
TRIM COSTS			
TRIM	AMOUNT NEEDED	COST PER ITEM	TOTAL
		TOTAL TRIM	

(*continued*)

Table 11.1 (Continued)

LABOUR COSTS		
ACTION	DESCRIPTION	COST
CUT		
SEW		
DYE		
PRINT		
EMBROIDERY		
MARKING/GRADING		
	TOTAL LABOUR	
SUNDRY COSTS		
		COST
LABELS		
PACKAGING		
	TOTAL SUNDRY	
	TOTAL OF MATERIAL, TRIM, LABOUR, SUNDRY	
	WHOLESALE PRICE	
	RETAIL MARKUP	
	RRP	
	DIRECT TO CONSUMER PRICE	

The number of details included on the cost sheet will depend on the complexity of the garment. Using product cost sheets can ensure that the process is managed efficiently and collaboratively across the whole team, and makes it easy to compare and analyse costs and make necessary adjustments prior to production (Kochar, 2020).

Many cost sheets only cover the direct cost of goods, but the business also has overheads that need to be considered as well, such as rent, staff and machinery. Direct costs can easily be assigned to individual products, but overhead costs are often forgotten even though it is advised to include them in the cost of individual products and to take them into account when determining their final value (Business, 2019). Some brands will absorb the overheads in the margins they set from the cost prices, whereas others will calculate an overhead rate that they will add to their pricing formulas. This overhead rate may be calculated by adding up the total of all the business overheads and dividing by the estimated product created, or the brand may decide to use a fixed markup percentage to add to all products such as 30 per cent.

When completing the product cost sheet, brands have the opportunity to consider how effectively they are managing production costs. The cost sheet can be used to consider challenges such as minimum order quantities in materials and production to ensure they are producing as efficiently as possible. They can also use the cost sheets to identify areas where they can reduce production costs, if necessary, by simplifying patterns or reducing additional elements such as frills, trims or removing pockets.

Add value rather than cut prices

Having worked out the pricing, some brands may then realize that their prices are higher than they initially predicted and consider how they can reduce their prices. Discounting and sales are damaging the industry, as mentioned above, with the high street full of brands struggling to survive despite their cheap product and constant discounting and sales. For emerging or luxury labels, sales can really devalue and affect the brand's credibility and profile. A smaller or luxury brand will often worry that their prices are too high and consider offering discounts to draw in a customer. For these labels, their prices will always be high as their costs are higher due to buying fabrics and manufacturing in smaller quantities, which increases the end price of the product. There is little they can do about this, other than do their best to keep their costs down, as it is too risky to start cutting their profit margin or, worse still, selling at cost price as this will lead to certain failure of the brand. Instead of discounting, these brands need to build the value in their product, selling the brand values of exclusivity and scarcity through limited edition collections, higher brand experience and unique designs and packaging.

Accounting

As well as securing money and investment to grow the brand and setting the pricing strategy, the brand also has to develop systems for projecting and managing their finances. The simplest accounting method used by fashion brands is cash book accounting, a chronological record of income when cash is received and expenses when cash is paid out, taking information from the bank statement. In accounting terms, cash refers to all the payments that come in and out of the business bank account including bank transfers, standing orders, direct debits and cash deposits. While a few small companies still use physical cash book ledgers, most brands now use software programmes for their cash book accounts, which gives them the added benefits of being able to interrogate the data, automate invoices and provide images, tables and charts for management reports. Digital accounting now includes cloud accounting, the use of AI and numerous apps for small businesses to manage their finances. As well as being the simplest system, another benefit of cash book accounting is that businesses do not pay income tax on revenue until they receive it, which also helps with cashflow.

From the cash book data, the brand is able to generate the three financial statements that all businesses need – the profit and loss sheet, the balance sheet and the cashflow forecast (Figure 11.3).

Profit and loss

A profit and loss statement is often referred to as the P&L and is a financial report that provides a summary of the brand's income and expenses and the subsequent profits and losses for a set period of time, usually a year. The P&L statement shows a company's ability to generate sales, manage expenses and create profits (CFI Team, 2022). The statement is an indicator of the company's health and is one of the main documents used to raise finance as it allows potential investors or banks to see how much income the brand has generated, how much debt they have and how stable the business is.

Balance sheet

The balance sheet statement details the brand's total assets and how they are financed. It is often referred to as a statement of net worth and details the assets of the business (what it owns that has future economic benefit) and its liabilities (what the business owes to other people). The balance sheet is divided into two sides, with the company's assets on the left, and on the right the liabilities with the shareholder equity, or money invested in the business. The balance sheet should balance with the equation assets = liabilities + equity. Elizabeth Macauley explains, 'by making sure your assets equal your liabilities plus your shareholders' (also called, owners') equity you will avoid having difficulty paying your operating expenses' (Macauley, 2018).

Figure 11.3 Cash book accounting

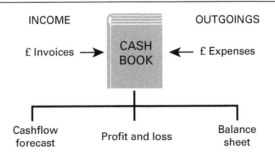

Cashflow forecast

Cashflow is the life blood of every business and how it is managed will make the difference between the brand succeeding or failing. Businesses need significant cashflow to pay their suppliers, employees and overheads – in a volatile market, with seasonality and ever-changing costs, failing to anticipate a worst-case scenario can cripple even the most highly profitable brand.

A cashflow statement is the most basic level of accounting and gives an idea of the business's current financial health. While this has value as part of the accounting process, for fashion brands the most valuable cashflow process is a cashflow forecast or prediction, which estimates the money the brand expects to flow in and out of the business over the next 12-month period, including all income and expenses (Kappel, 2019). A cashflow forecast is an essential tool to help a brand identify shortfalls between the amounts coming in and the money needed to cover the expenses of running the business and paying for services. For start-up fashion brands, developing a cashflow forecast before they start their business will ensure they don't fall into the trap that so many start-up brands do of running out of cash before the end of their first year.

To conduct a cashflow forecast, the brand will need to gather information from various sources including suppliers and previous year's accounts in order to predict the next year's business. They need to research exact figures to include and not use guesswork or random figures. There is no point adding numbers because they look better, nor should they try to balance the incomings and outgoings, as the point of the cashflow forecast is to identify when there could be problems or cash shortages. The numbers need to be as accurate and realistic as possible. For a first cashflow forecast for a start-up business, it can feel like the brand is picking figures out of thin air, but, with detailed research, in future years they will be able to estimate more realistic figures.

Table 11.2 gives an example of a typical cashflow forecast template for a fashion brand, and below is an explanation of the different sections.

Income

The biggest error brands make when writing their cashflow forecasts is including unrealistic sales predictions. While being optimistic about the sales may be a motivator, for the purposes of a cashflow forecast it is necessary to consider the worst-case scenario.

The income is split into different sections so that it is clear which sales channels are working best, as well as recording where additional income has come from such as from investment or the bank. The brand needs to predict their sales based on the different channels they are selling through. For wholesale they need to estimate the number of sales at wholesale price they think they will make, whereas online sales will be the pieces that they predict selling at RRP. Retail sales will predict how many

Table 11.2 Cashflow forecast

Cashflow forecast

	Pre-start	Month	Month	Month	Month	Month	Month	Month	Month	Month	Month	Month	Month
INCOME													
Wholesale sales													
Retail sales													
Online sales													
Loan													
Personal													
Investor													
TOTAL													
COST of SALE													
Fabric													
Trims													
Manufacturer													
Labour/salaries													
Packaging													
Sales agent													
TOTAL													
EXPENSES													
Rent													

(continued)

Table 11.2 (Continued)

Utilities											
Staff salaries											
Insurance											
Consultants											
Travel											
Website											
Telephone											
Office supplies											
Postage											
Advertising											
Marketing materials											
Photo shoots											
Events											
Loan repayments											
Tax											
Capital purchases											
Contingency											
TOTAL											
Cashflow surplus or deficit -/+											

sales they think they will make through their own direct retail opportunities such as stores, pop-up shops, events or a trunk show. It is important to split online sales from direct retail sales so that the brand can work out the profit margins after the expenses of shop rent or hiring space, to see if it brings in a healthy return on investment.

The income section is where the brand will list the money that comes into the business from the owner, from a bank loan, government grant, or money from an investor. This is usually a lump sum, listed as a one-off amount in the month the money is received by the brand.

Cost of sales/direct costs

The cost of sales, also known as direct costs, relates to the costs that the brand incurs in making the product that is for sale. The cost of sales includes materials, labour or factory, packaging and shipping. It can also include the commission charged by a sales agent. The cost of sales helps the brand measure their ability to design, source and manufacture goods at a reasonable cost and have a healthy profit margin. The cost of sales does not include indirect expenses such as office and marketing costs etc, a percentage of these may be added depending on the brand's pricing strategy.

Expenses/indirect costs

Expenses are often referred to as indirect costs or the overheads of the business. In other words, they are the expenses that are not assigned to the production of a particular product. The expenses include rent, advertising, office supplies, accountancy services and utilities. The expenses can be fixed costs that are paid regularly each month such as the rent or insurance bill, or can be variable expenses such as electricity bills, which may fluctuate monthly or quarterly. Other expenses will only occur occasionally such as creating marketing materials or a product campaign shoot.

Managing the cashflow

Brands have to take every action possible to improve their cashflow, which involves tracking, managing and negotiating their direct and indirect costs to increase their profitability. They need to be always looking for potential areas of cost improvement. The brand may need to negotiate better terms with both suppliers and customers or improve their wholesale payment terms to ensure they are paid more efficiently. The brand can also consider exercising their rights to charge late payment penalties, charge interest on late payments or incentivize a store to pay promptly by offering discounts for early payment.

Specific ways that fashion brands can improve their cashflow includes minimizing returns by ensuring products are good quality and a good fit, as well as giving clear sizing and details on their websites. Brands also need to ensure they don't have cash tied up in surplus stock or fabrics, as overproduction and dead stock is wasted money and a brand will need to find ways to sell it to release capital. Brands may also need to increase their prices if they are finding that their costs are rising. This can be scary for many brand owners as they worry that no one will buy their pieces; however, if they don't increase prices to cover their costs and make a profit then there is a chance that they will go out of business anyway. Sometimes the brand has to take the risk and look at how they can add the value so that the customer will pay the increase in price.

Summary

At the time of writing this book, the economy and the fashion industry is in a time of crisis as it tries to recover from the Covid-19 pandemic, supply chain disruptions and shaky consumer demand. Every fashion brand faces a complex mix of challenges and opportunities, in which there is little room for missteps (Business of Fashion and McKinsey & Company 2022). As the fashion brands struggle to turn a profit, they will need greater focus on managing their finances and controlling their costs. At the same time, with growing consumer demand for increased engagement, sustainability and better online experiences, brands are needing to invest heavily in new technologies and innovation.

Brands that survive and grow will be ones that reshape their business models, streamline their operations and optimize their cashflow to develop more efficient and effective future-facing strategies.

Key terms

balance sheet	crowdfunding	license
business angel	debt	profit and loss
cash accounting	endowment	retail pricing
cashflow	equity	sponsorship
cashflow forecast	factoring	venture capital
cost of sales	grants	wholesale pricing
cost price strategy	keystone markup	

Activity

On Kickstarter, find a fashion brand campaign and look at the rewards they offer in return for financial pledges, and investigate which campaigns are more successful and why.

Online resources

Cashflow forecast and product cost sheet examples.

References

Baskin (2018) Why Chanel is raising prices on its most popular bags, *The Business of Fashion*, www.businessoffashion.com/articles/china/why-chanel-is-raising-prices-on-its-most-popular-bags/ (archived at https://perma.cc/58UA-EBBZ)

Baukh, O (2020) Difference between retail and wholesale in apparel industry, *Techpacker Blog*, techpacker.com/blog/design/difference-between-retail-and-wholesale-price-in-the-apparel-industry/#:~:text=Wholesale%20price%20is%20a%20rate%20charged%20by%20the,garments%20you%20sell%20the%20lower%20rate%20you%20quote (archived at https://perma.cc/P46E-7GNS)

Biondi, A (2020) Fashion's alternatives to the discounting trap, *Vogue Business*, www.voguebusiness.com/consumers/fashion-discounting-alternatives-supply-chain-overhaul (archived at https://perma.cc/U37F-49JL)

British Business Bank (n.d.) Business grants, *British Business Bank*, www.british-business-bank.co.uk/finance-hub/grants-finance/#:~:text=Business%20grants%20are%20payments%20provided%20by%20either%20the,away%20a%20share%20of%20your%20business%20in%20exchange (archived at https://perma.cc/PJ2E-UL77)

Business, G (2019) Overhead costs, *IONOS*, www.ionos.co.uk/startupguide/grow-your-business/overhead-costs/ (archived at https://perma.cc/AA2V-SGLK)

Business of Fashion and McKinsey & Company (2022) The state of fashion 2022, *McKinsey*, www.mckinsey.com/~/media/mckinsey/industries/retail/our%20insights/state%20of%20fashion/2022/the-state-of-fashion-2022.pdf (archived at https://perma.cc/WK53-DAYW)

Carroll, M (2012) How fashion brands set prices, *Forbes*, www.forbes.com/sites/matthewcarroll/2012/02/22/how-fashion-brands-set-prices/?sh=7ae4c682822d (archived at https://perma.cc/XT2R-JLVH)

CFI Team (2022) Profit and loss statement (P&L), *Corporate Finance Institute*, corporatefinanceinstitute.com/resources/knowledge/accounting/profit-and-loss-statement-pl/ (archived at https://perma.cc/8FH6-PT6J)

Chitrakorn, K (2014) 6 emerging fashion brands worth investing in, *The Business of Fashion*, www.businessoffashion.com/articles/finance/6-emerging-fashion-brands-worth-investing/ (archived at https://perma.cc/3GXL-S6PM)

Damen, A (2022) Product pricing: how to set prices for wholesale and retail, *Shopify*, www.shopify.co.uk/retail/product-pricing-for-wholesale-and-retail (archived at https://perma.cc/8Q8V-BN88)

Domenech, A (2021) How to set wholesale prices for brands new to wholesale, *Tradegala*, www.tradegala.com/blogs/wholesale-news/how-to-set-wholesale-prices-for-brands-new-to-wholesale (archived at https://perma.cc/HS8X-Y4VN)

Ewens, H (2020) The AliExpress app is fuelling fast fashion's race to the bottom, *Vice*, www.vice.com/en/article/884m55/aliexpress-app-fuelling-fast-fashion (archived at https://perma.cc/R8BT-HXUX)

Factor Funding Co (2012) What is apparel industry factoring?, *Factor Funding*, blog.factorfunding.com/blog/what-is-apparel-industry-factoring/ (archived at https://perma.cc/VRL2-FL4Q)

Farra, E (2021) What is the right price for fashion?, *Vogue*, www.vogue.com/article/what-is-the-right-price-for-fashion (archived at https://perma.cc/F5V9-K7MM)

Fashionista (2018) All the ways to finance a fashion Business in 2018, *Fashionista*, fashionista.com/2018/06/how-to-fund-finance-fashion-business (archived at https://perma.cc/LZ7F-HEY8)

Gaille, B (2018) 14 licensing advantages and disadvantages, *Brandon Gaille*, brandongaille.com/14-licensing-advantages-and-disadvantages/#:~:text=%20List%20of%20the%20Advantages%20of%20Licensing%20,place%2C%20then%20the%20licensor%20is%20able...%20More%20 (archived at https://perma.cc/42DL-CR3C)

Kappel, M (2019) Cash flow projection, *Patriot Software*, www.patriotsoftware.com/blog/accounting/how-to-project-your-cash-flow/ (archived at https://perma.cc/T6WJ-5PSV)

Kochar, S (2020) How to create a garment costing sheet, *Techpacker Blog*, techpacker.com/blog/design/apparel-and-garment-costing/ (archived at https://perma.cc/8HWY-C9RC)

Lovelace, T (2017) Tips for starting a successful clothing brand, *Start Up Nation*, https://startupnation.com/start-your-business/start-clothing-brand/ (archived at https://perma.cc/WAJ2-4PQT)

Macauley, E (2018) How does a balance sheet balance?, *Small Biz Ahead*, Sba.thehartford.com, sba.thehartford.com/finance/accounting/balance-sheet/ (archived at https://perma.cc/9MMA-3VV8)

McDowell, M (2020) Payment instalments are now a fashion marketing play, *Vogue Business*, www.voguebusiness.com/technology/fintech-fashion-marketing-pay-later-klarna-afterpay (archived at https://perma.cc/33AX-GRMR)

McDowell, M (2021) Fashion-tech's funding boom: who's being funded — and why?, *Vogue Business*, www.voguebusiness.com/technology/fashion-techs-funding-boom-whos-being-funded-and-why (archived at https://perma.cc/QN58-8HZS)

Miller, N (2022) Which businesses and industries are considered high-risk? (and what it means if you're on the list), *Merchant Maverick*, www.merchantmaverick.com/high-risk-business-company-industry/ (archived at https://perma.cc/GQ67-9R3M)

Tsolova, D (2016) Business crowdfunding for fashion brands, *Fashion Insiders*, fashioninsiders.co/toolkit/top-tips/business-crowdfunding-fashion-brands/ (archived at https://perma.cc/V3JW-VYA4)

Woods, D (2019) The role of accounting in business and why it's important, *CPA Firm Tampa*, www.pdr-cpa.com/knowledge-center/blog/role-of-accounting-in-business (archived at https://perma.cc/9EJV-85P6)

Case study
Yala Jewellery

Yala is an award-winning African jewellery brand, offering modern intricate designs created with sustainability, ethics, transparency and purpose embedded to its core. Yala was the first jewellery company in the UK to become a certified B-Corp, meeting the highest standards of social and environmental performance, transparency and accountability, and a finalist in the Great British Entrepreneur Awards for Sustainable Business of the Year 2022.

Yala is the vision of passionate entrepreneur Audrey Migot-Adholla, who was born in Kenya and the brand is named after the town where her late grandmother lived. Audrey now lives in Bristol but splits her time between the UK and Kenya, where the small-batch jewellery collections are made exclusively for the brand.

Audrey turned her passion for accessories and traditional crafts such as beadwork and wax prints into Yala, with her dream to create a business that works with local artisans to showcase their skills across the world. Audrey works directly with over 150 artisans in Kenya, ensuring they have safe and healthy working environments, receive recognition for their talent and are paid three times more than the average wages for jewellery artisans working in the informal sector in Kenya. She is passionate about ensuring true transparency across the production process and has a genuine connection with the artisans working on the pieces, regularly visiting them to ensure they have a safe and happy environment in which to create the jewellery. The Yala collections are designed with the intention to challenge the common misconceptions about Africa and its people through beautiful design, entrepreneurship and creative talent. As well as empowering the artisans, the brand seeks to also protect the planet, ensuring that all its raw materials are sourced ethically, with a focus on recycled and reclaimed elements, to create as little environmental impact as possible.

Audrey has also invested considerable time and energy into the brand's packaging, which is eco-friendly, made with components that are reusable, recyclable or compostable and printed with vegetable-based inks. With every order, the brand embeds rich storytelling in the packaging, with information cards that enable the consumer to discover the stories of the brand and its makers, establishing connection and community between the brand, the artisans and the customer.

www.yalajewellery.com

Future entrepreneurial advantage for fashion brands

12

LEARNING OBJECTIVES

After reading this chapter you should be able to:

- Understand the key characteristics of an entrepreneur
- Explain the difference between an entrepreneur, intrapreneur and entrepreneurial spirit
- Describe how fashion brands can build entrepreneurial advantage
- Identify the characteristics of a successful entrepreneur

Introduction

Throughout this book, the discussions have revolved around the 'broken' global fashion industry and the increasing challenges it is facing, with the old fashion rules no longer working and brands needing to do things differently to succeed in an ever-changing, volatile market. To solve these challenges the industry needs entrepreneurs and an entrepreneurial mindset to address social and environmental problems and boost economic growth through innovative technologies and business models.

This final chapter will consider how fashion brands need to create an entrepreneurial mindset, encourage a culture of innovation, initiative, confidence and passion to find creative solutions and new opportunities. Discussing the elements of entrepreneurs, entrepreneurial spirit or mindset, intrapreneurs and the entrepreneurial economy, the chapter will address how fashion brands who have a more entrepreneurial approach to designing, producing and marketing their brand, products and services will have more chance of survival and success during turbulent times.

Entrepreneur and entrepreneurship

As the fashion industry has floundered against the swell of environmental and economic issues, it has become apparent that entrepreneurship is of huge importance to turn the tide. In the industry there is already a rise of entrepreneurial activity by individuals or brands who seek to solve these problems. They are achieving this change either through their own more socially and environmentally conscious brands and projects or through groundbreaking collaborations, which demonstrates what is possible when an industry joins together for collaborative impact (Ashoka, 2014). In the fashion industry the term entrepreneur, entrepreneurship, intrapreneur and social entrepreneurship are starting to be used more frequently, therefore the starting point in this chapter is to understand these terms.

Entrepreneur

An entrepreneur can be described as someone who undertakes to provide products or a service to the market for a profit. 'The entrepreneur will usually invest capital in the business and take on the risks associated with the investment' (Law, 2009). Other definitions of the word 'entrepreneur' usually refer to it as a term for an individual who starts a business, who in creating their own company will take on the financial risk in the hope of making profit. Though the concept of an entrepreneur has existed for centuries, it was only in the middle of the 20th century that economists, including Joseph Schumpeter, Frank Knight and Israel Kirzner, started to incorporate the term 'entrepreneur' into their models. They each had their own perspective on entrepreneurs, with Schumpeter suggesting that it is entrepreneurs, not just companies, who were responsible for the creation of new things in the search for profit, whereas Knight focused on entrepreneurs as the bearers of uncertainty and believed they were responsible for risk premiums in financial markets, and Kirzner discussed entrepreneurship as a process that led to discovery (Today Headline, 2021). In today's world, many newspaper column inches are given to high-profile entrepreneurs such as Elon Musk, Bill Gates and Steve Jobs, who have disrupted and transformed the world and the way we live in it. These leading entrepreneurs have been seen as the forces behind the 'creative destruction' needed for major industrial progress and economic growth, and as Schumpeter identified there is an important difference between the 'inventor who produces ideas and the entrepreneur who gets things done' (Young, 2019).

Fashion industry entrepreneurs

The fashion industry, despite being a highly competitive market, has always been alluring for budding entrepreneurs who have a passion to showcase their talent and designs, or disrupt the industry with new business and/or social models. The fashion industry is full of new talent who have studied design and want to start their own fashion labels, and for many years designer-entrepreneurs have been the lifeblood of the fashion industry. 'Sometimes they were secretive virtuosos like Antwerp's Martin Margiela, or emotional *enfants terribles* like self-described 'East End yob' Alexander McQueen. Back in 2003, just three years after Gucci Group acquired 51 per cent of McQueen's brand in a deal that gave him full artistic licence, he took part in a blunt interview with Polly Vernon that seemed to sum up the entrepreneurial spirit of his generation: 'I was never a big networker', he said, 'but I was a spin doctor – all those shock shows, that's how I got my first [financial] backers' (Young, 2019).

Start-up entrepreneurs

Along with the big names, the fashion industry is full of smaller, start-up brands and solo entrepreneurs who are disrupting the industry with new agile business models that can sometimes give them advantages that the more well-known labels cannot achieve. In the UK, the small business arena makes a hugely significant contribution to the economy, forming 98 per cent of private-sector businesses (I W Capital, 2019). The entrepreneurialism of start-up founders drives the fashion private-sector forward. In Vogue Business Future Edit, Lucy Maguire looked at the fashion start-up trends in 2021 and identified that, 'The brands and start-ups shaking up the fashion industry of tomorrow prioritized ethical values and tech innovation' (Maguire, 2021). This same article identified that many of the smaller brands were led by entrepreneurs who were more interested in responsible growth, community connectedness and scaling at a slow pace, rather than trying to compete with the megabrands (Maguire, 2021). These entrepreneurs are harnessing their advantages to ensure they have the lasting direct customer relationships that will mean their businesses survive in the long term (Power, 2019).

Skills needed by fashion entrepreneurs

Fashion entrepreneurs today need to have more than great design skills, and increasingly, the trailblazers among fashion entrepreneurs don't come from fashion schools (Young, 2019). Whatever their background though, all fashion entrepreneurs need to have ambition, focus, instinct for opportunity and an appetite for calculated risk. 'Fashion entrepreneurs [today] are expected to be the leading force, advancing and disrupting the industry,' says Jazia Al Dhanhani, chief executive of Dubai Design and Fashion Council in a Business of Fashion article on how modern entrepreneurs are made: 'Investing time and effort on innovation, connecting to the needs and aspirations of consumers and embracing technology are just the basic ingredients' (Young, 2019).

Fashion consultant James Hillman describes the need for fashion entrepreneurs on his blog, 'In order for the market to be reactive and versatile, it needs business leaders that have a good understanding of what consumers want. Since all companies have different goals and aspirations, being able to change with the times according to styles and industry demands is crucial for success. Fashion entrepreneurs will continue to be important post 2022 because the industry is constantly changing and evolving. Brands need someone to help establish their identities and guide them in the right direction' (Hillman and Hillman, 2022). Later in the chapter we look at the characteristic traits of entrepreneurs to discover what makes certain individuals more inclined to take an entrepreneurial path or makes them successful in their endeavours.

Entrepreneurship

Entrepreneurship, or being entrepreneurial, expands the definition of an entrepreneur beyond someone starting their own business to include an approach to management or running of a business. Being entrepreneurial is a way of thinking and acting, it is the art of critical questioning, the ability to generate and implement innovative ideas, and involves having the leadership qualities to build a successful team to meet the brand's vision. Entrepreneurship in fashion is just like entrepreneurship in any other field, where the organization through a visionary leadership team will develop innovative ideas for economic, environmental and social development. Fashion entrepreneurship combines the creative elements of the brand with the administration side of the business, and it has gained significance within the industry as competition became fiercer across the globe. In a complex and dynamic world, innovation and entrepreneurship are essential for fashion and occupy a pivotal role in economic development.

In its traditional form, entrepreneurship was often considered an innovation driver within our global economy; others perceived it as a model for exponential profits and wealth extraction, but in its ideal form, entrepreneurship can be an engine for galvanizing social change, preserving environmental sustainability and creating a prosperous economy (Bender-Salazar, 2021). In today's fashion industry, there is a demand for entrepreneurship to be positioned as more of a problem-solving process to address systemic challenges, rather than a wealth generator. In Rahmin Bender-Salazar's article for the World Economic Forum, they talked about the need for entrepreneurship to meet the needs of the 'great reset' and 'all venture- and value-creation approaches must integrate social justice and ecological systems. For entrepreneurship to incorporate ecological and social systems effectively, we must understand our collective responsibility for justice. We can no longer think of the world as a zero-sum power game, in which for some to win others must lose' (Bender-Salazar, 2021).

Entrepreneurship is a competence that needs to be developed in all brands. For fashion businesses there is a positive relationship between entrepreneurship and innovation (Ünay and Zehir, 2012) and brands need to find new business opportunities to survive market shifts. Entrepreneurship will improve a fashion brand's performance and, along with a unique creative edge or design aesthetic, it will lead to competitive advantage.

Intrapreneur

An intrapreneur is an employee with entrepreneurial skills who is tasked with developing innovative ideas, products, services or projects within a business. The term 'intrapreneur' was coined by Gifford Pinchot III in 1978, and when Steve Jobs quoted the term in a *Newsweek* interview in 1985, it began to be recognized around the world (Wallstreetmojo, n.d.). Intrapreneurship, also known as corporate entrepreneurship, denotes the concept of entrepreneurial thinking, which is not only applied within an organization but becomes a core part of the organizational culture. Every brand needs to find systems to support and encourage innovation and new business growth within their organization, and intrapreneurship can provide a process within the company to create value and generate new revenue growth through entrepreneurial thought and action (Corporate Entrepreneurs, 2022).

To develop intrapreneurship, brands need to embed and encourage systems that allow people to develop ideas, take action and provide an environment that is open to entrepreneurship, learning and growth across the business. In the research paper 'An interactive model of the corporate entrepreneurship process', it was identified that there are critical elements that are needed for both an entrepreneurial climate and to stimulate entrepreneurial thinking, which include goals and rewards as well as positive feedback, reinforcement and trust (Hornsby et al,1993).

In the fashion industry, brands need to start recognizing that they may have a potential resource of intrapreneurs within their own team who can drive change and not just look at external influences. However, there are challenges in adopting new cultures and it takes time, training and learning across the organization to create the systems and environment needed to encourage more intrapreneurial activity.

Social entrepreneurship

The definition of a social entrepreneur is a person who sets up a business with the aim of either solving social problems or effecting social change. Social entrepreneurship has some differences from the non-profit social enterprise model, as although they both seek to make profit, the social entrepreneur has more entrepreneurial tendencies towards risk and innovation. Social enterprises are more focused on achieving social goals rather than taking a disruptive approach to new ideas. In an article by Certo and Miller about social entrepreneurship, they state that even some of the most renowned capitalists have embraced and served as champions for social entrepreneurship, with one of the most notable examples being Bill Gates, the founder of Microsoft. Bill Gates has often discussed social entrepreneurship and in his speech on the subject at the World Economic Forum in Switzerland has been reported as saying, 'Such a system would have a twin mission: making profits and also improving lives for those who don't fully benefit from market forces' (Certo and Miller, 2008).

In the fashion industry, due to the growing concerns over environmental and social issues, many more fashion entrepreneurs have become interested in the social consequences of their economic activity. The Grow Ensemble discussed social entrepreneurship on one of their podcasts and the show notes shared the concept that the future of the fashion industry, our environment and our communities depend on adopting a new paradigm that opts out of the abhorrent practices currently and historically plaguing fashion. The only way forward is for fashion entrepreneurs to become a part of an entirely new conscious fashion economy: one that is rooted in responsible growth, sustainability and circular design (Grow Ensemble, n.d.).

Entrepreneurs of all kinds are critical for a buoyant economy, as they drive innovation, improve business processes, and develop new technologies and ways of working.

Entrepreneurial economy

The entrepreneurial economy refers to the economic environment in which entrepreneurs thrive. Nurturing entrepreneurship can have a positive impact on the economy, as the increase in new businesses, goods, services and employment creates a ripple effect in the economy resulting in further development. Entrepreneurship is considered crucial to a dynamic economy and governments can encourage greater entrepreneurial developments by providing conducive economic packages to encourage more entrepreneurs, including better tax, regulatory and bureaucratic systems to support rather than hamper entrepreneurial activity.

Characteristics of successful entrepreneurs

Entrepreneurs have become high-profile contributors to society and their names are often associated not only with great wealth, but also with high esteem. Leading entrepreneurs are the celebrities of the business world but many of them are now well known across society as well. Their appeal comes from their passion, tenacity and success, often giving hope to millions of others that they too can start an entrepreneurial journey. What sets an entrepreneur apart is not just their business plan, it is often the characteristics of the entrepreneur themselves that make them stand out. In the Business of Fashion article on 'How modern entrepreneurs are made', Young (2019) supposes that 'Instinct, ambition, a nose for opportunity, focus, grit and an appetite for calculated risk all play their part in the making of successful entrepreneurs. But it is unlikely that any single gene sequence or psychographic profile makes us significantly predisposed to life as an entrepreneur. And yet, the enduring notion that entrepreneurs are born, not made, adds to the pressure that many founders feel'. Setting up, managing and growing a fashion brand in today's volatile and ever-changing market needs a wealth of talent, skills, knowledge and boldness. Although there is not a magic formula for success, it is widely recognized that there are some common characteristics that many successful entrepreneurs share. These include:

- **Passion:** Passion is what drives entrepreneurs; their passion is the 'why' or 'purpose' behind what they do. Passion is what motivates the entrepreneur through the tough times and makes the long hours, the hard work and the sacrifices worth it. The entrepreneur's passion for their brand is also what excites the customer and makes the label seem more inspiring and compelling.

- **Determination:** Entrepreneurs have a determination to succeed, overcoming obstacles and challenges. Fashion brands take time to grow and success rarely happens overnight. A lot of perceived 'overnight' successful businesses have in reality been working for years towards that moment when they are discovered.

- **Vision:** Entrepreneurs have vision, looking to the future and developing a brand that will adapt to and lead change in order to be relevant in the future not just today. The entrepreneur can see the bigger picture, rather than getting tied up in the day-to-day small detail.

- **Resilience and risk tolerance:** Entrepreneurs have resilience and are not easily defeated. They see risk as a potential opportunity and are not afraid of failure. Successful entrepreneurs see failures as learning opportunities, a chance to get back up and do something better.

- **Confidence and strong communication skills:** Confidence is a huge part of an entrepreneur's success. They can communicate ideas clearly with passion and confidence, have great negotiation skills, and can inspire other people to believe in the vision and the brand. Successful entrepreneurs will find balance on the fine line between confidence and arrogance, knowing that there is a place for gratitude and appreciation for others in their teams. There is no place for ego or arrogance in a successful business, therefore entrepreneurs can communicate in assertive direct ways while remaining respectful.

- **Flexibility:** Successful entrepreneurs are flexible, ready to adapt to changing circumstances, creating agile businesses that can take advantage of new opportunities. Being flexible or agile is a mindset, it means entrepreneurs are capable of faster innovation, are prepared to take calculated risks, will learn from failure and quickly overcome the challenges.

- **Network:** Entrepreneurs know they cannot do everything themselves, nor do they need to be the smartest person in their business. They build great networks and surround themselves with talented people. Networking is essential and entrepreneurs invest time into building relationships, understanding the phrase 'your network is your net worth'. In other words, your value is that of the people in your network. Networking is also a form of research, where entrepreneurs learn about industry trends, successful traits of other business owners, identify potential partners, investors or collaborators and gain feedback on their ideas.

Entrepreneurial mindset

An entrepreneurial mindset can be defined as not only a set of skills but also the mental attitude that a person has that gives them a unique way of approaching problems and helps them identify opportunities, and overcome and learn from setbacks. It was economic theorist Schumpeter who coined the term in German *unternehmergeist*, which translates as 'entrepreneurial spirit' (Young, 2019).

Social psychologist Norris F Krueger (2007) claimed the difference between entrepreneurship and entrepreneurial thinking lies in the fact that entrepreneurship is about actions and intentions while entrepreneurial thinking is about attitude and beliefs: 'Behind entrepreneurial action are entrepreneurial intentions. Behind entrepreneurial intentions are known entrepreneurial attitudes. Behind entrepreneurial attitudes are deep cognitive structures. Behind deep cognitive structures are deep beliefs'. Entrepreneurial mindset or thinking is the ability to see things differently from the rest of the world. It is said to be the ability to harness passions, skills, experience, knowledge and insights, resources and networks to spot and take advantage of opportunities at the right time and in the right way.

Entrepreneurial mindset is not necessarily an inherited characteristic, and while some theorists argue that entrepreneurial spirit is nature not nurture, others feel it can be easily developed or improved. Professional services company Ernst & Young, in their report 'Nature or nurture? Decoding the DNA of the entrepreneur', stated that entrepreneurial leaders are made, not born (Gary, 2022). The report detected that though there are some inherent traits, entrepreneurs with the right mindset also need education, resources and the right environment to fulfil their entrepreneurial goals. Therefore, mindset alone is not enough.

With the fashion industry needing to adapt to turbulent markets, greater focus on developing entrepreneurial mindsets and thinking is important to identify new opportunities for improvement and growth. Fashion brands must encourage and support an entrepreneurial mindset across their organizations, developing their teams with decision making, confidence, accountability and agility skills. Creating a positive environment that supports entrepreneurial thinking and action changes a business, and will result in a dynamic and productive brand.

Entrepreneurship education

Education is an essential element in building entrepreneurs, an entrepreneurial mindset, and is a key component of developing an entrepreneurial economy. There is an ongoing debate about whether entrepreneurship can be taught or not, and a wide range of research that adds to the ongoing debate around nature versus nurture (Spruijt, 2017). However, in the Kauffman Foundation's 2009 report, 'The anatomy of an entrepreneur', the results of a survey of over 500 US company founders stated that there is a strong link between entrepreneurship and higher education, with over 95 per cent of the surveyed entrepreneurs having bachelor's degrees and 47 per cent having more advanced degrees (Young, 2019).

Entrepreneurial thinking is now described as one of the most relevant skills for the 21st-century workforce (Bacigalupo et al, 2016), therefore entrepreneurial education is essential. Teaching the important skills of innovative and creative thinking can help people develop a flexible 'growth mindset' that can adapt to new problems. It is not about teaching business skills such as accounting and pitching, but what it means to be entrepreneurial (Weicht, 2018). This teaching should not be constrained to only future entrepreneurs, as it is an essential skill for 'strengthening human capital, employability and competitiveness' (Bacigalupo et al, 2016).

The European Commission has proposed an Entrepreneurship Competence Framework, also known as EntreComp, which offers a tool to improve the entrepreneurial capacity of European citizens and organizations (European Commission, Directorate-General for Employment, Social Affairs and Inclusion, 2019). The framework aims to build consensus around a common understanding of entrepreneurship competence by defining three competence areas, a list of 15 competences, learning outcomes and proficiency levels, which current and future initiatives can refer to (Bacigalupo et al, 2016). The three competence areas are classed as ideas and opportunities, resources and into action. The further 15 competences under these banners include life skills as well as business skills to provide learners with the means to act upon opportunities and ideas and transform them into value for others, whether financial, cultural or social (Weicht, 2018).

The fashion industry needs to improve the access to entrepreneurial education, and fashion schools around the world are starting to address the need for entrepreneurship and entrepreneurial thinking to be an integral part of all learning. In particular, fashion design students need to be better prepared for business, with as much focus on entrepreneurial skills as on design, which would improve the viability of their brand.

An entrepreneurial approach to scaling a brand

Having an initial great business idea is a wonderful start, but the idea on its own is worth very little. A fashion brand needs all the elements of entrepreneurial mindset and thinking in order to start, develop and scale a business. Managing growth of a business also has its challenges as sudden unplanned growth can cause 'death by success' when the demand suddenly exceeds capacity and the brand cannot deliver the orders coming in. Examples of this have been a brand that finished Paris Fashion Week with a full order book but no finance in place to manufacture the product, or another brand that had grown to a significant point, but the investor suddenly pulled out, leaving the brand with no contingency plan to pay the staff wages or manufacturer fees. Both these brands ended in administration despite their potential success.

Scaling a business is a difficult balancing act and it takes a lot of skill, luck and support to get it right. Some brands may seek investors to build the resources within the company to take their label to the next level. Other brands may choose to scale their brands organically, growing the business slowly using the resources, skills and knowledge they have in-house, taking careful steps to grow ensuring they have the capacity to deliver orders and manage the business.

For more environmentally and socially conscious businesses, the process of scaling their brands is particularly challenging, as they need to ensure they do not move from their original aims and purpose. Many of the brands featured in the 2021 Vogue Business Future Edit were less interested in scaling to compete with megabrands. These brands were instead looking at maintaining responsible growth and connecting with communities, scaling at a slow but steady pace to ensure their employees are treated fairly, they do not overproduce, and product quality is maintained (Maguire, 2021).

Whichever strategy the brand takes to growth, it needs to create strategies to ensure the business stays agile and does not become rigid in its approach or blinkered to opportunities that arise from a changing market. An agile entrepreneurial business is one that is innovative, flexible, ready to adapt and respond to market changes and opportunities, and constantly reflecting on and evaluating the market, competitors and business processes.

Entrepreneurial success

Many entrepreneurs and brands are so obsessed with the future and achieving their goals that they forget to take time out to celebrate their successes along the way. For entrepreneurs it is important to recognize everyday accomplishments and celebrate each small win, instead of constantly chasing the next goal. If they do not take time out to recognize and celebrate achievements, then there is a much higher probability of burnout. Celebrating wins increases motivation, positive attitudes and trust within teams, and gives time to reflect and recharge. While it is important to take time out to celebrate achievements, success can be short-lived if a brand does not keep ahead of the competition, stay agile and continue to develop new skills. For a successful entrepreneur there is no endgame, they just keep looking for new opportunities, taking steps every day towards the next goal, as businesses grow by taking lots of small steps rather than waiting to take one massive leap forward.

Entrepreneurial failure

There is risk for every brand, whether start-up or scaling, and success is never guaranteed. Some entrepreneurs make the decision to start a business based on their intuition, because they have an idea that they really believe in. Most entrepreneurs will calculate the risks involved in starting a business and weigh them against the potential rewards they might receive. They are also prepared to fail but will look to fail quickly in order to learn from mistakes and move on. Something going wrong does not have to mean total failure, unless the brand doesn't learn from their mistakes or take action to fix problems or change and adapt the business accordingly. However, there are times when a great concept, excellent product and hard work just are not enough, and things just don't work out. Success takes a lot of hard work and a lot of luck. Sometimes that luck just runs out.

Dealing with things as they start to go wrong is where a true entrepreneur comes into action. They will take positive, brave steps to turn the business, they will be agile and respond quickly to make necessary changes, even if that means the decision to close the brand and pursue new opportunities. Many of today's most successful fashion entrepreneurs and businesses failed, sometimes more than once, before they succeeded. Brands including Chanel, Tommy Hilfiger, Christian Dior, Gucci, Calvin Klein and Michael Kors all filed for bankruptcy protection or had to shutter part of their businesses before rising to the success they are today.

Sometimes the failure for start-up fashion labels happens right at the start and the brands never even make it to market. This is often due to the whole business concept being reliant on external investment. In the fashion industry getting outside investment is the exception, not the rule. Investors will only ever look at brands that have some traction and experience in the market, so the fashion start-up has very little appeal. As previously mentioned in this book, a great concept is one thing but making it a reality is the main challenge.

Entrepreneurial vision

The entrepreneurial vision for the future of the fashion industry is a rebirth of the sector that balances profit, people and the planet. That vision perceives a sector that will be full of visionary brands and entrepreneurial leaders seeking new business models, and innovative products and processes that meet the consumer's needs. The new ways forward include all the different models discussed in this book, including new circular business models, increasing awareness of and actions taken on social and environmental issues, greater authenticity and transparency in the supply chain, greater use of technology across the sector and omnichannel retail to improve customer experience.

Summary

This chapter has identified the elements of entrepreneurs, entrepreneurial mindset, intrapreneurs, entrepreneurial characteristics, education and need for entrepreneurial endeavours to create a new, more conscious fashion industry. The industry has some huge historic challenges to overcome as well as dealing with future market volatility, uncertainty, continuing geopolitical conflicts and shifts in the global economy. To meet these challenges, there needs to be more focus on entrepreneurial activity and mindset to increase the culture of innovation, initiative, confidence, and passion to find creative solutions and new opportunities. Fashion brand managers need to encourage entrepreneurial approaches in every element of the business, including design, supply chain, production, human resources, retail and marketing if the brand wants more chance of survival and success during turbulent times.

Key terms

entrepreneur	entrepreneurial mindset/ spirit	entrepreneurship
entrepreneurial economy		intrapreneur
	entrepreneurial thinking	social entrepreneurship

Chapter review questions

- Explain the difference between entrepreneurship and intrapreneurship.
- List the main characteristics that entrepreneurs often share.
- Explain why there is a need for greater entrepreneurial education in the fashion industry.

Activity

Research a high-profile fashion entrepreneur who you admire and share with the class why they inspire you.

References

Ashoka, (2014) revolutionizing the fashion industry's impact: four insights from a top social entrepreneur, *Forbes*, www.forbes.com/sites/ashoka/2014/04/11/revolutionizing-the-fashion-industrys-impact-on-the-planet-four-insights-from-a-top-social-entrepreneur/?msc lkid=de938393c09411ecb90256229539463d&sh=591608f17372 (archived at https://perma.cc/6BPL-RSEK)

Bacigalupo, M et al (2016) European Commission, Joint Research Centre, EntreComp: the entrepreneurship competence framework, *Publications Office*, data.europa.eu/doi/10.2791/593884 (archived at https://perma.cc/4AQJ-K4VM)

Bender-Salazar, R (2021) 3 things to consider when adapting entrepreneurship for the post-Covid world, *World Economic Forum*, www.weforum.org/agenda/2021/03/3-key-considerations-when-adapting-entrepreneurship-for-the-great-reset/ (archived at https://perma.cc/9ZDU-B7KH)

Certo, S and Miller, T (2008) Social entrepreneurship: key issues and concepts, *Business Horizons*, 51(4), pp 267–71

Corporate Entrepreneurs (2022) Corporate entrepreneurship, *Corporate Entrepreneurs*, corporate-entrepreneurs.com/welcome/corporate-entrepreneurship/?msclkid=57cdb508c0 d011eca486fbdb5ebf5aee (archived at https://perma.cc/YH5A-8LW9)

European Commission, Directorate-General for Employment, Social Affairs and Inclusion, (2019) EntreComp: the European Entrepreneurship Competence Framework, *Publications Office*, data.europa.eu/doi/10.2767/88978 (archived at https://perma.cc/2X6U-KGTB)

Gary, B (2022) Nature or nurture? Born an entrepreneur? (E&Y report), *Business English with Prof Gary*, profgary-business-english.com/nature-or-nurture-born-an-entrepreneur-ey-report/?msclkid=55ff2fc0c14311ecaeb122921fd7fc0d (archived at https://perma.cc/VM3Q-RNLG)

Grow Ensemble (n.d.) The new fashion entrepreneur: what leadership in fashion must look like for the next generation, *Grow Ensemble*, growensemble.com/fashion-entrepreneur/?msclkid=88abf306c0da11ec8c40501414327398 (archived at https://perma.cc/FZ7N-US6G)

Hillman, J and Hillman, J (2022) The fashion entrepreneur skills you need in 2022, *James Hillman Fashion Consultancy*, www.jameshillman.co.uk/blog/2021/1/24/the-fashion-entrepreneur-skills-you-need-in-2022?msclkid=58b5e4e5bff211eca30cfe51669879bd (archived at https://perma.cc/7UAX-HC32)

Hornsby, J S et al (1993) An interactive model of the corporate entrepreneurship process, *Entrepreneurship Theory and Practice*, 17(2), pp 29–37, doi: 10.1177/104225879301700203 (archived at https://perma.cc/9QTF-BBXL)

I W Capital (2019) The importance of entrepreneurship to the UK economy, IW Capital, iwcapital.co.uk/the-importance-of-entrepreneurship-to-the-uk-economy/?msclkid=07d37544c0a511ecb5c53b0cf7d5be95 (archived at https://perma.cc/Y85N-XLJ4)

Krueger, N F (2007) What lies beneath? The experiential essence of entrepreneurial thinking, *Entrepreneurship Theory and Practice*, 31(1), pp 123–38

Law, J (2009) *A Dictionary of Business and Management*, 5th edn, Oxford University Press, Oxford

Maguire, L (2021) Fashion's start-ups trends for 2021, *Vogue Business*, www.voguebusiness.com/companies/fashions-startups-trends-for-2021 (archived at https://perma.cc/42GS-PWUR)

Power, R (2019) How entrepreneurs can take on the big players, *Forbes*, www.forbes.com/sites/rhettpower/2019/10/20/how-entrepreneurs-can-take-on-the-big-players/?sh=326ae8de65d7 (archived at https://perma.cc/KV59-TKHX)

Spruijt, J (2017) Paradoxes of entrepreneurial thinking: why entrepreneurship can hardly be taught, *ResearchGate*, https://www.researchgate.net/publication/317150787_Paradoxes_of_Entrepreneurial_Thinking_Why_Entrepreneurship_Can_Hardly_Be_Taught (archived at https://perma.cc/HTF7-MRQK)

Today Headline (2021) Who coined the term 'entrepreneur'?, *Today Headline*, todayheadline.co/who-coined-the-term-entrepreneur/#:~:text=Entrepreneur%20is%20a%20French%20word%20probably%20coined%20by,was%20a%20serious%20flaw.%20Say%E2%80%99s%20View%20on%20Entrepreneurship?msclkid=66442f6ac0a111eca20d33d21d766815 (archived at https://perma.cc/6VWP-W4EU)

Ünay, F and Zehir, C (2012) Innovation intelligence and entrepreneurship in the fashion industry, *Procedia – Social and Behavioral Sciences*, 41, pp 315–21

Wallstreetmojo (n.d.) Intrapreneur, *WallStreetMojo*, www.wallstreetmojo.com/intrapreneur/?msclkid=fd5f522dc0b511ec9613e06c9ba730f1 (archived at https://perma.cc/4BFK-JSUY)

Weicht, R (2018) Education systems can stifle creative thought: here's how to do things differently, *World Economic Forum*, www.weforum.org/agenda/2018/04/education-systems-can-stifle-creative-thought-here-s-how-to-do-things-differently/ (archived at https://perma.cc/BB7U-7WE6)

Young, R (2019) How modern entrepreneurs are made, *The Business of Fashion*, www.businessoffashion.com/articles/technology/how-modern-entrepreneurs-are-made/?msclkid=f14a1e31c0a011ec8e3108c1327bded8 (archived at https://perma.cc/P8W3-9Y7A)

GLOSSARY

3D design: using computer modelling software to create an object.

advisory board: a group of experts who guide a business.

aesthetic: the artistic principles of an artist or brand.

affiliates: a person who partners with a brand for commercial gain.

AIDA: advertising model referring to Attention, Interest, Desire and Action.

altruism: a charitable action that a brand takes that benefits others, not themselves.

artificial intelligence: computer systems that perform tasks that normally require human intelligence.

atelier: a workshop or studio used by a designer or brand.

augmented reality: a technology that enhances the physical world through visuals, sounds or other sensory stimuli.

authenticity: the quality of being honest and genuine.

avatars: a computer-generated image or figure that represents a person.

balance sheet: a financial statement that reports the brand's assets, liabilities and shareholders' equity.

bill of materials: a document that brands give to the manufacturer that lists all the raw materials, components and the instructions on how to make a particular garment.

blockchain: a digital ledger that records all the transactions of making an item that is securely linked together and time-stamped.

brand activations: an experiential event that brings the brand to life and engages with the customer.

brand DNA: the essence of the brand that defines its credibility and uniqueness.

brand equity: a marketing term to describe a brand's value.

brand essence: a marketing term that refers to the heart of the business.

brand experience: how the brand makes the customer feel.

brand identity: the visual components of a brand.

brand messaging: the words and language that the brand uses to describe what they do.

brand perception: what the customer thinks and feels about the brand or its product and the value they place on it.

brand pillars: the foundations that the brand uses to develop their unique characteristics.

branding: the process of sharing the brand's values with the customer.

bridge/diffusion line: a level of fashion that sits between ready-to-wear and mass-market collections.

business angel: an individual who invests their own money and time to support a brand.

business model: the way that a brand does business.

business plan: a strategic plan that sets out the brand's aims and objectives.

business strategy: a long-term plan that sets out the way the brand will conduct business based on comprehensive research.

business structure: the legal formation of a brand.

buyer: an individual who purchases fashion products either for personal use or for their store.

CAD: computer-aided design software that is used by designers.

cash accounting: an accounting method that records when payments are received and expenses are paid.

cashflow: the money that comes in and out of a business in its day-to-day transactions.

cashflow forecast: a document that records the estimated income and expenses of the business.

circular fashion model: a system where garments are designed and circulated with the aim of using them for as long as possible before being broken down to be repurposed into future products.

collection: a range of fashion products that are created together at the same time.

commercially viable: a product or business that can compete in the market and make money.

competitive advantage: a position that a brand has in the market that is superior to other brands.

competitive landscape: the environment in which the business is operating and how it is positioned in that market.

connected store: a store that combines digital and physical elements to provide advanced customer experience.

consignment: products that are provided to stores on a sale-or-return basis.

consumer: the customer who purchases fashion for their own use.

consumer behaviour: the way that customers behave depending on economic, social and psychological factors.

consumer insight trends: new ways that customers will behave in the future or the motivations that will make them purchase particular goods or in a certain way.

consumer motivation: the conscious or subconscious reasons that customers will purchase fashion.

consumer profile: a factual description of a customer based on research that identifies characteristics according to behaviour, geography and psychographics.

content: the production of marketing materials such as social media posts, blogs or newsletters.

converters: companies that specialize in finishing fabrics to a brand's requirement.

copyright: a legal right that is assigned to a pattern, design or content.

core competences: refers to key skills that a brand has within their organization such as design skills or business acumen.

cost leadership: a strategy that a brand uses to achieve competitive advantage through low-cost positioning.

cost of sales: a record of all the costs it takes to make a product or collection.

cost price strategy: a business model that sets the prices of the products by multiplying the costs by a set markup percentage to reach the sales price.

critical path: a timeline that records all the key dates and times it takes to complete tasks.

crowdfunding: funding a project and raising money through lots of people giving small amounts.

cut, make, trim (CMT): a manufacturing process used by brands that provide all the materials and components to the factory, who then cut, make and trim it.

debt: money that is owed.

design rights: a legal process to protect the visual appearance of a design through registration.

differentiation: the process of making a brand different from others.

digital design: a design that is made in a digital format.

direct competitors: a business that is similar or offers similar products to the same consumer group.

direct retail: selling products face-to-face with the customer.

direct to consumer: selling products to customers through own physical and digital channels.

drop model: a marketing and sales process of releasing products on set dates rather than using seasons.

dropship: an e-commerce retail strategy that allows a platform to promote the brand's products, but they do not keep the inventory and the brand ships the orders to customers.

e-commerce: selling products through digital channels such as a webstore.

endowment: a donation of money to a business.

entrepreneur: a person takes a risk to start a business or action a solution to a business challenge.

entrepreneurial economy: the environment that is favourable to the development of new enterprises and growth of businesses and innovation.

entrepreneurial mindset/spirit: a way of thinking and a set of skills that people have to identify and take advantage of opportunities.

entrepreneurial thinking: the ability to see things differently to identify opportunities for commercial gain.

entrepreneurship: a mindset that involves the creation or development of economic value.

environmental scan: gathering information and identifying challenges and opportunities in the marketplace of a business.

equity: the value of a brand shared into parts.

ethics: the moral principles that guide a brand's way of working.

experience: the way the consumer feels after an interaction with a brand.

extended reality: an umbrella term for the merging of virtual reality, augmented reality and mixed reality.

factoring: a financial process where a company buys the invoices of another company to release the money to the brand for a fee.

fashion cycle: the time it takes for a fashion trend to emerge, be adopted and then go out of style.

fast fashion: mass-produced, trend-focused, cheap clothing products.

focus: a marketing process that means a brand will concentrate on a narrow and specific segment of the market.

full production package (FPP): a type of manufacturing provider who manages the whole process including patterns, sourcing materials and making the product.

gamification: applying the elements of a game such as rewards or points to encourage people to participate in the digital realm.

GDPR: the General Data Protection Regulation is a legal framework for the collection and processing of personal information.

grants: a sum of money given to a brand from an organization for a specific purpose.

greenwashing: falsely promoting or giving misleading information about how sustainable fashion products are.

haute couture: the accredited luxury design houses that create exclusive luxury garments for individual customers.

hyper-personalization: a marketing approach that uses AI and data to offer advanced personal content and product suggestions.

ideation: the process of forming ideas in a business environment.

indirect competitors: another business that offers a different solution to the same target customer.

influencer marketing: a marketing process that involves a person on social media who has influence to a particular following to endorse the brand's product.

intellectual property protection: the process of legally protecting a brand's name, designs and products.

interactive: the exchange of information where all parties can be involved in the process.

internal environment: used in marketing to relate to the internal workings of a brand that they control such as human resource or technology.

Internet of Things: connecting and exchanging data though sensors being embedded in physical objects.

intrapreneur: someone who works within a company who acts like an entrepreneur.

iterative process: a design process that goes through different testing stages to result in product that meets customer and market need.

jobbers: fabric suppliers who find and sell surplus or dead-stock fabrics.

keystone markup: a pricing process that is used to add a margin to the cost of a product.

landfill: a waste disposal site that buries rubbish.

licence: a legal document that allows a business to operate in a certain way.

limited liability: a form of legal business structure that protects the owners' assets.

line: a range or collection of a particular category of fashion products that a brand produces.

line sheet: a document used in the sales process that details the brand's products including styles, sizes and colours.

live shopping: a selling technique using video live streaming on social media channels to talk through the products and interact with potential customers.

location advantage model: a business model that looks at the benefits of basing a brand in a certain country or city.

logistics: the management of how goods are transported and warehoused in different locations.

look book: a document used by brands to showcase their collections to wholesale buyers using imagery.

macro environment: refers to the external forces within an economy that can affect how a business performs.

marker: a guide used in the cutting process to show how the pattern pieces fit on the fabric.

market segments: a group of customers who have similar behaviours and likes.

marketing: a business activity of promoting and selling a brand and its products.

marketing myopia: a short-sighted approach to business that does not consider the customers' needs.

marketplace: a place where products can be sold either online or in a physical place.

mass market: the widest group of customers as possible.

m-commerce: buying or selling products through handheld devices such as phones or tablets.

metaverse: an immersive virtual world where people connect, play and work.

micro-environment: a marketing term that relates to the area of the environment that a brand can control including its suppliers, customer segments, competitors and distribution.

mills: a factory that makes fabrics.

minimum order quantity (MOQ): the lowest quantity of products that can be ordered.

mixed reality: an immersive digital environment that combines physical and virtual reality.

multi-functional: clothing that has more than one function or can be used or styled in different ways.

nearshoring: transferring business processes to a nearby country to benefit from local economic, political and geographic trading conditions.

neuromarketing: using neuroscience and cognitive science to understand how people behave in response to advertising and brand messages.

NFTs: non-fungible tokens are pieces of digital content, artwork or designs linked to blockchain, which cannot be copied or substituted.

non-disclosure agreement (NDA): a legally binding agreement that establishes confidentiality on information shared.

omnichannel: an integrated approach that links the shopping experience across all channels.

overproduction: making more products than the brand needs or can sell, leading to waste product.

PACE model: a changing consumer behaviour model that describes how customers look for brands that offer protection, acceptance, connection and engagement.

patent: a legal grant for inventors that determines they are the owner of the concept with sole rights to make, use or sell.

perception: the way a consumer feels when they see or hear a brand.

PESTLE: a business model used to scan the macro-environment that a business operates in, looking at the political, economic, social, technological, legal and environmental factors.

positioning: the process of placing a brand in the market in comparison to its competitors.

PR: public relations, which refers to the process of building relationships with the brand's public and providing them with information about the business and its products.

primary research: the process of conducting own research rather than using data collected by other people.

product star: a business model used in fashion to add value in the development of products.

production: the making process of fashion in quantities.

production docket: a document that is given to the manufacturer, which gives precise details of all the production requirements.

production management: the management of all the steps in the sourcing and making process to ensure they are completed on time and to the quality requirements.

profit and loss: a financial statement that details the total revenue and expenses to record if the company has made a profit or a loss.

proof: a marketing process that uses reviews and recommendations to generate new customers.

psychographic: a market research approach that looks at the attitudes, values, interests, etc, of customer groups.

psychology of fashion: the use of psychology to understand why customers behave in a certain way and consideration of how fashion affects their identity and makes them feel.

purpose: the reason a business exists and the intentions they set on what they want to achieve.

range plan: a document that provides an overview of a collection.

ready-to-wear: products that are made to be sold off the shelf, rather than made to each individual customer.

representation: the portrayal of different individuals.

retail: the sale of products directly to consumers.

retail pricing: the price of goods that are sold directly to consumers.

RFID: radio frequency identification systems that use wireless communication that transmits signals to share data.

sales funnel: a visual representation of the customer journey.

saturated market: a marketplace that already has a lot of competitors selling to the same customer segments.

seasonal: a set time of year when products are sold.

seasonal collections: collections that are designed and made to be sold within a certain time period such as spring/summer.

secondary research: research that involves gathering existing data from numerous sources.

see now buy now: a sales process that means the products being shown are available to buy straight away.

segmentation: groups of customers that have the same behaviours or interests.

SEO: search engine optimization – a process for improving traffic to a website.

signature: the unique design element of a brand that appears in every collection, or on every product.

smart mirrors: a two-way mirror with an inbuilt display function that uses digital technology to provide additional information or experiences.

social enterprise: a business that is created with the aim of promoting and achieving social or environmental good.

social entrepreneurship: the process of identifying and pursuing opportunities that create social value.

social PR: a process that uses social media to build relationships with the brand's public.

social selling: a sales strategy that uses social networks, both digital and physical, to sell products.

sole proprietor: a type of business that is owned by one person and is not incorporated.

sourcing: the process of finding all the elements and materials for the production of fashion garments.

specification sheet: a technical document that is given to a factory, which includes all the technical construction information for a garment.

sponsorship: an agreement with a partner organization that gives money in return for agreed benefits.

storytelling: the art of telling stories that engage the audience with the brand.

subcontracting: the process of assigning a contract, or outsourcing an activity to another factory.

supply chain: a network of suppliers that a brand uses to make and distribute their products.

sustainability: the process of making goods that are produced in a way that does not impact on the environment or community.

SWOT: a business model that is used to determine the strengths, weaknesses, opportunities and threats of a brand.

tech pack: an instruction manual of the exact steps and materials needed to make a garment.

threshold competences: the basic knowledge and skills that a business needs to be able to run the business.

timeless: relates to classic fashion that does not go out of style over time.

tone of voice: the way the brand expresses its personality through language.

touchpoints: the places that a consumer comes into contact with a brand.

trademark: a legally identified mark that is used to identify a brand and distinguish it from others such as the name or logo.

transparency: an approach that brands use to communicate openly and honestly with their customers.

trend: a change or development that is popular for a certain amount of time.

trunk shows: a sales event where a brand shows customers their products in a different setting, such as in an office, within another brand's store, or hotel.

user-generated content: content that is created by consumers and shared on social media channels.

value chain: the activities that a brand does that add value to the customer.

value fashion: discount fashion that is mass produced and sold cheaply.

value proposition: a statement of the values that the brand promises to the customer.

venture capital: a form of finance that is provided in return for equity in the brand.

virtual reality: an artificial environment that is experienced through digital technology.

Web3: the next generation of the worldwide web.

wholesale: a sales process that involves selling bulk orders of products to a store.

wholesale pricing: the pricing strategy for setting the price to sell products to a store, so there is a profit margin for both partners.

zero waste: an approach a business takes to reduce waste through fabric cutting, reuse or recycling.

INDEX

NB: page numbers in *italic* indicate figures or tables